U.S. MEDIA AND MIGRATION

Using oral history, ethnography, and close readings of media, Sarah C. Bishop probes the myriad and sometimes conflicting ways refugees interpret and use mediated representations of life in the United States throughout their resettlement. Guided by 74 refugee narrators from Bhutan, Burma, Iraq, and Somalia, *U.S. Media and Migration* explores answers to questions such as: What does one learn from media about an unfamiliar place? How does media help or hinder refugees' sense of belonging after relocation? Why and how does the U.S. government use media to shape refugees' understanding of American norms, standards, and ideals? With insights from refugees and resettlement administrators throughout, Bishop provides a compelling and layered analysis of the interaction between refugees and U.S. media before, during, and long after resettlement.

Sarah C. Bishop is an Assistant Professor in the Department of Communication Studies at Baruch College, City University of New York.

U.S. MEDIA AND MIGRATION

Refugee Oral Histories

Sarah C. Bishop

NEW YORK AND LONDON

First published 2016
by Routledge
711 Third Avenue, New York, NY 10017

and by Routledge
2 Park Square, Milton Park, Abingdon, Oxon OX14 4RN

Routledge is an imprint of the Taylor & Francis Group, an informa business

© 2016 Taylor & Francis

The right of Sarah C. Bishop to be identified as author of this work has been asserted by her in accordance with sections 77 and 78 of the Copyright, Designs and Patents Act 1988.

All rights reserved. No part of this book may be reprinted or reproduced or utilised in any form or by any electronic, mechanical, or other means, now known or hereafter invented, including photocopying and recording, or in any information storage or retrieval system, without permission in writing from the publishers.

Trademark notice: Product or corporate names may be trademarks or registered trademarks, and are used only for identification and explanation without intent to infringe.

Library of Congress Cataloging-in-Publication Data
Bishop, Sarah C., 1984– author.
 U.S. media and migration : refugee oral histories / Sarah C. Bishop.
  pages cm
 Includes bibliographical references and index.
 1. Mass media and immigrants—United States. 2. Refugees—United States. I. Title.
  P94.5.I482U6545 2016
  302.23086'9120973—dc23
  2015029561

ISBN: 978-1-138-94746-7 (hbk)
ISBN: 978-1-138-94747-4 (pbk)
ISBN: 978-1-315-67007-2 (ebk)

Typeset in Bembo
by Apex CoVantage, LLC

CONTENTS

List of Tables and Figures   vii
Acknowledgments   ix

Introduction   1

1 Refugees as Audiences of U.S. Media in
Pre-Arrival Contexts   20
Gaining Access to U.S. Media 28
*"The Reality Check": Sorting Fact from Fiction in
Popular U.S. Media 37*
Complicating Enculturation through Media 43

2 Refugees' Use of Media in Pre-Departure
Preparation and Orientations   55
Pre-Departure Overseas Orientations 58
Importance of Visuality in Orientation Media 63
The Relationship between Orientation Content and Context 64
The Power of Orientation Media 67
A Closer Look at One Orientation Text 69
*Limited Access to and Disappointment with Orientations and
Their Media 84*
Relocation Preparation outside of Orientation 88

3 Voluntary and Mandated Media Encounters during
   Refugees' First Days in the U.S.   96
   Navigating "Home": Making Sense of American
      Living Arrangements and Media Access 98
   Perspectives on the Importance of Post-Arrival Media Acquisition 104
   Expectations Meet Reality during the First Days of
      Living in the United States 109
   Post-Arrival Orientations and Orientation Media 116
   The Infallible Helpmate: Government Agency
      Self-Representation in Post-Arrival Contexts 125
   Print Media as a Means to Develop, Standardize, and
      Ensure Fulfillment of Post-Arrival Orientation 129
   Post-Arrival Media Facilitates Deprivatization 131

4 Media and Refugees' Ongoing Resettlement   142
   Media about Refugees in the United States 144
   Refugees in U.S. News 145
   Refugees and Americans Respond to News about
      Refugees in the United States 151
   Media, Language, and Religion 164
   Media, Friends, and Family 169

Conclusion   180

Appendix   *185*
References   *187*
Index   *207*

TABLES AND FIGURES

Tables

0.1	New refugee arrivals in fiscal year 2012 by four top nations of origin	9
0.2	Affiliated organizations and interview details	10
0.3	Incoming refugees by top-four states in fiscal years 2010–2012	12

Figures

2.1	Cultural orientation in Thailand	59
2.2	Still taken from "Welcome to the United States"	61
2.3	An instructional diagram on the door of a bathroom at a refugee camp in Nepal	65
2.4	Orientation attendees watch a film at the Dadaab camp in Kenya	66
2.5	Refugees respond to a question during pre-departure orientation	71
2.6	Page 40 of the *Guidebook for Refugees* orientation text	80
2.7	Page 226 of the *Guidebook for Refugees* orientation text	81
3.1	Page 145 of the *Guidebook for Refugees* orientation text	108
3.2	Page 149 of the *Guidebook for Refugees* orientation text	117
3.3	Page 26 of YMCA Houston's *Reception and Placement* orientation text	118
3.4	Page 15 of YMCA Houston's *Reception and Placement* orientation text	119
3.5	Page 53 of YMCA Houston's *Reception and Placement* orientation text	122
3.6	Page 143 of *Making Your Way* orientation text	126
3.7	Page 277 of *Making Your Way* orientation text	127

ACKNOWLEDGMENTS

This project was made possible through an oral history grant from the Arthur and Elizabeth Schlesinger Library on the History of Women in America at Harvard University, a teaching fellowship from the Department of Communication and the Dietrich School of Arts & Sciences at the University of Pittsburgh, a summer research award from the Dietrich School of Arts & Sciences at the University of Pittsburgh, and a research grant from the Waterhouse Family Institute for the Study of Communication and Society at Villanova University. I have been humbled by the amount of time that the directors and administrators at refugee resettlement agencies in Pennsylvania, New York, Texas, and California have willingly given to facilitating this project and owe a debt of gratitude to Kheir Mugwaneza of Northern Area Ministries in Pittsburgh; Leslie Aizenman of Jewish Family & Children's Services of Pittsburgh; Dylanna Jackson at the International Institute of Erie; Marc Fallon at CAMBA NYC; Lisa Guitguit, Jeff Klein, Melody Brown, and Ron Rea at YMCA Houston; Meg Goodman Erskine and Esther Diaz at the Multicultural Refugee Coalition Austin; Meghann Perry at Journey's End Refugee Services; Sahra Abdi at United Women's East African Support Team; Said Abiyow at Somali Bantu San Diego; Mike McKay at Catholic Charities; and Lily Alba at the International Institute of Los Angeles. To all of the interpreters, thank you for your patience and attention to detail. To the narrators, thank you for sharing your stories. I am forever grateful. To Jonathan Crane, thank you for driving, listening, editing, and to my advisor at the University of Pittsburgh, Ron Zboray, and to Jonathan Crane, Brent Malin, Olga Kuchinskaya, and Kent Ono, I offer my sincerest thanks; your guidance at each state of this project was invaluable. Finally, special thanks to Mary Zboray for her close attention to my work, infinite patience, and encouragement.

INTRODUCTION

The United States accepts around sixty thousand immigrants with refugee status each year. These "forced migrants"[1] fled or were driven from their homes because of some social, political, or natural threat to their safety. While some refugees know a good deal about the United States when they arrive, many have moved directly from refugee camps that often lacked access to television, the Internet, and other mass media. When refugees arrive in the United States, they not only confront a new nation about which they may have limited prior knowledge but also a media-saturated environment in which successful orientation and resettlement depends on their ability to engage with such media. Because refugees throughout their relocation process need to interact with U.S.-made films, television, and news, as well as with U.S.-government-produced print matter, to help them navigate their new environment, studying such encounters offers a previously underdeveloped perspective of media's role in refugees' lived experiences and, more broadly, of U.S. media's variable capacity to provide crucial information to these individuals.

This book looks into the ways refugees use and interpret multiple forms of U.S. media throughout their long-term relocation. With the aid of firsthand perspectives provided by seventy-four oral history interviews I conducted with refugees in the United States, as well as twelve interviews with refugee resettlement administrators, I work to answer the following questions: How is relocating refugees' knowledge about their new host country influenced by their encounters with media from the United States during the relocation process? How does mediated communication help or hinder refugees' sense of belonging in the United States? What role, if any, do media play in refugees' attempts to adopt or resist perceived American norms, standards, and ideals? Finally, how do media produced by local, state, and federal governments shape refugees' understanding and experiences during relocation, and how do governments attempt to use these media toward particular ends? By analyzing refugees' encounters with U.S. media before, during, and after their relocation to multiple parts of the United States, this book directly addresses each of these questions.

One cannot gain a thorough view of media's role in refugee resettlement by considering only the media that refugees encounter before they are displaced; likewise, a view that takes into account only the ways that media and refugees interact post-resettlement would prove too narrow to offer insight about the ways that refugees transition from one nation to another with the impact of pre-resettlement media encounters lingering in their deep memory. For this purpose, this book is organized according to the ways media's impact unfolds sequentially through three general stages of migration: (1) *before* long-term resettlement, when refugees' encounters with U.S. media are determined and limited by the availability of this media within their countries of origin or secondary countries of asylum; (2) *during* resettlement—that is, immediately before and after relocating to the United States—when much of the U.S. media refugees hear, see, and read is mandated, produced, and disseminated by the U.S. government or governmental organizations during mandated pre-departure and post-arrival orientations; and (3) *after* resettlement, when, once having settled into the media-saturated United States and gaining more independence from the U.S. government's direct involvement in their daily lives, refugees' media engagements diversify according to tastes, desires, and/or academic and professional requirements. As this book demonstrates, the ways refugees use U.S. media in each of these three stages is different from the other two. A chronological format will thus allow for the clearest unfolding of these distinctions, while simultaneously mimicking the sequential narrative arc of the interviews themselves.[2] In short, in this book, I argue that the influence of media on the relocation process is far more wide reaching than is currently on the radar of both media scholars and resettlement professionals, and that studying refugees' interpretation and negotiation of media can advance understanding of media's power and limitations in transnational contexts.

The oral history methodology of this book works to counter asymmetries in power and control of the topic by providing an experiential, narrative-driven account. In the heavily mass-mediated United States, self-reports of refugee media use provide insight into a crucial locus of interaction between refugees and their host country. Studying that locus promises to suggest how media-dependent cultural citizenship is imbricated with more conventional government-sponsored pathways to citizenship that have been part of the standard immigration narrative.[3] As a narrative that has become a key fixture of American ideology, the overly positive story of "a nation of immigrants" adapting to abundance (as Andrew Heinze argues in his book of the same title) is challenged by the study of forced migrants' media use, which shows a much more nuanced and often conflicted picture of forced migrants' experiences.[4] Thus, this book sheds new light on the refugee experience in the United States, U.S. media as an avenue of immigrant enculturation, and U.S. state power exercised through media upon forced migrants.

While communication scholars, sociologists, and anthropologists have studied the interaction of media and migration, refugees are often underrepresented in such research because of the diversity of their narratives; their general status as a vulnerable, and transient, population; and the obstacles refugees and scholars face in comprehending each other's languages. As a result, most of the existing scholarly narratives about media and migration foreground voluntary, rather than forced, immigrant perspectives.[5]

The goal of this book is to advance understanding of refugee interaction with U.S. media while maintaining sight of the heterogeneity of refugees and their narratives. Because refugees in the United States are not a generic, homogenous cultural group, their media experiences are not generalizable but, rather, vary due to factors such as the divergent geographic contexts of their countries of origin and areas of settlement in the U.S. differential exposure to media when growing up, disparate levels of literacy and English-language comprehension, and dissimilar positions on the socioeconomic ladder. To emphasize such heterogeneity, this book (1) employs oral-history-based investigation that eschews standardized questionnaires of a group in favor of open-ended questions that encourage reports of personal and unique experiences; (2) involves people of different social statuses from four distinct refugee-producing nations that represent the largest recent refugee streams into the United States; and (3) adopts a multisited approach involving key cities in the four states that have recently received the greatest numbers of refugees: California, New York, Texas, and Pennsylvania. This research design permits analysis of the many ways that refugee encounters with media may vary by ethnicity, socioeconomic status, area of origin, and area of resettlement.

I am aware that by referring to these four groups according to their nations of origin instead of their ethnicities or some other characteristic that I risk perpetuating the nationalistic nature of refugee research. However, because refugee resettlement is determined and facilitated by nation-states, because the 1951 United Nations Refugee Agency's very definition of "refugee" utilizes national categorization, and because the refugee narrators were not always explicit about their ethnicities during interviews, I will refer to refugees throughout this book according to their nation of origin. In cases where the narrators mentioned their ethnicity as a salient aspect of their narrative, I have noted it in the text.

This book is based upon the belief that underprivileged, forced migration should receive the same scholarly attention as more privileged forms of migration. The lack of attention in American immigration scholarship to forced migration has normalized the experiences of more privileged migrants, so that voluntary migrants become the yardstick of invidious distinction against which other migrants are measured. By attending to forced immigration, this book offers to revise the prevailing mythologies concerning immigration that tend to be overly positive, while simultaneously providing insights that may be useful to those who facilitate migration. The objective here is thus both theoretical and pragmatic, and the resulting work should lend scholarly insight into the ways communicative encounters with U.S.-produced media inform refugee relocation and, at the same time, provide useful, pertinent analysis for any individuals or groups involved in, or affected by, refugees relocating to the United States.

At the end of one of the first oral history interviews I conducted in early 2013, I asked the participating refugee narrator, Tek Rimal, "Is there anything you would like to tell me that I haven't asked you about?"[6] I included this question at the end of each interview, and the responses were often fruitful—participants sometimes wanted to clarify something they mentioned earlier, or remembered something they meant to say before. But Tek's reply was unique. Instead of continuing with his narrative after this prompt, he paused, and then asked simply, "How will your research help refugees?" I set down my notebook. While I had presupposed even in the earliest stages of developing this research that my work would be helpful to those involved in the relocation of refugees, I realized in that moment the gravity of what Tek was asking. He had invited me to interview him in his home that evening after working back-to-back shifts at his two full-time jobs because he trusted that telling his own story might have a tangible, positive effect for others who bear the burden of displacement.

Tek's question became an imperative for me. I offer these narratives and my analysis in the faith that this work will blur the line that too often separates the academic from the pragmatically useful and ethically sound. Repeating Tek's question as a mantra at each stage of this work, I pursued this research with academic rigor for the sake of positive social change. I believe that the most valuable contribution of this book will be a richer understanding of the wealth of knowledge to be gained by anyone willing to listen to firsthand—rather than secondhand or presupposed—accounts of media's role in forced migration.

To investigate the scope of the interaction of refugee migration and media, I have conducted seventy-four oral history interviews with refugees from the top-four nations of origin for recent refugee arrivals in the U.S.—Bhutan, Burma,[7] Iraq, and Somalia—in order to compare and contrast the myriad ways refugees encounter, interpret, and understand mediated representations of life in the United States.[8] In addition to the seventy-four interviews with refugees, I also interviewed twelve refugee resettlement administrators. An oral history methodology entails conducting and recording qualitative, long-form interviews using open-ended questions and has proven germane for my project in that it fostered a firsthand, in-depth view into refugees' sense of meaning-making about their mediated perceptions of relocation. My interviews took place in the four leading states of residence for refugees admitted to the United States in 2012: Texas, California, New York, and Pennsylvania.⁹ In addition, I completed close readings and visual/textual analysis of several relevant texts that were brought to my attention by the participating narrators. Finally, in this book, I call upon my observation of the several refugee classes, orientations, and other refugee-related meetings I attended in order to analyze the ways these meetings' visual, oral, and written components inform refugee resettlement. In the following pages, I discuss each of these three methods in detail.

The oral history method I used throughout this project allowed firsthand, refugee voices to guide the research in a way that standardized questionnaires could not. Refugees' resettlement experiences are permeated on all fronts with mediated representations of America, nationalism, patriotism, and, sometimes, xenophobia. But the ways refugees interpret or use these media vary widely. For this reason, it is imperative to my project that the narrators were able to testify, in their own words, to their own unique experiences.

The Oral History Association (OHA) explains that oral history "refers both to a method of recording and preserving oral testimony and to the product of that process."¹⁰ Through dialogic exchange, oral histories traverse ground unavailable via other methodologies by creating inimitable environments for individual reflections on highly personal narratives, and by providing a means for the recording and storage of voices that may otherwise not be preserved. Sherna Gluck suggests that oral history allows researchers to gather underrepresented histories by "challenging the traditional concepts of history, of what is 'historically important,' and . . . affirming that our everyday lives *are* history."¹¹ This methodology is overseen and internally governed by the OHA, established in 1966, which "seeks to bring together all persons interested in oral history as a way of collecting and interpreting human memories to foster knowledge and human dignity."¹² The genesis of contemporary oral history has been attributed to the post-World War II "renaissance of memory as a source for 'people's history,'" and has undergone several transformations and incarnations since that time, but the role of individual narrations of history has remained consistently central and valuable to the philosophy of this work.¹³ Scholars from multiple disciplines employ an oral history methodology, and it exists in communication and media studies as one of many methods of research. The foundational assumptions of this technique include the belief that some personalized, historical knowledge cannot be gained quantitatively, but only through a process of open-ended reflection and the recovery of memory in which the researcher does not anticipate the responses of the participant prior to the interview. The resulting findings are both unanticipated and not reproducible, because they are allowed to emerge organically throughout the interview instead of through predetermined research questions and hypotheses. Because oral history is a methodology of experience, one that should not anticipate its findings before the interviews take place, researchers must guard against the tendency to give priority to only what they suspect they will find or to ask leading questions in hopes of confirming what they already assume is true. The philosophy of oral history privileges the narrators' accounts over the researchers' presuppositions, so the responsible interviewer must provide time and opportunity for whichever responses a narrator chooses to exhibit. Such a position remains limited, however, by the reality that the researcher has predetermined which event to study, which narrators to seek out, and which perspectives to leave out of the final project. In this way, as renowned oral historian Alessandro Portelli reminds us, "the control of the historical discourse remains firmly in the hands of the historian," and assuming otherwise would provide oral history an impossible advantage over every other kind of historical research.[14] Indeed, just as the narrator will inevitably include his/her interpretations alongside the account of history, so will the researcher inevitably interpret his/her findings according to personal understanding and intent. In this way, throughout an oral history, the narrator and the interviewer work as partners, collaborating to create a record of a particular history. Portelli suggests, "oral sources are always the result of a relationship, a common project in which both the informant and the researcher are involved, together."[15] Instead of ignoring this inescapable reality, many oral historians recommend addressing it head on, taking on a "reflective, critical approach to memory and history"[16] so that "by reflecting on our practice we can move toward a more sensitive research methodology."[17] A self-reflexive approach can work to keep the narrators' perspectives more central to oral history research.

An important distinction exists regarding the unit of study within the oral history research included in this work. For this project, the unit of study is not some historical event itself, but rather the *memory* of a particular time in the narrators' history. I refer to past events as "histories" instead of "history," as this minor semantic change allows for the possibility of multiple or conflicting experiences around singular past events. Here, the significance lies not in the "reality" that some event occurred, but rather that the event was experienced by an individual or group of individuals who responded with highly variable reactions based on any number of factors. This reality speaks to a viable intersection of oral history with communication studies.

Contemporary communication theory leans heavily on the dynamic nature of the self, found in the works of scholars such as Roland Barthes and David Harvey. Barthes worked to advance the view that every experience is subject to personal dynamic interpretation called connotation, or, "the imposition of a second meaning."[18] In this view, no individual can experience an event objectively, because his/her experience depends highly on contextual and personal factors. Taking this view further, David Harvey asserts that individuals create meanings that may shift or change "depending on the situation."[19] Though a self-proclaimed Marxist,

Harvey rejects the Marxist idea of a coherent self in favor of the notion of the "fragmented" selves that make up each individual and allow for the existence of simultaneous event divergent meanings.[20] Carrying these views into this oral history project allowed me to consider any narrator's account not as an official or stagnant explanation of "truth," but as a reality, nonetheless, that is dynamic and situated within a particular temporal and spatial context.

The multisited, multilingual oral history interviews I completed for this work presented some unanticipated challenges that compelled me to maintain a constant view of my own positionality while interviewing. For example, while some of the refugee narrators were well educated and quite comfortable with academic research, others who had little or no history of education were unsure of what academic research was or how it might be used, so I had to spend a good deal of the relatively little time we had together explaining my intentions and affiliations and working through the deed of gift forms—which granted me permission to use the narrators' words—line-by-line.[21] Some members of the refugee populations living in Texas, California, New York, and Pennsylvania had formal lessons in English before their arrival in the United States, and many had access to extensive free English classes after their arrival. All twelve of the resettlement administrators I interviewed spoke English fluently. Therefore, I was able to conduct about half of the interviews in English. While several of the narrators were happy to speak with me through an interpreter in their native language, others were eager to use their newly acquired language skills and participate in the interview in English with no interpreter present. While I conceded whenever this request was made, I was challenged in a few instances by the mid-interview realization that the narrator and I were having difficulty understanding each other clearly. In these instances, due to the extra time it took to ensure bidirectional understanding, the interviews covered comparatively less ground than others.

The presence of an interpreter did not eradicate difficulty, but instead changed its nature. Throughout this project, I faced questions such as, how can I be sure the interpreter is repeating clearly what the narrators and I have said? How should I proceed when interpreters who are also refugees begin—perhaps due to the informal nature of the interview conversations—to share their own experiences in addition to translating the narrators'? How should one transcribe language that is not grammatically correct, and how should this strategy change when the errors are an interpreter's rather than a narrator's? I faced each of these questions several times, and rather than developing a standard protocol by which to handle them, I instead dealt with them on a case-by-case basis that took into account the narrators' preferences, my own desires, and the interpreters' willingness and skill.

Especially sensitive in this project was the prevailing reality that many refugees are asked consistently and repeatedly by their case managers or other resettlement personnel to talk with strangers who are often affiliated with the government in some capacity. Refugees' case managers may require them to meet with representatives from Health and Human Services, immigration lawyers, state-funded counselors, and other resettlement agency or government personnel at multiple points after their relocation. Whether out of respect for their case managers or an understanding that compliance with case managers' requests often leads to the availability of aid or resources, I gained the sense during this project that refugees are sometimes willing to agree to a meeting even when they are not entirely sure of its purpose or outcome. Because I worked with refugee case managers to solicit narrators for this project, this realization led me to believe that it was important at the beginning of the interviews to take the time to establish with the narrators that I had no ongoing affiliation with their resettlement agencies, that speaking with me would have no impact on their ability to receive aid or their standing with their resettlement agency, and that their decision to participate could be reversed if they wished. Once I made these qualifications, I was overwhelmed by how many refugee narrators were still eager to tell their stories and often wanted to continue talking even beyond the time we had scheduled for our meeting.

Beyond the aforementioned challenges, there were others that made this project a frustrating but ultimately rewarding venture. For example, some of the narrators did not know their addresses or how to write words other than their names, so that completing the deeds of gift became a multiperson and time-consuming affair. Others did not know the day or year they were born or the names of the places they had lived before they were displaced, so that information that is often standard or easy to obtain in many interviewing projects became cumbersome or impossible in this one. Additionally, interviewing narrators who had sustained bodily torture—many of whom were from Somalia—posed a challenge that was quite the opposite of what I had expected. I knew that it was likely that I would encounter some narrators who had experienced torture; it is all too common in refugee experiences. While I did ask all of the refugee narrators to explain to me their understanding of the reasons they were displaced, I was clear that they did not need to recount memories that may be too painful to revisit. I assumed most would not want to discuss the intricate details of their hardships with a near stranger. Instead, I found that the refugees who had sustained bodily torture were often intent on sharing those parts of their narratives at length during our interviews. In those moments, I felt pulled between my academic concerns and my human ones; the graphic verbal descriptions of rape, murder, and mutilation sometimes rendered me speechless, so that I was unable to or uninterested in maintaining my side of the conversation. Since completing the interviews, I have revisited and wrestled with these survivor narratives repeatedly. Like the narrators, I have sometimes found it difficult to concentrate on the other parts of this research in light of the massive and ongoing reality of violence. In deference to this particular group of narrators and their fervent commitment to making an American researcher aware of the prevalence of violence in refugees' pasts, I have attempted to provide as much context as is possible regarding the narrators' pre- and mid-displacement experiences. Indeed, even when these experiences appeared at first to have no relation at all to refugees' use and interpretation of media, I often learned well into some interviews that a history of torture has a direct and ongoing effect on the ways refugees function as audiences of media and discuss this revelation in detail at multiple points in this work.

To seek out the narrators for this project, I relied on refugee arrival data from the U.S. Department of State; the Bureau of Population, Refugees, and Migration; and the Worldwide Refugee Admissions Processing System. In fiscal year 2012, 58,179 refugees were admitted to the United States (31,380 men; 26,799 women).[22] Seventy-nine percent of these admissions were from Bhutan (26 percent), Burma (24 percent), Iraq (21 percent), or Somalia (8.4 percent).[23] Table 0.1 reveals the dispersion of newly arriving refugees from these four groups in 2012 across the four states involved in this project.

I interviewed twenty-four Bhutanese refugees, twenty Iraqi refugees, nineteen Somali refugees, and eleven Burmese refugees. In keeping with the Oral History Association's (2012) guidelines for best practices, I prepared an interview guide of some questions that I asked each narrator. These questions included inquiries such as, "Where were you born?" and "How old are you?" While these questions are standard in oral history research and may be assumed to provoke simple answers; in fact, because many refugees were displaced from their homes when they were quite young and because many have no record of their birth, sometimes the factual answers to these questions were unattainable. For example, about ten of the seventy-four narrators told me they were born on January 1 of some year, which is likely an indication that refugees or resettlement personnel use this date as a default during resettlement processing when refugees are unsure of their birth date. The interview guide evolved during the interviewing stage of this project to include the adaptation or addition of some questions and the removal of others, so that each interview comprised a unique event with its own findings. During each interview, I allowed ample time for any new directions the narrator might lead me. Many times, these new directions arose when narrators'

TABLE 0.1 New refugee arrivals in fiscal year 2012 by four top nations of origin[24]

	Bhutan	*Burma/Myanmar*	*Iraq*	*Somalia*
Texas	1,216	2,142	960	456
California	107	409	2,912	238
New York	1,204	1,074	324	411
Pennsylvania	2,166	255	167	23
Total admitted to U.S. in FY 2012	15,070	14,160	12,163	4,900

responses evoked follow-up questions that led the narrator to discuss additional, unanticipated topics in detail.

I contacted the majority of the narrators in this project through liaisons at the refugee resettlement agencies in each of the four involved states. Additional narrators were recruited by way of the "snowball effect," wherein narrators recommended I talk with their friends or family members and helped to facilitate meetings with them. In order to gain a fuller grasp on the ways changes in the local culture may have impacted my findings, I interviewed narrators living in two distinct areas within each state: New York City and Buffalo in New York, Los Angeles and San Diego in California, Houston and Austin in Texas, and Pittsburgh and Erie in Pennsylvania. Table 0.2 provides the names and locations of all participating refugee resettlement organizations, the dates of my interviews, and the number of narrators affiliated with each organization.

TABLE 0.2 Affiliated organizations and interview details

Refugee-Related Organization	Location	Dates of Interviews	Number of Narrators
Jewish Family and Children's Services	Pittsburgh, Pennsylvania	February 5, 2013 February 20, 2013 March 4, 2013	5
International Institute of Erie	Erie, Pennsylvania	February 7, 2013	4
Northern Area Multi-Service Center	Pittsburgh, Pennsylvania	March 5, 2013 March 22, 2013	3
CAMBA NYC	New York, New York	June 4, 2013	2
International Institute of Los Angeles	Los Angeles, California	July 9, 2013 July 11, 2013 July 12, 2013	12
Journey's End Refugee Services	Buffalo, New York	August 6, 2013 August 7, 2013	12
International Institute of Buffalo	Buffalo, New York	August 7, 2013	1
YMCA Houston	Houston, Texas	November 13, 2013 November 14, 2013	13
Multicultural Refugee Coalition	Austin, Texas	November 15, 2013	6
Catholic Charities	San Diego, California	November 18, 2013	12
Somali Bantu Association of America	San Diego, California	November 20, 2013 November 21, 2013	13
United Women's East African Support Team	San Diego, California	November 21, 2013	3
Total: 86 narrators (74 refugees, 12 administrators)			

I conducted the interviews either at the agencies with which the narrators were affiliated or in the narrators' homes, and the interviews lasted approximately fifty minutes on average. I audio recorded each interview using an application on my iPhone or iPad, excluding two interviews where the narrators declined to give permission for such recording. Because some refugees in the United States need to protect their identities for the safety of family members still living in their home countries or country of asylum, five of the narrators preferred that I use a pseudonym to identify them in this work. In these cases, the interviews are cited using the pseudonym as well as the statement "name changed at the narrator's request." After the interviews and observations of refugee-related meetings and events were complete, I had approximately sixty-three hours of recorded material. I indexed the recordings by dividing their content into themes of media interaction before and after relocation and employed professional transcriptionists to transcribe twenty-two selected interviews that I selected on the basis of relevancy to the project's themes.[25] I transcribed selected parts of the other interviews myself.

While I have addressed some errors and omissions in the transcripts by providing brackets for clarity of reading, I have not invisibly corrected refugees' or translators' grammar when they are quoted in this book. For example, a narrator's quote in chapter 2 appears as "my dream and [what] I faced so different." The original transcriptions of the interviews are verbatim and include vocalized pauses, false starts, and other nonverbal utterances. Because none of the refugee narrators spoke English as a first language, and because several of the refugee narrators preferred to speak with me in English, many times they would use vocalized pauses, such as "um," "ahh," or "you know," as they searched for a word or confirmed my understanding. In this book, I have removed many of these nonverbal utterances for two reasons: (1) because the utterances were sometimes the interpreters' rather than the narrators' and (2) for the sake of brevity and clarity.

I chose the four geographic sites for this project not only because they provided access to the greatest number of refugees[26] but also because (1) they represent the four regions of the United States: West Coast, East Coast, North, and South; (2) a USCRI-sponsored refugee resettlement agency exists in each; (3) the directors of refugee resettlement at the four respective USCRI-sponsored agencies volunteered to facilitate the project by reaching out to narrators and facilitating interpreters;[27] and (4) each of the four house large populations of Burmese, Bhutanese, Iraqi, and Somali refugees. Table 0.3 reveals the numbers of all incoming refugees to these top four states for resettlement in fiscal years 2010, 2011, and 2012.

Throughout this work, I use the insights I gained from the oral history interviews I conducted to take up the methodology of close reading and criticism of several pieces of print, video, and digital media. My goal, as it relates to the

TABLE 0.3 Incoming refugees by top-four states in fiscal years 2010–2012[28]

	Incoming Refugees FY 2010	Incoming Refugees FY 2011	Incoming Refugees FY 2012
Texas	7918	5627	5905
California	8577	4987	5167
New York	4559	3529	3525
Pennsylvania	2632	2972	2809

examination of these media, is not to suggest that the texts hold meaning in and of themselves, but rather to explore the ways they promote certain versions of reality while concealing others. In order to avoid a viewing of these media as isolated, finite pieces of information, I examine the texts situationally and contextually, considering the varieties of ways they may appear within, and interact with, refugees' lives.

Rhetorical criticism is an interdisciplinary approach to the study of language and power that recognizes the ability of communication to facilitate the advancement of knowledges and realities, and recognizes that discourse acts not only as a carrier of ideology but also as a social action in and of itself.[29] Taking up a mandate of close attention to both language and context, rhetorical criticism involves examination of implicit and explicit strategies in language and visual artifacts, and considers critically how these strategies may provide insights into relationships of power and truth production. By utilizing rhetorical criticism to examine the ways truth is created, negotiated, and/or maintained in any text or talk, one can gain a better understanding of the ways the production of these "truths" affect the lived realities of individuals.

In the parts of this work that utilize close readings of media and rhetorical criticism, I take up Sonja K. Foss's notion of *ideological* criticism, which recognizes that "evaluative beliefs" are encoded into rhetorical (and, in this case, mass-mediated) messages that "serve as the foundation for knowledge, attitudes, [and] motives."[30] By homing in on the implicit ideologies that appear in mass media, I am able to tease out the discourses of power and knowledge that run like a current through the kinds of media that refugees encounter before, during, and after their arrival in the United States.

While the critical analysis of talk and text is a prevalent methodology in communication studies generally,[31] its use in examinations of artifacts relating to migration media specifically has been limited.[32] In light of this, my decision to focus on individual artifacts (instead of whole genres or groups of related artifacts) in each of the chapters that employ critical analysis is based on Michael Billig's view that at an early stage in an area's theoretical development, a single case study can be especially useful . . . Whilst no claims for sample representativeness can be made from a single case study, it is hoped that in-depth analysis can reveal features and complexities, which have a wider generality.[33]

This approach has allowed me to examine a handful of key texts with a good deal of detail rather than including superficial reviews of an indiscriminate amount of media.

Because refugees encounter a wide range of media throughout their relocation, and because refugees' encounters with media vary depending on area of origin, number of years spent in a secondary country of asylum before arriving in the United States, age, language skill, interest, and other factors, I followed the lead of the narrators in deciding which media to analyze. When a particular piece of media was mentioned during an interview, I asked the narrators to describe their memory of the media. After the interview, I would read, watch, or listen to the media myself in order to complete an analysis of its style, format, and content. This process was complicated by the fact that in several cases, narrators could not recall the names of the films, books, television shows, or websites to which they referred. Though these instances prevented me from being able to analyze these unnamed pieces of media myself, I still include the narrators' descriptions of them in several parts of this book. Refugees' descriptions of unnamed media reinforce the significance of the lingering yet partial impact of media on audiences.

At several of the locations involved in this project, I had the opportunity to observe and/or participate in meetings and events at refugee-related organizations. These events served several purposes in this project. First, they allowed me to become familiar with the daily goings on and structure of refugee resettlement agencies and other refugee-related organizations. Second, they provided me with an opportunity to meet and network with refugees and resettlement administrators. Third, they gave me a firsthand view of the ways that refugee-related organizations acquire, display, and disseminate media. In some cases, such as when I attended an English as a Second Language class for newly arrived refugees affiliated with Journey's End Refugee Services in Buffalo, New York, my role was merely observational. I sat to the side of the class taking notes and photographs. In other cases, such as when I attended a board meeting of resettlement staff at the YMCA in Houston, Texas, I was asked to share my goals, findings, and/or recommendations, and thus acted as both observer and participant.[34] The meetings and events I attended varied in purpose, attendance, length, and format. Beyond the English as a Second Language class and board meeting I mentioned earlier, I attended a formal refugee orientation in Pittsburgh, a monthly community meeting of the San Diego Refugee Council, and a yearly digital webinar about the current state of pre-departure orientations delivered by the Cultural

Orientation Resource Center. In addition to these formal events, I was also given the chance to tour and photograph the twelve refugee-related organizations that cooperated with me in my research and to enjoy several afternoon teas and meals with refugees and resettlement staff in multiple locations. While I do not write at length about every one of these experiences in the following pages, I cannot overemphasize how integral they were to this work. The opportunity to attend these formal and informal meetings and events in the four states involved in this project provided context, background knowledge, and perspective for each of the following chapters.

I do not presume that my attendance at the aforementioned events and venues has provided me with a complete view of refugee resettlement. Rather, I am keen to agree with James Clifford, who emphasizes that any participant/observer must address the issue of cultural representation directly, recognizing that any interpretation of a place or event is contestable and contingent on the researcher's beliefs, values, and preferences.[35] I am aware that resettlement personnel invited me to some events and not to others, and that the set of refugee-related organizations that I contacted are not representative of all of the others. My goal in observing or participating in these events was not to predict or provide generalizations about the behavior of any certain group or culture but rather to gain context for my project with attention to detail and meaning.[36]

This book is divided into four chapters, followed by a brief conclusion: Chapter 1 investigates the ways refugees interpret the U.S. media that they encounter long before their arrival in the United States and how they may understand these media as representations or distortions of the reality of life in the United States. Moreover, the first chapter considers how these media may affect refugees' decisions to apply for resettlement to the United States and any apprehension or anticipation related to those decisions. In chapter 2, the narrators discuss the types of digital, print, and video media they were given during the weeks and months leading up to their relocation, in United Nations' mandated pre-departure cultural orientations, and/or in personal preparations for resettlement. I analyze the ways this new knowledge informs refugees' move to the United States by providing detailed analysis of the most widely used pre-departure orientation text, titled, *Welcome to the United States: A Guidebook for Refugees*, and by chronicling and analyzing the media that refugees may encounter outside of these orientations in personal preparations for their relocation. In the third chapter, I inquire into the realm of learning and experience by concentrating on refugees' first days in the United States. Specifically, because refugees carry impressions and memories of pre-arrival media with them into the United States, chapter 3 provides instances in which the narrators compare what they learned in pre-arrival media encounters about the United States to the reality of their experiences upon resettlement. This chapter also discusses refugees' acquisition of media technology after their arrival in the United States and the varying degrees of importance this acquisition had for the narrators. Additionally, chapter 3 considers how local resettlement organizations in the United States use print and digital media in an attempt to guide refugees through their first days after relocation and how these post-arrival orientation media represent the United States government, act as a means of standardization, and foster the imposition of governmental control into the realms of health, hygiene, and family. The fourth and final chapter turns to consider the ways refugees use media in processes of ongoing resettlement after they have completed their post-arrival orientations and after their contact with their resettlement agencies begins to wane. Here the narrators interpret instances in which members of their community are portrayed in U.S. media and how these portrayals affect their sense of belonging in the United States or their knowledge about Americans' perceptions of refugees. I undertake a close reading of several such media to reveal how messages regarding belonging and/or nationalism are embedded within the texts' style, language, and format. The conclusion offers a discussion of the implications of this research, recommendations for resettlement personnel, and suggestions for future study. The chronological format in which this work appears attempts to maintain a narrative arc that mimics the sequential manner of the accounts provided by the narrators as well as the chronological progression of refugee resettlement itself.

I believe this work accomplishes several tasks, and the usefulness of each will depend on the readers' expectations and desires. First and foremost, this work provides firsthand accounts from the top four incoming refugee groups as they describe, in their own words, the role of media in the progression and trials of resettlement. The narratives work to undercut the perception—evident across U.S. news and entertainment media—of refugees as a faceless wave of helpless outcasts by demonstrating the ways they constantly employ agency and determination even in the midst of forced migration to critically engage their new home. This work challenges those who believe that all refugees wish to come to the United States or that they are all satisfied once they arrive.

This work reveals the differences that exist within the refugee community in terms of its range of interests in and uses of media, contentedness with life after resettlement, willingness to enculturate, and multiple other social and personal variables. Moreover, this book allows for a consideration of the ways popular media—such as films, television shows, or newspaper articles—may inform refugees' expectations about a future destination and, in turn, how these expectations impact refugees' integration into U.S. cultures after their arrival. In this way, this book provides a space for the continued future questioning of media's (in)ability to affect a group of people in a particular way and for a consideration of the multitude of responses a single piece of media may incite in a group whose members share some external circumstances in common. Indeed, an exploration of refugees' media encounters may inform current popular and scholarly knowledge about intercultural integration and the role of media in transnational migration more generally. Finally, this book questions the benefits and detriments of government deprivatization in refugees' lives by offering narrators' responses to the multiple criteria for success laid out in government media. It paves the way for continued future study of the multiple kinds of government media produced for and disseminated to immigrants, both voluntary and forced.

This project reflects a slice in time. Individuals from other parts of the world have already begun to surpass the groups included here in numbers of incoming refugees. Moreover, advances in the international availability and affordability of media technologies may render obsolete some of the kinds of media I discuss in the coming pages. As a result of the unpredictability of war, famine, natural disasters, governmental regulations, and economics, refugee resettlement will always be subject to unforeseen fluctuations. Thus, the reader should not consider the project contained in these pages a long-standing, determinate statement on the welfare of refugees in the United States, but rather a partial, temporal view into the ways seventy-four refugees described their interactions with media throughout their resettlement. While these seventy-four narratives represent just a fraction of the current refugee population in the United States, their significance should not be minimized. These voices reveal the hope, fear, curiosity, and frustration that refugees' encounters with media provoke and open a view into the fascinating intersection of media and resettlement.

When I set out on this project in January 2013, I simply wanted to understand more about how incoming refugees' knowledge about the culture, norms, and values of their eventual U.S. destinations were formed and negotiated through engagements with media during the relocation process. But as I met with and talked to refugees in New York, California, Texas, and Pennsylvania, I slowly came to see the complexity of my question. This book is the result of asking questions with surprising answers. It is the manifestation of a pursuit driven by curiosity, determination, and some very patient refugees. Along the way, my understanding of the potential and limitations of media has been, in turn, questioned, dismantled, rebuilt, and negotiated. I don't suppose that the view into refugees use of media that this book provides will make the plight of forced migrants any less precarious, but I do suppose that by listening to the voices included here, readers may gain a view into the powers that act on resettlement from all sides, as well as the determined creative agency refugees must summon to withstand the dire process of resettlement.

Notes

1 The International Organization for Migration (IOM) defines forced migration as migration "in which an element of coercion exists, including threats to life and livelihood, whether arising from natural or man-made causes" (See http://www.iom.int/cms/en/sites/iom/home/about-migration/key-migration-terms-1.html#Forced-migration). While refugees are sometimes referred to as "involuntary migrants" in popular and scholarly discourse, some have charged that this term does not allow for a recognition of refugees' agency or desire to leave their homes when those homes are under threat from unwanted political, social, or natural forces (see, for example, Alden Speare, "The Relevance of Models of Internal Migration for the Study of International Migration, in G. Tapinos, ed., *International Migration: Proceedings of a Seminar on Demographic Research in Relation to International Migration* (Buenos Aires: CICRED, 1974); Samir Amin, *Modern Migrations in Western Africa* (London: Oxford University Press, 1974); and William Peterson, "A General Typology of Migration," *American Sociological Review* 23, no. 3 (1958): 256–66. This book will provide multiple examples of the varying degrees of choice present in refugee migration, and supports the IOM's suggestion that "Population mobility is probably best viewed as being arranged along a continuum ranging from totally voluntary migration, in which the choice and will of the migrants is the overwhelmingly decisive element encouraging people to move, to totally forced migration, where the migrants are faced with death if they remain in their present place of residence." Graeme Hugo, *Migration, Development and Environment* (Geneva: International Organization for Migration, 2008): 16.

2 This sequential organization also mimics a framework frequently employed in the United Nations High Commissioner for Refugees' own reports of refugee resettlement. For example, see Laura Hammond, "History, Overview, Trends and Issues in Major Somali Refugee Displacements in the Near Region," *New Issues in Refugee Research* (Geneva: United Nations Refugee Agency, 2014, Research Paper No. 268 (1-19)); Christine Goodall, "Moving Together: Involuntary Movement and the Universal Dynamics of Moving, Meeting and Mixing," *New Issues in Refugee Research* (Geneva: United Nations Refugee Agency, 2013, Research Paper No. 262 (1-31)); and Ann Evans Barnes, "Realizing Protection Space for Iraqi Refugees: UNHCR in Syria, Jordan and Lebanon," *New Issues in Refugee Research* (Geneva: United Nations Refugee Agency, 2009, Research Paper No. 167 (1-34)).

3 See Toby Miller, *Cultural Citizenship: Cosmopolitanism, Consumerism, and Television in a Neoliberal Age* (Philadelphia: Temple University Press, 2006).

4 See Andrew R. Heinze, *Adapting to Abundance: Jewish Immigrants, Mass Consumption, and the Search for American Identity* (New York: Columbia University Press, 1990).

5 See, for example, Youna Kim, *Transnational Migration, Media and Identity of Asian Women: Diasporic Daughters* (New York: Routledge, 2011); Myria Georgiou, "Media and the City: Making Sense of Place," *International Journal of Media and Cultural Politics* 6, no. 3 (2011): 343–50; Regina Branton and Johanna Dunaway, "English- and Spanish-Language Media Coverage of Immigration: A Comparative Analysis," *Social Science Quarterly* 89, no. 4 (2008): 1006–22; Jonathan Corpus Ong, "Watching the Nation, Singing the Nation: London-Based Filipino Migrants' Identity Constructions in News and Karaoke Practices," *Communication, Culture & Critique* 2, no. 2 (2009): 160–81; Christine M. Du Bois, *Images of West Indian Immigrants in Mass Media: The Struggle for a Positive Ethnic Reputation* (New York: LFB Scholarly Publishing LLC, 2004); Rita J.

Simon, *Public Opinion and the Immigrant: Print Media Coverage, 1880–1980* (Lexington, MA: Lexington Books, 1985); and Athanasia Batziou, *Picturing Immigration: Photojournalistic Representation of Immigrants in Greek and Spanish Press* (Bristol, UK: Intellect, 2011).
6. Tek Rimal, interview by Sarah Bishop, Pittsburgh, March 18, 2013, archived at the Schlesinger Library at Harvard University.
7. Burma is also known as Myanmar. For the sake of consistency, and alignment with my narrators' preference, I will refer to this nation throughout this work as Burma.
8. At the University of Pittsburgh, oral histories are excluded from IRB oversight as outlined in a 2004 agreement between the IRB and Pitt's Communication Department. In light of this exclusion, my own research methods follow the "Principles and Best Practices of the Oral History Association" (2009), http://www.oralhistory.org/about/principles-and-practices/.
9. U.S. Department of State; Bureau of Population, Refugees, and Migration (PRM); Worldwide Refugee Admissions Processing System (WRAPS). "Annual Flow Report" (2012): 4, accessed June 1, 2013, http://www.dhs.gov/sites/default/files/publications/ois_rfa_fr_2012.pdf.
10. "Principles and Best Practices," Oral History Association, http://www.oralhistory.org/about/principles-and-practices/#intro.
11. Emphasis original. Sherna Gluck, "What's So Special about Women?: Women's Oral History," *Frontiers: A Journal of Women Studies* 2, no. 2 (1977): 3.
12. "About OHA," Oral History Association, accessed March 4, 2013, http://www.oralhistory.org/about/.
13. Alistair Thomson, "Four Paradigm Transformations in Oral History," *Oral History Review* 34, no. 1 (2007): 49.
14. Alessandro Portelli, "The Peculiarities of Oral History," *History Workshop*, 12 (1981): 105.
15. Ibid., 103.
16. Thomson, "Four Paradigm Transformations," 57.
17. Katharine Borland, "'That's Not What I Said': Interpretive Conflict in Oral Narrative Research," in *Women's Words: The Feminist Practice of Oral History*, eds. Sherna Berger Gluck and Daphne Patai (New York: Routledge, 1991), 63.
18. Roland Barthes, *Image, Music, Text* (New York: Hill and Wang, 1978), 20.
19. David Harvey, *The Condition of Postmodernity: An Enquiry into the Origins of Cultural Change* (Hoboken, NJ: Wiley-Blackwell, 1991), 46.
20. Ibid., 53.
21. See the deed of gift in Appendix A.
22. U.S. Department of State, Bureau of Population, Refugees, and Migration (PRM), Worldwide Refugee Admissions Processing System (WRAPS), accessed on April 13, 2013, http://www.dhs.gov/sites/default/files/publications/ois_rfa_fr_2012.pdf, 1, 4.
23. Ibid., 3.
24. "Refugee Arrival Data," U.S. Department of Health and Human Services, accessed on April 13, 2013, http://www.acf.hhs.gov/programs/orr/resource/refugee-arrival-data.
25. http://www.mediascribe.us/
26. According to the Department of Homeland Security, Texas, California, New York, and Pennsylvania were the four leading states of residence of refugees admitted to the United States in FY 2012. See Table 0.3.

27. Kheir Mugwaneza at Northern Area Ministries in Pittsburgh, Marc Fallon at CAMBA in New York City, Lisa Guitguit at YMCA Houston, and Lilian Alba at the International Institute of Los Angeles.
28. Daniel C. Martin and James E. Yankay, "Annual Report: Refugees and Asylees 2012," Department of Homeland Security, accessed on April 13, 2013, http://www.dhs.gov/sites/default/files/publications/ois_rfa_fr_2012.pdf. Note: This Department of Homeland Security report cites "U.S. Department of State, Bureau of Population, Refugees, and Migration (PRM), Worldwide Refugee Admissions Processing System (WRAPS)" for its incoming refugee statistics. However, minor unexplained discrepancies exist in the number of refugee arrivals by state between the Department of Homeland Security report and the annual statistics released by the Department of State. In each category, the discrepancy is less than ten individuals. For example, the Department of State reported 5,173 incoming refugees to California in FY 2012, while the Department of Homeland Security reported only 5,167. The Department of State's refugee arrival data for fiscal years 2010, 2011, and 2012 can be found at http://www.acf.hhs.gov/programs/orr/resource/refugee-arrival-data.
29. Sonja K. Foss, *Rhetorical Criticism: Exploration & Practice* (Long Grove, IL: Waveland Press, 2004).
30. Ibid., 239.
31. See, for example, Teun Adrianus van Dijk, *News Analysis: Case Studies of International and National News in the Press* (Hillsdale, NJ: L. Erlbaum, 1987); Philip Wander, "The Rhetoric of American Foreign Policy," *Quarterly Journal of Speech* 70 no. 4 (1984): 339–61; Michael McGee, "In Search of 'The People': A Rhetorical Alternative," *Quarterly Journal of Speech* 61 no. 3 (1975): 235–49; Raymie E. McKerrow, "Critical Rhetoric: Theory and Praxis," *Communication Monographs* 56, no. 2 (1989): 91–111; Janice Hocker Rushing, "Power, Other, and Spirit in Cultural Texts," *Western Journal of Communication* 57, no. 2 (1993): 159; Lawrence Grossberg, "Marxist Dialectics and Rhetorical Criticism," *Quarterly Journal of Speech* 65, no. 3 (1979): 235–49; and Celeste M. Condit, "The Rhetorical Limits of Polysemy," *Critical Studies in Mass Communication* 6, no. 2 (1989): 103–22.
32. See Sara McKinnon, "Rhetorical Dimensions of Forced Migration" and Don Waisanen, "Bordering Populism in Immigration Activism: Outlaw–Civic Discourse in a (Counter)Public," *Communication Monographs* 79, no. 2 (2012): 232–55.
33. Michael Billig, "The Argumentative Nature of Holding Strong Views: A Case Study," *European Journal Of Social Psychology* 19, no. 3 (1989): 204.
34. For more on participant observation methodology, see Yvonna S. Lincoln and Egon G. Guba, *The Constructivist Credo* (Walnut Creek, CA: Left Coast Press, 2013) and Kathleen Musante DeWalt and Billie R. DeWalt, *Participant Observation: A Guide for Fieldworkers* (Lanham, MD: Rowman & Littlefield, 2011).
35. James Clifford, "Introduction: Partial Truths," in *Writing Culture: The Poetics and Politics of Ethnography*, eds. James Clifford, George E. Marcus, and Kim Fortun (Berkeley: University of California Press, 1986).
36. For a detailed description of the ways in which interpretive research varies from social science or critical research, see Judith N. Martin and Thomas K. Nakayama, *Intercultural Communication in Contexts* (Boston: McGraw-Hill, 2007).

1
REFUGEES AS AUDIENCES OF U.S. MEDIA IN PRE-ARRIVAL CONTEXTS

Sancha Rai remembers seeing *The Pursuit of Happyness* (2006), an American film about a man who loses his job, home, and wife after making a poor business decision, while living as a refugee in the city of Dharan in southeastern Nepal shortly before he was resettled to the United States:[1]

> From that movie I learned the reality of the ordinary people in the U.S. If you don't pay rent you'll be evicted from [your] house and divorce is common. Also I learned that when people are lonely, there won't be another person in the neighborhood to help you.[2]

Though Sancha saw this film before he became aware that he would be resettled to the United States, *The Pursuit of Happyness* served as an introductory, informal education about life on the other side of the world.

Sancha was born in 1974 in the Samtse district of southern Bhutan. At sixteen, he was forced to leave his home and resettle in 1990 in the Khudunabari refugee camp in Nepal when the Bhutanese government began evicting persons of Nepali origin from Bhutan during a widespread implementation of the Bhutanese Citizenship Act of 1985. At the camp, Sancha was assigned to a hut that included a small space for cooking and eating and a place to sleep. Because education beyond grade ten was not available in the camp, Sancha received permission in 1997 from the government of Nepal and the United Nations High Commissioner for Refugees (UNHCR) to leave Khudunabari and complete grades eleven and twelve at a Nepali school a couple of hours away.[3] Sancha told me, "I was in the leave-or-take situation—either stay in the refugee camp or do something to pursue education further." To manage his living expenses during this time, Sancha found work as an assistant teacher in a private school. After finishing grade twelve, and while continuing to work full time, he completed bachelor degrees in geography and English literature, as well as a master's degree in sociology from Tribhuvan University in Nepal. Sancha's formal education at Tribhuvan allowed him to become fluent in English and to read the works of several American scholars.

In 2006, former head of the U.S. Department of State's Bureau of Population, Refugees, and Migration Ellen Sauerbrey announced the U.S. government's willingness to resettle 60,000 of the approximately 106,000 refugees who were currently living in the Nepal camps.[4] When he was approved for resettlement in the United States, Sancha took part in a five-day, pre-departure cultural orientation led by the International Organization for Migration (IOM). IOM describes the key objectives of their cultural orientations for refugees in Nepal as being threefold: to provide factual information about the countries where the refugees may be settled, to teach practical skills necessary for succeeding in these new locations, and to explore refugees' attitudes having to do with family roles, values, and proactivity about the future.[5] In addition to this orientation, Sancha also relied on the informal education he received from films he saw in Nepal, such as *The Pursuit of Happyness*.[6] Sancha watched *The Pursuit of Happyness* in his apartment in Dharan after borrowing the DVD from a friend who, he remembers, "thought this could be one good resource to learn the American society." Sancha believes that this film, as well as other films about America that he saw in Nepal—including *Journey from the Fall* and *Black Hawk Down*—helped him to form a picture of what U.S. life was like.[7] Watching these films, Sancha participated in a form of enculturation, or, the process by which individuals intentionally or unintentionally begin to understand and become familiar with the values, norms, behaviors, and identities of a culture other than the one into which they were born.

Enculturation differs from and complicates the idea of *acculturation*, or, the process by which one sets aside facets of a former culture while learning and accepting a new cultural context.[8] Enculturation suggests that cultural learning is not one-directional and that any individual may choose to accept, resist, question, or deny certain facets of a new culture, while simultaneously maintaining, negotiating, or blending his or her former culture into a new context.[9] Scholars in the fields of education, psychology, and sociology have long been familiar with the many manifestations of enculturation that occur during cultural interactions one encounters after physically arriving within a new cultural context,[10] but Sancha's experience reveals something different: His enculturation into American values, norms, and behaviors began long before he arrived in the United States as the result of seeing U.S. media—especially films—that portrayed some parts of U.S. life. The range of information Sancha managed to learn from these films testifies to the complexity of the processes of enculturation that may occur during interactions with digital, video, sound, or print media from an unfamiliar place.

Sancha believes that the films he saw taught him the "basic social etiquette" of Americans and helped him become familiar with some of the hardships they face if they do not have enough money. Still, the films that had such an impact on Sancha were often misleading and certainly not comprehensive in describing U.S. life; indeed, they only provided a partial picture. For example, these media failed to inform him that in Pennsylvania, leaves fall from the trees during winter. As his plane landed in Scranton in early 2009, Sancha looked out the window and thought, "The trees are dying out! This place is soon going to turn into desert."

Today, four years after his arrival in the United States, Sancha works as a case manager in the Refugee Resettlement Office of Jewish Family and Children's Services (JFCS) in Pittsburgh, Pennsylvania, where he spends each day addressing the multitudinous needs of newly arrived refugees—many of whom fled the same oppression his own family experienced. From his well-lit, paper-crowded office in Pittsburgh, Sancha takes calls from two different phones that seem to ring so often it is hard to imagine how one could find time to do anything other than answer them. Most days Sancha manages to take these calls while simultaneously translating important documents for Nepali clients, arranging airport pickups for new refugee arrivals, planning the curriculum for the "Happy Family" marriage and communication seminar he teaches at JFCS, and, sometimes, sitting down with curious, inconveniencing researchers.

I met Sancha in his office for the first time on January 29, 2013 and was somewhat surprised when he quickly volunteered to set aside what I assume would have been a very busy afternoon the following week to talk with me so that I could ask him more questions about his experiences living in Bhutan, Nepal, and Pennsylvania and about the role films and other U.S. media played in his relocation. A couple of weeks after our second meeting, Sancha invited me to his home to meet his family and interview his sister, Kumari, and his sister-in-law, Buddhi. The following month, I met Sancha at one of the weekly JFCS orientations for new Bhutanese refugee arrivals led by an English-speaking AmeriCorps volunteer in downtown Pittsburgh, where he acted in turn as a teacher, translator, facilitator, and driver. Four years after his own relocation, Sancha has become a walking encyclopedia of refugee challenges and resources. Like most refugees arriving in the United States from Nepal, Sancha learned the minutiae of this necessary knowledge not through formal training but, instead, through the arduous day-to-day process of learning through experience and informal education.

The films that Sancha watched before relocating to the United States remained in his memory after his arrival. A few days after his family settled in Scranton, Pennsylvania, Sancha's fifteen-month-old son started choking during the night. Sancha explained that because he had seen American films and attended the compulsory cultural orientation for five days in Nepal,

> I knew there is 911 service, ER service, but [I didn't have a] telephone or any phone services available and it was middle of the night. Who could

help me to call 911? I know it is not okay to disturb any people, but at that time, I thought if there is a question of life and death, it is okay to knock [at some] body's apartment.

Films also helped Sancha understand his financial situation during his first couple of weeks in the United States. "I was hopeful that my resettlement agency would pay rent at least for two, three months or at least until I get a job," he explained to me. "But when I had been to resettlement agency's office on May 3rd or 4th, they asked me whether I paid rent or not. And I didn't believe my ears because that is something unexpected. It was like nightmare," he recalled. "Really, at that time, I was frustrated. Because, same thing came in my mind, you know like in *Pursuit of Happyness*—people get evicted from home if you don't pay rent." This was the second time Sancha mentioned the film he saw in Dharan. The first time he mentioned this film, it seemed clear that Sancha had utilized it to construct some expectations about what his life in the United States might be like. But when he alluded to *The Pursuit of Happyness* again to describe the financial trouble he experienced in Scranton, Sancha revealed something more: His memories of this film continued to serve him as a way to process or interpret his experiences in the United States and to anticipate what might happen to him should he fail to manage what was required of him. I wanted clarification about the function of this film in his life and asked Sancha whether he found, after arriving in the United States, that the information he learned from *The Pursuit of Happyness* seemed correct. He replied, "Ahh, very much true, yeah, very much true." Sancha believes this film showed him that the United States is an individualistic culture, one where "if you have money, you have everything; if not, [it's] very tough to get food and shelter." *The Pursuit of Happyness* correctly reveals, according to Sancha, that "life in America is not that easy."

Sancha's narrative provides compelling motivation to take a closer look at the ways refugees may interpret particular types of media that they encounter before their relocation and how these media might influence refugees' expectations about the acceptance, assistance, or challenges they may face upon their arrival in the United States. To understand how a refugee might use popular U.S. media as a means for enculturation, or as a kind of informal education about life in the United States, one must ask, what exactly is it possible to learn through media and what are the implications of this kind of learning? To answer these questions thoroughly demands a consideration that any single person's migration process involves much more time than it takes to fly from one country to another. Indeed, the processes of migration begin long before an individual boards a plane for his or her new home and do not end when he or she arrives.

For this reason, this chapter elucidates the ways refugees' encounters with U.S. media during a "pre-relocation" phase reveal both the ability and limitations of learning through digital, video, sound, and print media. Because of the diversity of refugees' experiences prior to their resettlement in the United States, it is necessary for me to explain that I identify pre-arrival media encounters as those that occur before refugees physically relocate to the United States. For further clarity, I have divided my discussion of pre-arrival media encounters into two parts. First, in this chapter, I will draw from refugees' memories of the U.S. media that they watched, heard, or read before the United Nations High Commissioner of Refugees approved them for resettlement in the United States. In the next chapter, refugees from Bhutan, Burma, Iraq, and Somalia will discuss the second stage of pre-arrival media encounters, or those that occur after refugees apply for resettlement to the United States, either during formal cultural orientations that typically take place sometime during the last few months preceding refugees' resettlement or in refugees' personal preparations before their departure date.[11]

While this division between the two "stages" of pre-arrival media is somewhat arbitrary, it testifies to the reality that the effects of pre-arrival media are long-lasting; after their resettlement, refugees may evoke or employ an interpretation of a piece of media that they encountered even many years ago. Indeed, by considering both media that refugees may have encountered before they were displaced, as well as the media refugees saw or heard or listened to during any interim stay in a secondary location prior to their resettlement in the United States, one can gain a fuller view of the ways different types of international media may be utilized to greater or lesser extents during certain periods of a refugee's life and also how refugees may recall certain films, songs, texts, or images at multiple points throughout the migration process in order to make sense of their experiences.

Sahro Nor, a Somali refugee, described to me one manifestation of the nuanced manner in which individuals may intentionally or unintentionally store away the memory of U.S. media seen before their arrival in the United States to be used for the interpretation of their experiences after their relocation. Sahro grew up in Mogadishu, the coastal capital of Somalia, in a family of sixteen girls. She married a wealthy man and lived in a beautiful home in Mogadishu where several servants helped her with daily household tasks. When the effects of the Somali Civil War reached too close to home, Sahro and her family fled to a refugee camp in Kenya, where they lived for one year and three months before relocating to San Diego in 1994. Sahro fondly remembers her life in Mogadishu, where she and her husband entertained guests frequently and often had friends and family over for evenings spent watching films. She recalled,

> Before eighties, we go to the cinema. And then after eighties, we get the cassette, and DVD, and that stuff, so we watch—we go to the rental place, and we rented the movie, and we coming home, and we watch it . . . Family or friend, or always we have a couple, group. We never watch movie one single person. Usually mother and father and children, which is the

people who working in the house, maids, family, friends . . . we together watching the TV.[12]

Sahro had a difficult time remembering the names of the U.S. movies she saw before she was displaced, but she remembers vividly some of the images she saw and how they made her feel. Describing the U.S. Westerns she saw in Mogadishu, Sahro recalled,

> It's windy, and the wind whistling, and they have hat, and they have horse . . . Some of them cowboy. Some of them they stole, the kill or something, they manage to get the ladies, like. I think when I see and hear the Halloween time, the scary movie, they always—you see someone in a vampire, or they bite the people here, and then blood and that stuff. So watching that kind of movie, scary . . . And when we watched the movies, we see always the killer movie, the something you don't like it, the somebody—somebody killing, the guy, like, get the woman, like nicely, and while when he doing everything, then he killing her, cutting her breasts, or something like that.

I assumed that the gruesome nature of these films influenced Sahro's beliefs about U.S. culture in some way and asked her whether this was the case. Her answer surprised me.

> Really that time, because I'm not thinking I'm going to go America, so I didn't feel any feeling of that. But when I came, even when I in the processing of this and you go to America, even that I didn't remember the movie I watch. But when I came America, first night when I see the guy who dig in the trash, I say, "Oh, my goodness! The people you watch in movies—that kind of people—long hair." So that I'm thinking a lot. But when I'm processing, when I'm moving that time, no picture at all in America. Just, it's a big country, nice country; that's it . . . In the morning I see the white guy, blue eyes, digging in the trash, get in some cans, and that's that. I say, "Oh, my goodness! The people who belong to here, they're doing that stuff!" And you come from Africa, you never seen someone who dig in the trash. Oh, my goodness—maybe the people, the reason they did bring you here, it's not to get a life. Maybe they cut your organ, and sell it!

Sahro's narrative is revealing of the potential of media's long-standing and nuanced effects; when she saw U.S. films in Somalia, they did not influence her ideas about the United States, because she did not yet know she would need to move there. Even during her pre-departure processing and during her physical relocation to the United States, as she clearly states earlier, Sahro did not remember the American films she had seen in Somalia. But the "white guy, blue eyes, digging in the trash" she encountered on her first morning in the United States served as a trigger, drawing the memory of the frightening scenes from American films she had seen years before back into her mind and causing her to fear for her life.

By taking the time to consider narratives such as the one Sahro describes here, where media encounters that occur even several years before arrival in the United States clearly and significantly affect refugees' post-arrival beliefs and expectations, one may better understand the extent of the relationship between media and enculturation and gain a fuller grasp of the long-term effects of migrants' encounters with pre-arrival international media. Still, the contexts in which refugees live before their arrival in the United States vary greatly, and so it is not possible to talk about this "pre-arrival phase" as monolithic. Many of the refugees I interviewed—especially from Bhutan, Burma, and Somalia—lived for several years or even decades in refugee camps in interim countries after their original displacement and before arriving in the United States. In these camps, the refugees had varying access to media. Some camps, such as Khudunabari in Nepal, exist in relatively safe areas and allow refugees to come and go with permission. Indeed, several of the Bhutanese refugees I interviewed, such as Sancha, reported receiving approval to leave their refugee camps and, as a result, gained fairly extensive access to U.S. media in Nepali cities. For other groups of refugees, such as those from Burma, who have been living in nine camps along the western border of Thailand since the 1980s, access to media outside the camps is not an option. Thai camps are typically closed, and the Thai government considers Burmese refugees living outside of them as illegal aliens subject to arrest and deportation. Thus for most refugees who have fled Burma, the ability to encounter media about the United States before their cultural orientation is solely dependent on the resources available inside the refugee camps.

As a refugee encounters mediated representations of the United States, s/he may begin to form an opinion about what s/he has seen and create an imagined picture of the United States as a whole from even a few books, films, or photographs of the United States. As the narrators in this chapter reveal, media provide refugees fodder for opinion making about multiple aspects of American culture, including, but not limited to, romantic relationships, parenting styles, work, education, gender roles, religion, food, styles of housing, leisure, transportation, health care, conflict management, and U.S. history. Generally speaking, the more mediated depictions of U.S. life the narrators I interviewed had encountered before their arrival in the United States, the more complete view they believed they had of U.S. life and, in some cases, as the following chapters will reveal, the more their expectations clashed with the reality they found upon their arrival to their U.S. destinations.

Some refugees have memories of seeing media about the U.S. before they fled or were driven from their homes. But thousands of other refugees, like thirty-year-old Kler Htoo, whose family fled Burma and whom I interviewed in Buffalo, New York, were born as refugees and lived in refugee camps from the time of their birth until their resettlement in the United States.[13] For these individuals, any access to media about the outside world is particularly impacting, as it may be one of very few sources of information about life beyond the refugee camp that the residents encounter. In Dadaab, a massive refugee camp currently housing over four hundred thousand Somalis in eastern Kenya, international nonprofit groups like Internews have recognized the significance of media to refugees and have taken great pains to make media about the outside world available to residents. Internews established a radio broadcasting system in Dadaab to transmit both camp-specific and world news, including current U.S. events, and to provide information regarding resettlement. At a recent teleconference with members of a United Nations panel on promoting humanitarian innovation, Mohamed Bashir Sheik, one of Internews's refugee journalists living in Dadaab, explained why radio proves an effective means of communication:

> I am a blogger, and have been blogging for a number of years, but the problem that I had was that people in the camps could not read my stories. I would write stories for them . . . but the people in my own community could not read them—either because they were illiterate or because they could not access them. With the radio you can reach everyone in the camps; everyone will listen. With a computer, some will see it but most will not. It is as simple as that.[14]

Indeed, any consideration of the role of media in refugees' lives must consider not only what kinds of media are available in particular contexts but also whether potential audiences have the knowledge and resources they need to access available media.

Some refugee groups, such as Iraqis, may not spend any time at all in refugee camps before their cultural orientation. As of April 2013, about eighty-four thousand Iraqi refugees have been resettled in the United States.[15] Most of the Iraqis I interviewed for this project had spent time living independently or with friends or family in interim countries such as Jordan or Syria after they fled their homes and before they arrived in the United States.[16] While some refugees have comparatively less access to media during their interim stay in a secondary country and before their resettlement in the United States, for Iraqis, this interim location may provide more access to international media than was previously available. For example, Zahraa Eskander, an Iraqi refugee I interviewed in Los Angeles, remembered seeing only U.S. films and no U.S. television in her hometown in Iraq.[17] But during the three years that she and her family spent living in Jordan after fleeing Baghdad because of threats to her husband's life, Zahraa had ample access to both U.S. television and film.

Though their experiences varied greatly in the years leading up to their resettlement in the United States, the refugees I interviewed for this project consistently testified to the idea that audiences may utilize media for all kinds of purposes other than those the media's author may have intended. This active role of the audience has been well noted in the existing work of notable media studies scholars such as John Fiske, Don Kulick, Margaret Willson, and Radhika Parameswaran.[18] Beyond watching for simple entertainment, the refugees in this study recognized media as a way to learn about aspects of life in the United States ranging from proper dating behavior, to how to speak to authorities, the number of people who typically live in a home, the American criminal justice system, and the rules of American sports. By gaining understanding about the ways media works in refugees' lives as an informal education about life in the United States, one can better understand both media's power to depict certain versions of reality and the potentially limited sources of information that are available to migrants as they seek to make sense of a future home. Studying the memories that refugees from Bhutan, Burma, Iraq, and Somalia have about their encounters with pre-arrival, American-produced popular media such as films, books, radio, and television may allow one to become more acutely aware of how these experiences interface with more formal modes of education pertaining to the United States—such as learning about American history in elementary school—and to consider some of the implications of extracurricular enculturation through media.

Gaining Access to U.S. Media

Refugees are a unique group of immigrants, and their pre-arrival circumstances hold much sway over the means through which they engage in cultural learning. As a result of the nature of their migration, refugees may have less control than voluntary migrants over the amount and type of information they receive about their location of future resettlement. A few of the Bhutanese and Somali refugees I interviewed even told me that they had seen no U.S. media and knew absolutely nothing about the United States before they began their UNHCR-mandated cultural orientations.[19] But these cases were unusual; the vast majority of narrators I spoke with testified to having encountered some kind of American-produced popular media before their arrival, and even those who claimed to know nothing about America, such as one Bhutanese refugee named Nirmala Khanal, sometimes had relatives who remembered seeing, reading, or hearing varying amounts of U.S. media.[20] For instance, Nirmala's son, Govinda, who lived in the same refugee camp as his mother from the time he was five to when he was old enough to relocate outside the camp for college, and who worked as my interpreter during my time interviewing refugees in Buffalo, reported seeing U.S. media ranging from the 1974 film *The Great Gatsby* to the *Ellen DeGeneres Show*, reading the play *Cat on a Hot Tin Roof* and a biography of Abraham Lincoln, and listening to radio programs about the United States before his arrival in the United States.[21] When I asked Govinda how it happened that he encountered so much media before his relocation when his mother encountered none at all, he explained,

> I saw American movies while I was staying away from my mother. That time I was renting room to attend my college because there were no colleges near refugee camp. Another [reason] that my mother didn't see American movie [is] because of education too. I saw American movies while I was in college. In the [movies], I found a different society than mine. The movies were more advanced in technology and in performance. It looks like people were more open and advanced in scientific invention, and rich too. I saw American movies with my friends. I decided to watch as I was eager to learn about America and American people.[22]

Although his mother did not mention it, Govinda remembers that a few people did have televisions and VHS players in the refugee camp and would sometimes get access to American movies, including the 1997 blockbuster, *Titanic*, that they would watch with a group.[23] Govinda also recalled hearing the music of Michael Jackson and Justin Bieber in the Nepali refugee camp. The differences between Govinda and Nirmala's memories about U.S. media reveal the diversity that exists even within groups who arrive in the United States from the same nation, refugee camp, or family. Moreover, these narratives reveal that in some cases, media about the United States was nonetheless present even in contexts wherein some of the narrators were not aware.

Some of the refugees I spoke with remembered living in areas where governmental restrictions or sanctions limited the availability of media. Even in these cases, many of the narrators managed to gain access to some U.S. media before their arrival in the United States. For example, Shiraz Minasaqen, an Iraqi refugee living in Los Angeles who worked as a jewelry maker near Baghdad before he was forced to flee to Damascus, Syria, after receiving death threats from an unknown extortionist, encountered stern governmental restrictions on media.[24] Nonetheless, Shiraz watched many American films and listened to a good deal of American music from the time he was young. "My favorite actors are Sylvester Stallone and Arnold Schwarzenegger," Shiraz told me. "The best is *The Terminator* and *Rocky*."[25] He explained, "We don't have American televisions in [Iraq]. But we listen to American songs, English songs. I like Lionel Richie, Enrique Iglesias, and Bon Jovi." But when I asked Shiraz if he ever watched American news in Iraq, he answered, "No. There is no[ne]." Shiraz laughed, and continued,

> I can't. Everything about American we can't . . . how will you say it? We can't listen it or wear it, even if it's a t-shirt or everything with American flag or American, you know, words or anything. We can't wear it in there. That

means you are for the Americans, you don't love your country, you know? It's not that they—They're thinking in their mind, that it's our enemies, you know.

Here Shiraz testifies to a larger phenomenon. As has been especially documented in Middle Eastern countries such as Iraq and Iran, governmental authorities may fear that viewing media from other nations may lead to the dissolution or pollution of one's culture. Indeed, in unstable political environments, anxious concerns regarding the relationship of media to cultural imperialism are well documented in the work of scholars such as Marwan Kraidy, Don Kulick, and Margaret Willson.[26] One notable manifestation of this concern existed in Iraq in the years before 2003, when Saddam Hussain's Ba'ath party strictly controlled and limited Internet in Iraq and banned satellite dishes so that citizens could not gain access to unapproved television channels or websites. Jala Yaqo, an Iraqi refugee who fled Iraq for Syria in 2008 where he lived for four and a half years before he was resettled to San Diego, remembers the days of those restrictions well. When I asked Jala if he had access to any U.S. media before he was displaced from Iraq, he answered,

Just the movies that we see in the home, or we have to go to the cinema. There was no Internet connection in my country at that time, because Saddam prevented people from getting Internet. In the media in my country, I was watching that they say [the United States is an] imperialist country and they are against [Iraqi] people, in the newspaper they were saying that America is not a good country—[that] it intervened in another country's situation.[27]

By limiting access to U.S. media, international governments may, as Jala described, retain more control over what kinds of messages residents hear regarding the United States and maintain nationalist ideologies through the negative representation of unwanted outside influences.

Today there are comparatively more international television and radio stations in Iraq and more opportunities to access international media than were available to Jala and Shiraz. However, the Iraq Communications and Media Commission still regulates what may or may not be broadcasted through the granting of mandatory media licenses. While this practice works to control which kinds of television and radio Iraqis can access, a thriving market of pirated films and bootlegged music make procuring U.S. blockbuster films and popular music fairly easy for those with monetary means who live near Iraq's urban areas.[28] For example, on a single stretch of Al-Rubae Street in eastern Baghdad, near Jala's former home, shops selling pirated copies of U.S. DVDs and CDs line the sidewalks.[29] While many of the Iraqis I spoke with did not recall seeing U.S. television or hearing American songs on the radio before moving to the United States, like Shiraz and Jala, they had seen many U.S. films and were familiar with U.S. popular music.

Sometimes restricted access to media occurs as a result of shadowy and possibly related combinations of governmental restrictions and lack of resources. Tek Rimal, a Bhutanese refugee, told me,

> When I was growing up there were no electronic media in our country besides radio. To keep television we were suppose to have license. Also there was no electricity supply in our locality. I think the government did that to avoid people learn[ing] about political activities around the world.[30]

In this case, it is impossible to determine whether the Bhutanese government's desire to keep residents from knowing about international political activities directly resulted in Tek's lack of encounters with U.S. media in Bhutan. Still, Tek's mention of the possible relationship between the two points toward the oft-discussed question of the international cultural effect of—and response to—unwanted U.S. media.[31]

In order to understand the reasoning behind governmental fear of international media's effects, it may be useful to consider a pertinent account that advances an argument about the potential harm media may impose on a culture. Kinley Rinchen, of the Royal University of Bhutan, contributed in 2006 to a compilation of essays on *Media and Public Culture in Bhutan* in which he charged that because of the rise in popularity of and access to Western media in Bhutan, Bhutanese "society gets entrapped and inclined towards a culture which is non-Bhutanese, thereby eroding our own culture and tradition." The following are among the list of "negative effects" that Rinchen identifies as being related to this trend:

> [1] The Bhutanese language, not being supported by the media as anticipated, was found losing its priority within our society. Since whatever they [the audience] do, whether it is to search for information, to communicate, or to chat with friends, relatives or loved ones far away, they need to do it in English. Therefore, without the knowledge of English, they feel handicapped.[32]
>
> [2] Bhutanese traditionally consider someone beautiful based on the nature of the complexion and the shape of the face that is similar to the full moon. However, today emerging from the areas that are prone to media influences, it is usual that the Bhutanese girls and some boys come with all sorts of cosmetic touch-ups on their faces and hair as well . . . The coloring of their face and hair has become very common, which no longer makes them look like Bhutanese.
>
> [3] Since the film stars are more popular than national leaders in the society at large, the audience, specially the youth tend to believe in the behavior of those stars, which most of the time is vile and undesirable.[33]

Richen concludes by calling on the government of Bhutan to "enhance the media censor[ship] that will prohibit the view of certain harmful programmes."[34] This call provides evidence of the belief in the power of international media to affect the beliefs, values, and behaviors of a group to such an extent that governmental censorship may seem the only viable deterrent.

Where there are no governmental restrictions, a lack of reliable electricity in some cities or refugee camps; low levels of literacy and English language proficiency; or few professional, family, or neighborly connections to people with access to media technologies can limit some refugees' ability to see mediated representations of life in the United States before their resettlement. Even in these unfavorable conditions, many refugees find creative ways to gain access to various forms of media. For instance, in the Dadaab refugee camp in Kenya, Mohammed Ahmed Bashir, a Somali refugee, purchased a diesel generator in 2004 with money from remittances sent by his relatives[35] and from selling soda to camp residents. Since then, Bashir has been running a successful electricity supply company in Hagadera, which provides the necessary power for several Internet cafes in the camp.[36]

Megeney Ramazani, a Somali refugee, also lived in Dadaab before she was relocated to the Kakuma refugee camp in Kenya before being resettled in San Diego. Like many of the Somali refugees I interviewed, Megeney does not know what year she was born or how old she was when she was forced to leave Somalia, but she told me that she was already married with children when she arrived at Kakuma. There was no electricity in Kakuma at that time, and Megeney did not know how to read or write, and so there was little opportunity for her to consume media. Still, once a month, Megeney remembers, a truck from the International Organization for Migration (IOM) would drive into Kakuma and show a video about living healthily in the United States after relocation. Megeney explained that though the adults living in the camp did not have time to go watch the film, many kids would run toward the truck when they saw it coming and enjoyed watching. Even though she did not view the footage herself, Megeney seemed to know a lot about the IOM film:

> It will show you, like—it's not about the culture. It's about how you get healthy and all that . . . When we come to America, some people like be bad, like HIV, be bad like high blood pressure, be bad like cancer . . . they were showing . . . how you can survive all that.

After hearing a lengthy description of the video's content, I asked Megeney to confirm again that she had not seen the film. She answered,

> Only the kids saw that one. But you just—you know, the kids when they saw, they all talk about it, you know? When a little kid see something,

they will talk about it, and say, "Oh, we saw this one. We saw this one. It was like this." It's English. You don't understand. And the kids also don't understand, but you know, the way the movie act, you can tell.

Megeney's experience reveals that even refugees who do not have resources such as literacy, wealth, or electricity may be likely to encounter U.S. media—if not firsthand, then by way of another audience member's descriptions before their resettlement to the United States. This phenomenon is a unique manifestation of Elihu Katz's "two-step flow" of communication, wherein individuals encounter and interpret some media and then act as information mediaries to communicate that interpretation to a wider population that forms its opinions based on such interactions.[37]

Habiba Jama, who interpreted my conversation with Megeney and who is also a refugee from Somalia, remembers seeing what sounded like the same IOM film in Kenya.[38] Habiba was nine years old in 2001 when she arrived in Kakuma for a three-year stay before being resettled in the United States, and every month when the IOM truck would arrive with the video, she would go out to watch. I asked Habiba how many times she thought she saw the film. She answered, "Well, I was there almost like three years, and I didn't even miss one time." Habiba told me that the same film was screened every single month, and I asked her, "After you had seen the movie a few times, why did you keep coming back to watch it, if it was the same?" Habiba explained, "It was the same, but you know, as a childhood, it looks fun. You're just walking around, jumping, and all that. You know, when you are a little kid, you can do anything." She remembered that the film would start at 7:00 p.m. and last for about three hours. People would crowd in to sit on the ground around the outdoor screen—Habiba did not want to guess how many people would typically attend, but she knows it was at least more than five hundred. Sometimes the kids would fall asleep watching the film and stay the whole night sleeping by the traveling theatre even after the film was over.

Although it has been about ten years since Habiba saw the IOM film, she was recently able to describe to me in detail some of its content:

> It was about America, how they use a computer, and how they use electricity . . . It just teach me, like, electricity. One night, I saw a guy was fixing, like a handyman, you know, was fixing electricity. And then, it was raining, so the electricity got water, and then this explode, and he get hurt, you know. And then they dial 911, so ambulance will arrive. That's how that was teaching.[39]

Like Megeney, Habiba did not know English when she saw the film and had to interpret the content according to the action that she saw onscreen. In order to understand the significance of this film in Habiba's life, one should consider that because she was too young to attend a pre-departure orientation,[40] the film provided the first mediated representation of the United States that Habiba encountered in her life.

Govinda, fluent in English, translated for me as Laxmi Adhi Kari, a fifty-four-year-old refugee from Bhutan, described another creative solution for gaining access to media amid a challenging lack of resources.[41] Laxmi lived in a refugee camp in Nepal from 1991 to 2009, and although he did not have a television in his own hut, his children found out about a few people who had access to a TV and who would accept a payment of two Nepali rupees[42] from those who wanted to watch an American, or sometimes Indian, film of the television owner's choosing. "It's not the choice of the people," Laxmi remembers. "The people [who own] the TV will [decide] what they want to see." Typically, Laxmi remembers, "fifteen or twenty, sometimes ten" people would gather in the television owner's home to watch, and while he never attended any of the viewings himself, he would sometimes give his children money to participate.[43]

Govinda recalled the same kind of television setup in the refugee camp where he grew up and described how charging money for a film screening was necessary because watching films was only possible if a resident in the refugee camp could gain access to a large cell battery.[44] Because there was no electricity in the residential huts inside the camp,

> They need to take [the battery] to outside the camp to charge [and] to charge this battery they need money, so they charge the people for that . . . People watched American movies. *Titanic*, that I remember, and other were Indian movies, Nepali movies, and serials too.

In refugee camps, where many residents feel as though they are waiting for a resettlement assignment that sometimes seems like it will never arrive, filmed entertainment may be a welcome reprieve.

Like Govinda, Balaram Gurung also fled Bhutan and spent fifteen years living in a Nepali refugee camp. After resettling in Pennsylvania, and until recently, Balaram worked as a case manager at the Northern Area Multi-Service Center (NAMS), a resettlement agency in Pittsburgh. During a conversation I had with Balaram in March 2013 at NAMS, he explained, "I think [the] first English movie that most Bhutanese saw was . . . *Rambo*."[45] Balaram saw the film himself in grade three at a friend's house before his family was displaced and remembers: "In Bhutan, we had posters of Rambo in everyone's house and small postcards. We thought—what is the actor's name? Sylvester. We used to think that his [real] name was Rambo. Only rich people used to have TV . . . and about, I think, 40 to 50 people [would come together to watch *Rambo*] in a house." *Rambo* is one of the U.S. films that seemed particularly memorable for several of the Bhutanese narrators I interviewed; among the others mentioned frequently were *Black Hawk Down, The Pursuit of Happyness, The Great Gatsby, Terminator,* and *Jurassic Park.*[46] But for other Bhutanese narrators, such as Tek Rimal, U.S. films were secondary in significance to extensive interactions with U.S. news and social media.[47] Tek fled from Bhutan to India in 1991 when he was in grade five and was involuntarily driven from India to the Beldangi II Extension refugee camp in Nepal in a dump truck after the Indian government refused to accept some Bhutanese refugees. After completing grade ten in Beldangi II Extension, Tek had the opportunity to move out of the camp to pursue his bachelor of science degree at Tribhuvan University in Nepal, where he had access to both television and the Internet. He remembers,

> when we see [films in] English, and compare with India or Nepali movies, the stage they have—the quality of the picture—we would be like, astonished, you know, like, 'How could they even shoot in such a way?' So everybody would have a dream of if we could go to U.S.

Tek watched CNN and BBC while living outside the camp whenever he got a chance. He would keep regular tabs on the United States' gross income and remembered ongoing coverage of "the 9/11 incident [and] the affair of Bill Clinton, and . . . about the war with Iraq." Tek explained his curiosity about the United States:

> U.S. is like a country of concern for everyone. I mean because of superiority, because people think that it is one of the richest countries in around the world. They have all like–everything, like advanced things, like the technologies, everything. So I used to do some Internet research about the U.S. Not just for the process of resettlement but just to know about how the countries are getting rich around the world. In that sense I used to do some kind of Internet research and I know something about U.S. but not a lot. Going through the Internet search I found that, like, people in the U.S. they are very strict about the time. They follow the time very strictly. And they are always concerned about their work. They are not concerned about whatever things like their leisure time or enjoyment or anything. So that was my impression.

Here Tek reveals that while Internet research about unfamiliar areas may result in a better understanding about a nation's wealth or technological advancements, it may also lend clues about the lifestyle choices and concerns of individuals.

Social media also played an important role in helping Tek learn about his future home in America. As residents of his former camp began to resettle in the United States, Tek heard from them.

We have some communication sometimes—like the phone communication, or having an Internet chat through the Facebook, Yahoo, Gmail, like that. And then we hear that . . . the situation in the third countries it is far more better than in the refugee camp. So people told us it is far more better here [in the United States] because we have lot of opportunities. And then my family along with my parents and my siblings, we plan to take part into the resettlement.

In Tek's case, what he learned through social media conversations with friends, U.S. news, and general Internet searching directly influenced his and his family's decision to apply for relocation to the United States. Still, Tek's access to these resources contrasts with the experiences of others from his country who did not have the opportunity to leave the refugee camps and subsequently had more limited access to U.S. media before their relocation.[48] Indeed, the dissimilarity in the amount and type of U.S. media consumed even by refugees from similar ethnic and geographic backgrounds speaks to a larger diversity in refugee narratives. Though portrayals of refugees in U.S. media sometimes suggest that refugees are a homogeneous group; in fact, as Shiraz, Jala, Sancha, Megeney, Habiba, Govinda, Balaram, Tek, and others made clear, even within populations originating from the same nation, refugee camp, or family, refugees' experiences vary widely due to literacy, unequal access to technological resources, and governmental restrictions. Still, these are not the only factors that determine what media a refugee may encounter.

Several of the narrators I interviewed revealed how their own beliefs and preferences led them to avoid some types of U.S. media, even when it was readily available. For example, in Austin, Texas, I met a Burmese refugee named Paw Htoo Raw. She grew up in Dawei, in the Taninthayi region of Burma, where her neighbor had a television and charged her five Kyat[49] to watch U.S. or Burmese films. Paw Htoo fled from her home in Burma in 1997 when she was twenty years old, because a military regime attacked her village, and lived unsheltered in the jungle for ten months before finding her way to a refugee camp in Thailand. She explained to me that in the camp, "I see some [American movies], but I didn't—I didn't think that this is good to watch."[50] I asked her why she felt this way. "Just sometimes, I don't know . . . the movie that I watched is fighting—like—war, fighting and shooting . . . sometimes I feel pity and sometimes I cry." One time, Paw Htoo remembered, "Angelina Jolie, she went to the camp, and she donate[d] a TV to school . . . the school showed [a] movie every Friday evening, but I didn't go." In this instance, Paw Htoo was not restrained from encountering video media because of governmental restrictions or a lack of resources—indeed, U.S. films were available both in her neighbor's home in Burma and in the refugee camp in Thailand—but rather by her own belief that watching U.S. films was a detrimental practice.

Likewise, Hussein Al Dohi, an Iraqi refugee I met in San Diego, explained that when he was a teenager growing up in Baghdad he enjoyed listening to U.S. musicians, including Cyndi Lauper, Madonna, and Michael Jackson. He also told me, "In the '80s I loved *The Untouchables*, like, Kevin Costner, I don't know, the college movies, high school movies . . . I still like action movies."[51] Several of the Iraqis I interviewed before Hussein also mentioned having a penchant for American action films, and during my conversation with Hussein, I was beginning to wonder why this theme was so consistent. I asked him, "Are action movies from the United States more available than other kinds of genres in Iraq?" Hussein answered,

> No, no, I just prefer the action movie. Well, you know, in the Middle East, there's always guns and fighting, so of course they're going to like fighting movie, not love movie, you know. People are stressed and they hate the government so usually they release their stress [by] watching action movies. They wish that they can fight the government . . . it's an escape from reality. That's why you like to watch action movies. We don't like war movies—I don't—it's not popular there [in Iraq] because we live in a war and so it's not very fun to watch people wearing khaki and fighting because it's daily life. Here, it's interesting, but there, it's awful, it's boring to me. . . . We live in a war zone so what's the point of watching a war movie?

With these words, Hussein reveals that beyond watching for entertainment, some individuals may use U.S. media to feed a social fantasy of resistance and escape. Indeed, for Hussein, watching U.S. films in Iraq was only a desirable action insofar as the narratives represented in the films remained distinct from his own experience, revealing that a penchant for violence in media may not always extend to war narratives.

These narratives point to the reality of refugees' proactive agency when choosing which media to consume. Refugees are not passive audiences and may not decide to read, watch, or listen to some media simply because it is available. Rather, their choices about what to consume and avoid are likely—as Paw Htoo and Hussein described—informed by preexisting beliefs and ideas about the effects of certain media. Certainly, any study of media audiences must keep in mind that external circumstances play only a partial role in determining what audiences encounter. Beyond these external factors, a whole host of desires, fears, and values lead certain audiences toward certain media and away from others.

"The Reality Check": Sorting Fact from Fiction in Popular U.S. Media

Even in cases of limited or spotty access, refugees use what little U.S. media they encountered before their relocation not only for entertainment but also to form a picture about and make sense of life in the United States. Like Tek, some decided whether or not to apply for resettlement in the United States based upon what they learned from U.S. media. To recognize the full extent of the potential U.S. media may hold to influence such decisions, one must consider that while some refugees are familiar with U.S. norms and customs when they arrive, many have never met an American before their relocation and may be unfamiliar with the range of social mores and cultural cues that often govern interactions in the United States. Just as the amount and type of refugee interactions with U.S. media vary widely, so too does the degree to which refugees believe that the U.S. media they encounter before their arrival represent real life in the United States.

Fadhail Ibraheem, an Iraqi refugee who fled to Syria before arriving in the United States with her three children after her husband was kidnapped during a brutally violent nighttime raid in her home in Baghdad, explained to me clearly one potential effect of pre-arrival media; viewing U.S. films instilled in Fadhail a belief that Americans were dangerous and unpredictable.[52] She had initially decided to apply for relocation in Australia, not only because she wished to be reunited with her brother, who had been resettled there after he, too, fled Iraq, but also because she feared what she would find in the United States. Fadhail learned that her application for resettlement in Australia had been rejected when she received a call from the UN, after waiting four months in Syria, informing her that she was going to be interviewed in preparation for resettlement in the United States. Fadhail was scared for herself and her children before departure:

> What we kn[e]w about the United States [was] only from the movies. I don't have any . . . friendship with anyone . . . who lived in America to get an idea about what's going to be there. It's just what we saw in the movie, and in the movie sometimes you see how [Americans] are aggressive people, sometimes in the middle of street, in the middle of the night, all these high-sky bombings, people they can easily get lost there . . . just things like that.

Indeed, the U.S. films she had seen while living in Iraq began to serve Fadhail as a foreboding warning about the life that awaited her and her family in the United States. She could not remember the names of any U.S. action films she had seen except *What Lies Beneath*—a thriller about an American professor who has an affair with a student he later murders by drowning her in a lake.[53] Because I had not seen this film when I first met with Fadhail, she provided a synopsis:

> The professor kills his girlfriend, and dip her in lake, down, and his wife after that she find out and, it's kind of scary. But, I mean, as a kind of life in America, you know, there is always a kind of threat from somewhere,

from somehow. There is always a scare from something, that's like really, honestly what I [thought].

As Fadhail continued to describe the plot of *What Lies Beneath*, it became clear why this and other action films she had seen affected her expectations of the United States so profoundly. Without knowing anyone in the United States on whom to rely for information or help, Fadhail was simply using the resources she had available to her in order to prepare for life in a new part of the world where, as a result of her husband's kidnapping, she would hold sole responsibility for keeping her family safe.

Fadhail's familiarity with American thrillers and action films is not unique. Rather, as I mentioned previously, American action and horror films were particularly popular with the Iraqis I interviewed. At the International Institute of Los Angeles, in Glendale, California, I met Edwin Bazikiam, who arrived in the United States as a refugee[54] and now works as a case manager serving primarily Iraqi and Iranian clients.[55] During our conversation, Edwin talked, as Fadhail had, about how American films exaggerate violence and how this exaggeration affects his refugee clients. I asked Edwin what he wished his clients knew before they arrived in the United States. He answered, "U.S.A. is not like they show in Hollywood movies." After he paused, I asked Edwin to clarify. He answered,

> I can say two different things. The one subject can be the violence, the other can be the luxury life. The shooting, the massacres, the serial killers, I don't know, that kind of stuff . . . well, I don't know . . . sometimes they hear things in the news or the recent things that happen, so they—it's like a flashback—they think, "Hey, is [the United States] like the movies we saw, is it real? Is it not?"

In contrast to exaggerations of violence in the United States, Edwin believes, American films also may work to inform refugees' unrealistic expectations regarding the lifestyle most Americans enjoy. "They think people here relax and work a few hours in a week and then enjoy the time," he told me.[56] "They don't know that you work full time and you have to plan for a few days of vacation, and everybody works hard, you know? It can be, sometimes, hard for them to adjust." I wondered if Edwin's experience was in some way specific to the Iraqi refugee population or to refugees' resettling in Los Angeles, and so in Buffalo, New York, I asked Meghann Perry, the director of Programs and Adult Education at Journey's End Refugee Services, whether she had encountered anything similar with her own clients.[57] She answered,

> Definitely . . . I call [it] "The Reality Check." The settling into the real world is—the houses they see on sitcoms and movies or in videos—I don't

know if they watch, like, music videos any more, but the homes that they see, the lives that they see are not, you know, the lives on the west side of Buffalo. So I think that's . . . that's a huge part of the disconnect. Huge. I've definitely heard people say, "Wow, it's not like it is on TV." And I know a lot of the young people are seeing a lot on Facebook and the Internet.

Indeed, many refugees have no reason to believe that the opulence or violence they encounter in pre-arrival media is anything other than representative of real life in the United States; without firsthand testimony or personal experience to provide a contrasting perspective, there exists little motive to refute these seemingly cohesive, consistent portrayals.

Meghann's clients reiterated the experience of the "reality check" she described. For example, Esther—a twenty-five-year-old refugee from Burma whose resettlement was facilitated by Meghann's agency and who requested that her surname not be used—reported that she was quite influenced by the vast luxury she saw in American films.[58] Like thousands of other Burmese citizens, Esther and her family are part of the Chin ethnic minority group who were forced to flee their home because of a crisis that began with a pro-democracy uprising in Burma in 1988, escalated during the next decade due to a repressive military dictatorship that incited a series of military offensives in 1995 and 1997, and subsists currently due to ongoing—primarily ethnic-based—unrest.[59] Esther's family had a television in their home before they were displaced from Burma, and while they could not watch TV broadcasts, they did watch movies on VHS. Esther remembers seeing James Bond films, *Terminator*, and *Independence Day*.[60] She told me,

> Truly we, honestly we feel like, oh, America is like a heaven, with this heaven when we see the movie, a Hollywood movie, they let us feel like heaven you know. Like the American living standard . . . we very admire them. Because we see the very high buildings, tall buildings. So you know, we admire the American life.

I asked Esther what her first impressions were when she arrived in the United States. She answered,

> To be honest, it's different I think. Because, uh, when we watch the movie like New York City, we thought that when we go to New York that we can, we have to live like very high movies, but when we arrive here [in Buffalo] it's, you know, it's a town [or] something like that. . . we feel depressed.

I asked Esther, "Were you disappointed?" She answered, "No, not disappointed. I just feel it odd, different a bit." She explained that even though she knew she would be arriving in a different area than New York City, "Movie[s] are very good advertisement, so we thought that everywhere is like same, same thing, like New York City." Even though they encountered vastly different circumstances before their relocation and even though they now live on opposite sides of the country, both Edwin's clients and Esther were surprised to find that the U.S. lifestyle was not nearly as luxurious as it seemed in the media they had encountered before their resettlement.

This sense of surprise that the United States did not measure up to mediated expectations characterizes many of the narratives of the refugees I interviewed. For example, I asked Shiraz—the Iraqi jewelry maker living in Los Angeles whose love of action films and American pop music I discussed earlier—whether there was anything he wished he knew before he arrived in the United States. "[I] saw the movies that America, when you will go to there it's beautiful and everything is easy, you know, but when you come here, you'll get shocked," Shiraz answered.

> Everything is difficult and you have to work hard to get everything, you know, and we don't know these new rules here . . . this is different for us. Everything is beautiful for you, but when you get in the real life, you see the difference and everything is difficult, you know?

Shiraz's experience is revealing of some wider trends in the refugee experience, and he is not exaggerating when he suggests that refugees "have to work hard to get everything." Refugees often arrive in the United States with very few material possessions.[61] In order to acquire basic necessities, they must learn quickly how to exchange a new form of currency. This process is further complicated by the reality that many refugees arrive without the ability to speak English and are unsure of how to navigate the large number of stores, health care facilities, and schools that occupy even small American towns. Likewise, regardless of previous education and work experience, refugees often have an extremely difficult time securing even entry-level employment upon their arrival in the United States.[62] Thus, refugees' lifestyles during the years immediately following their resettlement are likely to hold little resemblance to the opulent wealth and leisure often portrayed in U.S. media.

Although Shiraz's, Esther's, and Edwin's clients' interpretations of pre-arrival popular U.S. media were similar, it is clear that refugees' interpretations of the measure to which popular U.S. media represent reality are complicated. For example, Buddhi Rai, Sancha's cousin, remembered seeing *The Great Gatsby* in grade twelve in Nepal and recalled, "There [were] so many things to learn from there. I learned many things from there: how to act with [a] friend, [and] what to do with [a] friend."[63] This statement seems to suggest that because the film revealed some reality about friendships in the United States, Buddhi was able to apply directly what she saw in *The Great Gatsby* to her real life after her resettlement. But when I asked Buddhi whether what she encountered firsthand in the

United States seemed similar to what she had seen in the film, she told me, it is "difficult to compare movies to particular life, it's tough." I found variations of Buddhi's response among other narrators: though they consistently recognized the difference between U.S. films and real life in the United States, many narrators found in U.S. media hints about American culture, relationships, government, and social interaction that were still useful as a kind of informal education about U.S. life, while others seemed to watch for simple entertainment.

In November I met a Somali refugee who asked me to call her Zanuba. She told me about the U.S. media she saw before the war in Somalia:

> In my country, in Somalia, I used to watch some movies. I don't remember the actors' names, but I used to know, like, Madonna, Michael Jackson, and there was other movie actors, I don't remember their names, but I know their faces.

Zanuba did not know English while she lived in Somalia, but explained, "You know, the action—that's what you understand." I asked Zanuba whether she believed she learned anything about the United States from watching these films or listening to American music, but at this question she furrowed her brow, "Just what I learned is—that time I was young, and it was cool, these people and the Hollywood—to see them, it was like amazing." Though Zanuba consumed U.S. media to be entertained by what was "cool" rather than to gain some explicit information or education about the United States, when she arrived in her new home in City Heights, a suburb of San Diego, she revealed,

> It was different [than] what I thought—I thought [it would be] more beautiful than that . . . I said, 'Is this America?' So it was different . . . City Heights, there was all the, you know, apartments, houses, and you see even some cockroaches—I never thought America has cockroaches![64]

I asked Zanuba whether she had seen cockroaches in Somalia, and when she confirmed, I asked her why she did not think she would also see cockroaches in San Diego. She answered, "Because in America we thought—they have rich, in our mind, what we see, they are powerful country, rich—so we thought everyone is rich almost and clean everywhere, not those things." I pressed her further, and asked, "Why did you believe that everyone here was rich—where did that expectation come from?" She answered simply, "When you see the film."

Here Zanuba's responses reveal that her pre-arrival consumption of U.S. media created an expectation of wealth and beauty that she found to be incongruent with reality upon her arrival in the United States. Still, Zanuba did not point to this relationship between media and expectation when I asked her what she learned from the U.S. media she saw while living in Somalia and only acknowledged the connection between her expectations and pre-arrival media after I asked her to account for her surprise regarding the cockroaches and general lack of beauty in City Heights. In this way, Zanuba's reflections testify to the reality that refugee audiences may be enculturated through pre-arrival media even when they are not explicitly aware of it.

The nuanced descriptions of the effects of pre-arrival media discussed in this section reveal that the relationship between media and enculturation is multifaceted. Instead of accepting or rejecting the whole of some mediated text as simple fact or fiction, refugee audiences may perform complex and selective processes of interpretation and use the mediated portrayal of certain norms, relationships, rituals, or values to familiarize themselves with the intricacies of particular facets of a new culture, even when they are not aware that they are doing so. In the next section, I discuss this possibility in more detail.

Complicating Enculturation through Media

The more I spoke with refugee narrators, the more I found that I needed to complicate my original question of whether they believed that the U.S. media they saw before their resettlement represented the reality of life in the United States. I began wondering, what facets of culture can be learned by watching, reading, or hearing media, and started asking the narrators more direct questions, such as, "What did you know about romantic relationships in the United States before you moved here?" and "Why did you want to watch American films before your relocation?" and "Did you ever talk with anyone about the American media you saw?" Two areas of insight became clear from this new line of questioning: First, a significant relationship exists between refugees' consumption of pre-arrival U.S. media and the interpersonal interactions they have in regard to this media. Indeed, as I will demonstrate, the refugees I interviewed use comparisons of real life and U.S. media—especially film—in conversation to prepare other refugees for arrival in the United States or to interpret other refugees' experiences after their arrival, revealing the ways that media may work as a kind of frame through which to predict or interpret experience. Second, it became clear from the answers to these kinds of questions that the narrators I spoke with were not only using U.S. media to form their general expectations of the United States but also to make themselves familiar with all kinds of cultural norms and social cues that are typical in the United States—from the ways that people interact with each other in the workplace, to the ways that Americans respond to unexpected encounters with strangers. These kinds of accounts show how mediated depictions of unknown places may facilitate enculturation and act as what Arjun Appadurai calls "strips of reality," providing audiences with useful, albeit partial clues.[65] As is evinced by Esther, Shiraz, Zanuba, and other narrators who, as we have seen, found discrepancies between mediated and firsthand encounters with the United States, any piece of media works as what John Durham Peters calls "bridge and chasm," revealing some possibilities or interpretations of reality while simultaneously concealing others.[66] Indeed, refugees who encounter media are not simply watching in order to make determinations regarding whether what they see offers a real or imagined picture of the United States. Rather, the refugees in this study reported more nuanced viewing practices in which—even when they realized the mediated narratives portrayed only a partial picture or singular interpretation of U.S. life—they could still use the media to acquaint or familiarize themselves with some cultural aspects of life in the United States.

In some cases, narrators revealed how pre-departure, media related expectations were accompanied and contradicted by interpersonal interactions about U.S. media. For example, before his resettlement to the United States, Mohammed Mahmod, an Iraqi now living in Pittsburgh,[67] spoke at length with his parents because they had visited the United States previously. Mohammed remembers that to help him prepare for his resettlement, his father told him "not to believe everything in the movies."[68] Likewise, Abreer, a Iraqi refugee who fled to Egypt in 2006 because of threats to her Christian family, and who arrived in Houston, Texas, in 2012, explained that in Iraq:

> We saw, I mean, old movies and new movies, they [were] concerning—especially in New York—like thieves, like people, I mean, kidnap someone, and robbery and something like this, so this is the first impression that we have about States, depending on what we see from the films, because it's the only way that we can see States, through films.[69]

Later in our interview, however, Abreer revealed that she had Iraqi family members who were already living in the United States when she arrived. When she confirmed that she spoke with these family members to prepare for her own resettlement, I asked what they told her. Her family, she remembered, simply explained: "No, it's not like the movies." In these cases, "the movies" act as a kind of shared locus from which to present a contrasting view about life in the United States, revealing another manifestation of media's role in the relocation process. Refugees' consumption of media does not occur in a vacuum, and in order to understand the significance of pre-departure U.S. media in the lives of refugee audiences, one must take up the process of what cultural studies scholar Lawrence Grossberg calls "radical contextualization,"[70] considering every mediated encounter as occurring within a complicated milieu of personal experiences that may both affect—and be affected by—the processes of encountering and interpreting pre-arrival media. In this way, one may recognize that pre-arrival media consumption and the events and interaction surrounding this consumption, such as interpersonal conversation about pre-arrival media, are not altogether separate phenomena but rather interlocking parts that make up an intricate, layered experience.

Of course, the facets of this reality vary greatly from person to person. For example, some of the refugees in this project, like Govinda, did not have the luxury of interpersonal interaction with individuals who had seen the United States firsthand and with whom he could vet his interpretations of pre-arrival media. When I asked Govinda how he learned about the United States before his arrival, he answered, "I learn in the book, but I learn—I didn't even talk with the people." In fact, as he revealed earlier in this chapter, Govinda had relatively wide access to American books, films, and televisions shows when he was attending college in Nepal. But without friends or family members who had firsthand experience living in the United States with whom to talk about these experiences, Govinda was left confused. He explained,

> I didn't understand because comparing to here, like in my culture, we never stay with girlfriend together, never. And, if I have a wife, in my culture, we don't need to keep a girlfriend, so we don't have permission to love another girl. In Great Gatsby I saw that. I, I was so confused about all things, you know? So, it's kind of awkward at the beginning . . . I didn't talk anybody from my community in the United States. So just when I come to United States it's only a dream, like, it's like a dream. So I have I don't know anything about that, it's totally new things.

While opportunities to discuss pre-arrival U.S. media experience with individuals who have firsthand experience living in the United States do not guarantee a refugee less culture shock or an easier learning curve, it is clear that the refugees in this study found these conversations—when they were available—to be useful and comforting.

In addition to contradicting or disproving expectations learned through pre-arrival media, sometimes interpersonal interaction about such media serves to affirm one's belief that U.S. media depicts reality. For example, Shiraz maintains that the pre-arrival U.S. media refugees encounter is similar enough to reality to prepare them for what they will find in the United States. Shiraz's view became clear when he demonstrated his frustration with some Iraqi refugees who had chosen to return to Syria after living only a short time in the United States:

> They come [to the United States as] a refugee and came back. I told them, "Why? Okay. You get there and everything is okay. Why?" [They answered,] "Oh, we can't, we can't live in there because the, you know, the culture is different and everything is different. We can't live in there." [So I would say to them] "Okay, you knew about America and you saw the movies and you, you knew the type of life in there. Why you, why you came to America?" I don't know. I don't understand. They come in and after two months or three months, they came back to Syria. They didn't

like it. But [I said to them] "You saw the movies! The, you saw everything, you know how is life in there, if it's, if it's different from your culture."[71]

Whether interpersonal interactions confirm or disconfirm the similarity between U.S. media and reality, in every case, it is clear that the cognitive links between media and the potential reality in the United States are formed long before an individual physically arrives within a new cultural context. Linda Estefan, an Iraqi refugee I interviewed in Los Angeles, discussed this phenomenon with me at length.

Linda described the first forty-five years of her life in Baghdad as "normal."[72] As a child, she would go on weekly trips with her father to the cinema. "Most Most[ly] American film," she recalled. "There is sometimes, they bring Indian film, and Turkish film. But everyone go to the American film." After graduating from university, Linda married, had two boys, and began working in a government lab as a biologist, a job she enjoyed. In 2007, everything changed. She and her husband had to remove their boys from school, pack their home quickly, and flee the country. "There is a war in Baghdad. And there are strangers and no safe[ty] and we can't, I can't stay," Linda explained. "I ran away because I, they gave me, they gave us threat. They threatened us. 'If you don't leave the country, we will take your son or we will kill anybody of your family,' like that. When I came to Syria as a refugee, I decided that I can't go back to my home country. I decided to move on to U.S.A." January 28, 2011, Linda and her family boarded a plane bound for Los Angeles.

The Estefans had family who had already moved to Los Angeles and who acted as their anchor during the relocation process.[73] Linda told me that she already knew a lot about the United States before her arrival. I asked whether her opinions about the United States had come from her education. "No, from the movies," she replied. "The movies very [much] affect us. Because, through the movie, there are many things about the American[s], how they live, how they, how their families live and what is the relationship between them or what is going on the country between the people and the government." I asked Linda about her family's typical media intake and learned from her response that the U.S. media Linda encountered during her time living in Baghdad was somewhat unique—while many of the other Iraqi refugees I interviewed mentioned seeing mostly recent action films, Linda remembered,

> The black and white films . . . the famous one I see, it's all in my mind. The one—*Gone with the Wind*.[74] Because, she is Elizabeth Taylor, I think.[75] Elizabeth Taylor. Yeah. Her beauty and her dress is very beautiful and different. Everything beautiful, from the house, [to] the garden.

Linda also remembers seeing cartoons in Baghdad: *Tom and Jerry*, *Roger Rabbit*, *Mickey Mouse*, and *Superman*. I asked Linda to tell me more about what she saw in U.S. media that was notably different from the culture in Baghdad. She answered,

> The first thing, the first thing that is different between them and us, there is a freedom too much in U.S.A. I mean, everything. In our home country, no, it's limited. If you'll see . . . if for example, like in a speech, you wanted to talk about something [in Iraq], politic or religion or something. They discriminated you, you should be aware. But in this country, no. You have a freedom in the speech. You have a freedom and, yes, there is a law. There is an instruction you have to agree to, but there is . . . there is a freedom more than my home country . . . my country, the religion is very strict, very. But in this country, no.

Though the cartoons and the films Linda mentioned do not provide explicit lessons about the American government or freedom of speech, Linda picked up on and familiarized herself with the ways these cultural aspects appeared implicitly in the media she watched. Linda's narrative reveals that enculturation does not occur only when an individual becomes physically present in a new culture, instead, cultural learning may take place remotely, when an individual becomes an audience member for a mediated cultural narrative that is in some way different from the one in which she lives.

Moses Boghossian also reported being enculturated through U.S. media before his arrival in Los Angeles. Like Linda, Moses grew up in Baghdad and remembers his time there fondly:

> It was very good. I have a good life there. But after 2006, when I came to here to United States [for a visit as a tourist], I [went] back to Iraq, I received a letter they want to kill me. That I was, me and my wife, we've been here for a tourist then we receive a letter that [they think] we are working with America, they want to kill us so I ran away from Baghdad.[76]

Before his displacement, Moses did not see much American television. He remembers that there were no American television shows available on his television in Iraq before 2003, and after 2003, the only available American show was *Dallas*.[77] But Moses saw many American films while he was living in Iraq. Action films—especially cowboy movies—were his favorite. Moses believes that he learned a lot from the American films he watched:

> I think we have good impressions about the America from the films. Especially the language, the education and, lots of things, you know, about the sports, about everything. When I came here, especially the first time when I talk [to] the customs [officer for the] interview in the airport, they thought that I've been here a lot—many times. So when I told them this is my first time, they were surprised. So when I talk with them, when I [knew] lots of things about the American life, American cities, they were,

they told me, "Where [have] you learn[ed] from?" I told them from our TV!—the television and the film.

For Moses, U.S. media was more than entertainment; it was a means for gaining useful information about education, language, and sports in the United States.

Moses's and Linda's narratives reinforce the notion that media is multivalent; instead of containing meaning in and of itself, any mediated text is decoded and interpreted uniquely by each member of the audience who encounters it.[78] Indeed, while some of the refugees I interviewed reported encountering some of the same media—such as *Rambo* or *The Great Gatsby*—it is clear that refugees' interpretations of these and other media are consistently tailored to the viewers' own lives and contingent upon their previous knowledge, experiences, and desires. In this way, these narrators function as members of an "active audience," interpreting media through their own, unique lenses of understanding.[79]

In any cultural context, the interpretation of media is highly personal, so that one cannot assume any media text holds an inherent or immanent meaning in itself independent of its audiences. For refugees in particular, as is shown by the narratives in this chapter, transnational media may serve as a kind of informal education—useful not only for the sake of forming an overarching picture about an unfamiliar place but also for the purposes of enculturating oneself into the social norms and customs of a future home.

Notes

1 *The Pursuit of Happyness*, directed by Gabriele Muccino (Culver City, CA: Sony Pictures Home Entertainment, 2006).
2 Sancha Rai, interview by Sarah Bishop, Pittsburgh, PA, February 5, 2013.
3 During Sancha's time in Nepal, the Nepali government restricted the residence of Bhutanese refugees to seven refugee camps, including Khudunabari. The rules of these camps dictate that residents must obtain passes to leave the refugee camps for durations of longer than twenty-four hours. Individuals who wish to go to school outside the camps, like Sancha, may apply for and receive renewable six-month leave passes for educational purposes. If a refugee remains outside the camp for longer than the duration of time that his or her pass allows, the camp authorities may suspend ration cards for food and living supplies upon the refugee's return. Moreover, the 1958 Foreigners Act permits the Nepali government to penalize refugees living outside of the camps without permission with fines of 2,000 rupees (approximately $20.00 USD) and up to two years in prison. See "Freedom of Movement and Resistance," *World Refugee Survey 2009: Nepal* (Arlington, VA: United States Committee for Refugees and Immigrants, 2009).
4 UNHCR Spokesperson Jennifer Paganos, "Nepal: Generous U.S. Resettlement Offer May Help Break Bhutanese Deadlock," *UNHCR Briefing Notes*, October 6, 2006, http://www.unhcr.org/45262b462.html.

5 For more about the curriculum, duration, and perceived benefits of IOM orientations in Nepal, see "United States Cultural Orientation in Nepal: Preparing Refugees for a New Life in the U.S.A.," *International Organization for Migration*, accessed October 19, 2013, https://www.iom.int/united-states-cultural-orientation-nepal-preparing-refugees-new-life-usa.
6 For more information about informal education, see Ahmed M. Baker, "Informal Education Programmes," *Journal of Refugee Studies* 2, no. 1 (1989): 98–107; Zvi Bekerman, Nicholas C. Burbules, and Diana Silberman-Keller, *Learning in Places: The Informal Education Reader*, vol. 249 (New York, NY: P. Lang, 2006); and Harry L. Strauss and J. R. Kidd, *Look, Listen and Learn: A Manual on the Use of Audio-Visual Materials in Informal Education* (New York: Association Press, 1948).
7 *Journey from the Fall*, directed by Ham Tran (Santa Monica, CA: ImaginAsian Pictures, 2007); *Black Hawk Down*, directed by Ridley Scott (Culver City, CA: Columbia Tri-Star Entertainment, 2001).
8 See, for example, Oscar Handlin, *Boston Immigrants, 1790-1880: A Study in Acculturation* (Cambridge, MA: Harvard University Press, 1941) and Fernando Ortiz, *Cuban Counterpoint, Tobacco and Sugar* (New York: Alfred Knopf, 1947).
9 For further explanation of enculturation, see Ronald Scollon, Suzanne B. K. Scollon, and Rodney H. Jones, *Intercultural Communication: A Discourse Approach* (Malden, MA: Wiley-Blackwell, 2012); Krum Krumov and Knud S. Larsen, *Cross-Cultural Psychology: Why Culture Matters* (Charlotte, NC: Information Age Publications, 2013); and Chul-Byung Choi, "Local Collective Identity Enculturation Within a Global Media Consumption Culture," *Asia Pacific Education Review* 3, no. 1 (2002): 1–17.
10 See, for example, Cheryl L. Currie, T. Cameron Wild, Donald P. Schopflocher, Lory Laing, Paul J. Veugelers, Brenda Parlee, and Daniel W. McKennitt, "Enculturation and Alcohol Use Problems among Aboriginal University Students," *Canadian Journal of Psychiatry* 56, no. 12 (2011): 735–42; Christine A. Walsh, Dave Este, and Brigette Krieg, "The Enculturation Experience of Roma Refugees: A Canadian Perspective," *British Journal of Social Work* 38, no. 5 (2008): 900–17; and Ashley D. Paterson and Julie Hakim-Larson, "Arab Youth in Canada: Acculturation, Enculturation, Social Support, and Life Satisfaction," *Journal of Multicultural Counseling and Development* 40, no. 4 (2012): 206–15.
11 In rare cases, such as when a refugee is granted a resettlement date that is earlier than originally expected, or when a refugee's life is in danger and s/he must relocate immediately, refugees may not attend a formal cultural orientation.
12 Sahro Nor, interview by Sarah Bishop, Buffalo, NY, November 21, 2013, archived at the Schlesinger Library at Harvard University.
13 Kler Htoo, interview by Sarah Bishop, Buffalo, NY, August 6, 2013.
14 "Refugee Journalists Emphasize the Importance of Community Radio in Dadaab at a High Profile United Nations Panel in Geneva," *Internews* (Dadaab, Kenya: August 13, 2013), http://internews.org/our-stories/project-updates/radio-you-can-reach-everyone-camps-everyone-will-listen.
15 "Iraqi Refugee Processing Fact Sheet," *United States Citizenship and Immigration Services*, updated June 6, 2013, accessed June 20, 2013, http://www.uscis.gov/portal/site/uscis/menuitem.5af9bb95919f35e66f614176543f6d1a/?vgnextchannel=68439c7755cb9010VgnVCM10000045f3d6a1RCRD&vgnextoid=df4c47c9de5ba110VgnVCM1000004718190aRCRD. The Iraqi refugee crisis is the result of multiple events

over the last forty years, including the Iran-Iraq War in the 1980s, the Iraqi invasion of Kuwait, the Gulf War, and the U.S.-led invasion in 2003.

16 Unfortunately, because of the recent escalating civil war in Syria, many Iraqis who fled there have been forced to return to Iraq or resettle in a third temporary location while they wait to receive their resettlement assignments from IOM. See Caroline Hawley, "Iraqi Refugees Flee Syrian Conflict to Return Home," *BBC News: Middle East*, http://www.bbc.co.uk/news/world-middle-east-20131033.

17 Zahraa Eskander, interview by Sarah Bishop, Los Angeles, CA, July 11, 2013, archived at the Schlesinger Library at Harvard University.

18 See John Fiske, *Understanding Popular Culture* (Boston: Unwin Hyman, 1998); Don Kulick and Margaret Willson, "Rambo's Wife Saves the Day: Subjugating the Gaze and Subverting the Narrative in a Papua New Guinean Swamp," *Visual Anthropology Review* 10, no. 2 (1994): 1–13; and Radhika Parameswaran, "Reading Fictions of Romance: Gender, Sexuality, and Nationalism in Postcolonial India," *Journal of Communication* 52, no. 4 (2002): 832–51.

19 Bishnu Khanal, interview by Sarah Bishop, Buffalo, NY, August 6, 2013, archived at the Schlesinger Library at Harvard University; Bishnu Maya Chapagain, interview by Sarah Bishop, Buffalo, New York, August 6, 2013, archived at the Schlesinger Library at Harvard University; Nirmala Khanal, interview by Sarah Bishop, Buffalo, NY, August 6, 2013, archived at the Schlesinger Library at Harvard University; Bishnu Maya Chapagain, interview by Sarah Bishop, Buffalo, NY, August 6, 2013, archived at the Schlesinger Library at Harvard University; Sitay Mbere, interview by Sarah Bishop, San Diego, CA, November 20, 2013, archived at the Schlesinger Library at Harvard University; Maynun Abdi, interview by Sarah Bishop, San Diego, CA, November 21, 2013, archived at the Schlesinger Library at Harvard University.

20 Some of the media that the narrators remembered did not rely on formal redistribution channels to circulate. For more information, see Barbara Klinger, "Contraband Cinema: Piracy, Titanic, and Central Asia," *Cinema Journal* 39, no. 2 (Winter 2010): 106–24; Phil Kiver, *182 Days in Iraq* (Pittsburgh, PA: Word Association Publishers, 2006); and Gregory F. Trevorton, *Film Piracy, Organized Crime, and Terrorism* (Santa Monica, CA: Rand Corporation, 2008).

21 Govinda Khanal, interview by Sarah Bishop, Buffalo, NY, August 6, 2013; *The Great Gatsby*, directed by Jack Clayton (Hollywood, CA: Paramount Pictures, 1974); *The Ellen DeGeneres Show* (Burbank, CA: Telepictures, 2003 [ongoing]); Tennessee Williams, *Cat on a Hot Tin Roof: A Play in Three Acts* (New York, NY: Dramatists Play Service, 1983).

22 Govinda Khanal, e-mail correspondence with Sarah Bishop, September 30, 2013.

23 *Titanic*, directed by James Cameron (Hollywood, CA: Paramount Pictures, 1997).

24 Shiraz Minasaqen, interview by Sarah Bishop, Los Angeles, CA, July 11, 2013, archived at the Schlesinger Library at Harvard University.

25 *The Terminator*, directed by James Cameron (Santa Monica, CA: MGM Home Entertainment, 1984); *Rocky*, directed by John G. Avildsen (Santa Monica, CA: MGM Studios, 1976).

26 Marwan M. Kraidy, *Reality Television and Arab Politics: Contention in Public Life* (Cambridge: Cambridge University Press, 2010); Don Kulick and Margaret Willson, "Rambo's Wife Saves the Day: Subjugating the Gaze and Subverting the Narrative in a Papua New Guinean Swamp," *Visual Anthropology Review* 10, no. 2 (1994): 1–13.

27 Jala Yaqo, interview by Sarah Bishop, San Diego, CA, November 18, 2013.
28 See Phil Kiver, *182 Days in Iraq* (Pittsburgh, PA: Word Association Publishers, 2006); Gregory F. Trevorton, *Film Piracy, Organized Crime, and Terrorism*, (Santa Monica, CA: Rand Corporation, 2008); Klinger, "Contraband Cinema," 106–24.
29 Zaid Sabah, "Pirated DVDs Among Hottest Items on Shelves," *U.S.A. Today* (January 20, 2006): A.12; Carolyn C. Guertin, *Digital Prohibition: Piracy and Authorship in New Media Art* (London: Continuum International Publication Group, 2012).
30 Tek Rimal, interview with Sarah Bishop, Pittsburgh, PA, March 18, 2013, archived at the Schlesinger Library at Harvard University
31 Raminder Kaur and William Mazzarella, *Censorship in South Asia: Cultural Regulation from Sedition to Seduction* (Bloomington: Indiana University Press, 2009); Michael Drewett and Martin Cloonan, *Popular Music Censorship in Africa* (Burlington, VT: Ashgate, 2006); Ann Hafften, "'Technical Difficulty' or Censorship?" *Washington Report on Middle East Affairs* 31, no. 2 (2012), 5; Michael Hutt, "Things that Should Not be Said: Censorship and Self-Censorship in the Nepali Press Media, 2001–02," *The Journal of Asian Studies* 65, no. 2 (2006), 361–92; Ramesh Subramanian, "The Growth of Global Internet Censorship and Circumvention: A Survey," *Communications of the IIMA* 11, no. 2 (2011), 69; Anne Cooper-Chen, *Global Entertainment Media: Content, Audiences, Issues* (New York: L. Erlbaum, 2005).
32 Because Burma was an English colony from 1886 to 1948, use of the English language in Burma is a particularly politically charged issue.
33 Kinley Rinchon, "Media and Public Culture: Media Whitewashing," in International Seminar on Bhutanese Studies, *Media and Public Culture: Proceedings of the Second International Seminar on Bhutan Studies* (Thimphu, Bhutan: Center for Bhutanese Studies, 2007), 221–28.
34 Rinchon, "Media and Public Culture," 235.
35 Anna Lindley, *The Early Morning Phone Call: Remittances from a Refugee Perspective*, Working Paper No. 4 (Oxford: University of Oxford Centre for Policy and Society, 2007).
36 Bosire Boniface, "Trade Booms in Dadaab Refugee Camps," *Sabahi*, May 14, 2012.
37 See Elihu Katz, "The Two-Step Flow of Communication: An Up-To-Date Report on an Hypothesis," *Public Opinion Quarterly* 21, no. 1 (1957): 61–78; Sonia Livingstone, "The Influences of *Personal Influence* on the Study of Audiences," *Annals of the American Academy of Political and Social Science* 608, no. 1 (November 2006): 233–50. As a few existing works have shown, children often play the role of mediaries, interpreting and communicating mediated information to their less-media-engaged elders. See, for example, Jennie A. Abrahamson and Karen E. Fisher, "Modeling the Information Behavior of Lay Mediaries," *Proceedings of the American Society for Information Science and Technology* 43, no. 1 (2006): 1–4; Ann Peterson Bishop and Lassana Magassa, "Using Design Thinking to Empower Ethnic Minority Immigrant Youth in the Roles as Technology and Information Mediaries," in *CHI '13 Extended Abstracts on Human Factors in Computing Systems* (New York: ACM, 2013), 361–66.
38 Because neither Megeney nor Habiba was able to read or speak English at the time they encountered the IOM film, it is impossible for me to verify which of the IOM films was made available to them. For an idea of the range of films that IOM brings to refugee camps for viewing in pre-orientation settings, see http://www.culturalorientation.net/providing-orientation/toolkit/providing-orientation-videos.

39 Though I have not been able to identify the film Habiba described, IOM's Media Library is available at http://medialib.iom.int/.
40 According to the Cultural Orientation Resource Center, refugees do not become eligible to attend an "overseas cultural orientation" until they are fifteen years old. I will discuss the implications of this age requirement more in the next chapter. For further information, see http://www.culturalorientation.net/providing-orientation/.
41 Laxmi Adhi Kari, interview with Sarah Bishop, Buffalo, NY, August 6, 2013, archived at the Schlesinger Library at Harvard University.
42 About 0.02 USD.
43 Group viewing is common among nonwestern populations. See, for example, James F. Kenny, "TV Viewing among TV Set Owners and Non-Owners in a Remote Philippine Province," *Journal of Broadcasting & Electronic Media* 40, no. 2 (1996): 227–42.
44 Cf. Jacob J. Podber, *The Electronic Front Porch: An Oral History of the Arrival of Modern Media in Rural Appalachia and the Meulgeon Community* (Macon: Mercer University Press, 2007), 70–83.
45 Balaram Gurung, interview by Sarah Bishop, Pittsburgh, PA, March 22, 2013, archived at the Schlesinger Library at Harvard University; *First Blood*, directed by Ted Kotcheff (Santa Monica, CA: LionsGate Home Entertainment, 1982).
46 *Jurassic Park*, directed by Steven Spielberg (Universal City, CA: Universal Pictures, 1993).
47 Tek Rimal, interview with Sarah Bishop, Pittsburgh, PA, March 18, 2013, archived at the Schlesinger Library at Harvard University.
48 See Cindy Horst, "*Buufis* amongst Somalis in Dadaab: The Transnational and Historical Logics behind Resettlement Dreams," *Journal of Refugee Studies* 19, no. 2 (June 2006): 143–57.
49 About 0.01 USD by today's conversion standards.
50 Paw Htoo Raw, interview by Sarah Bishop, Austin, TX, November 15, 2013, archived at the Schlesinger Library at Harvard University.
51 Hussein Al Dohi, interview by Sarah Bishop, San Diego, CA, November 18, 2013, archived at the Schlesinger Library at Harvard University.
52 Fadhail Ibraheem, interview by Sarah Bishop, Erie, PA, February 7, 2013, archived at the Schlesinger Library at Harvard University.
53 *What Lies Beneath*, directed by Robert Zemeckis (Glendale, CA: Dreamworks SKG, 2000).
54 Edwin was born and raised in Iran, and therefore his own experiences encountering U.S. media before his relocation are not included in this project. However, approximately half of Edwin's clients are Iraqi, making him an excellent resource for understanding the relationship of Iraqi refugees to U.S. media throughout their relocation.
55 Edwin Bazikiam, interview by Sarah Bishop, Los Angeles, CA, July 9, 2013, archived at the Schlesinger Library at Harvard University.
56 Here Edwin's assertions contradict Tek's earlier remarks regarding the ways that his Internet searches about U.S. news while he was living in India led him to believe that Americans "are always concerned about their work. They are not concerned about whatever things like their leisure time or enjoyment or anything." This discrepancy is likely due to the differences in genre and mediums to which Tek and Edwin are referring; while Edwin mainly discussed scripted blockbuster Hollywood films during our interview, Tek revealed his own penchant for American news found on websites run by CNN and BBC.

57 Meghann Perry, interview by Sarah Bishop, Buffalo, NY, August 7, 2013, archived at the Schlesinger Library at Harvard University.
58 Esther (last name not included at the request of the narrator), interview by Sarah Bishop, Buffalo, NY, August 6, 2013, archived at the Schlesinger Library at Harvard University.
59 "2014 UNHCR Country Operations Profile—Myanmar" (Geneva, Switzerland: United Nations High Commissioner for Refugees, 2014), http://www.unhcr.org/pages/49e4877d6.html.
60 *Independence Day*, directed by Roland Emmerich (Beverly Hills, CA: Twentieth Century Fox Film Corporation, 1996).
61 Refugees may fill what little luggage space they have with sentimental items and gifts from neighbors or family members. Not only are they deprived of personal property but, more importantly, of "common property resources" they may have relied upon not only for economic advantages but also for social sustenance. See Part 7 in Michael M. Cernea and Chris McDowell, eds., *Risks and Reconstruction: Experiences of Resettlers and Refugees* (Washington, DC: International Bank for Reconstruction and Development, 2000), 291–362.
62 For refugees arriving in the wake of the 2008 economic downturn, this process has proven especially challenging. In addition to the difficulties an American job seeker may face in a time when jobs are scant, refugees must often navigate the job search with less-than-fluent English and may encounter prejudice or xenophobia from employers opposed to immigration. See Office of Refugee Settlement, *Report to Congress 2009* (Washington, DC: U.S. Department of Health and Human Services, 2009).
63 Buddhi Rai, interview by Sarah Bishop, Pittsburgh, PA, February 20, 2013, archived at the Schlesinger Library at Harvard University.
64 "Zanuba," interview by Sarah Bishop, San Diego, CA, November 21, 2013, archived at the Schlesinger Library at Harvard University.
65 Arjun Appadurai, *Modernity at Large: Cultural Dimensions of Globalization*, Vol. 1 (Minneapolis: University of Minnesota Press, 1996), 35.
66 John Durham Peters, *Speaking into the Air: A History of the Idea of Communication* (Chicago: University of Chicago Press, 1999), 5.
67 Mohammed arrived in the United States with a Special Immigrant Visa (SIV)—a special kind of refugee status granted only, according to the U.S. State Department, to "persons who worked with the U.S. Armed Forces or under Chief of Mission authority as a translator or interpreter in Iraq or Afghanistan," and who faced some danger to their own or their family's livelihood because of this work. Iraqi special immigrants are eligible for the same entitlement programs, resettlement assistance, and other benefits as refugees admitted under the U.S. Refugee Admissions Program and often apply to the United States as refugees before being granted SIV status. See http://travel.state.gov/content/visas/en/immigrate/iraqis-work-for-us.html.
68 Mohammed Mahmod, interview by Sarah Bishop, Pittsburgh, PA, March 4, 2013, archived at the Schlesinger Library at Harvard University.
69 Abreer Bayara, interview by Sarah Bishop, Houston, TX, November 13, 2013, archived at the Schlesinger Library at Harvard University.
70 Lawrence Grossberg, *Cultural Studies in the Future Tense* (Durham NC: Duke University Press, 2010).
71 Shiraz Minasaqen, interview by Sarah Bishop, Los Angeles, CA, July 11, 2013, archived at the Schlesinger Library at Harvard University.

72 Linda Estefan, interview by Sarah Bishop, Los Angeles, CA, July 12, 2013, archived at the Schlesinger Library at Harvard University.
73 A refugee anchor is a family member living in the United States who agrees to sponsor an incoming refugee or refugee family.
74 *Gone with the Wind*, directed by Victor Fleming (Burbank, CA: Warner Home Video, 1939).
75 In fact, the lead actress in *Gone with the Wind* is not Elizabeth Taylor but rather another British-born actress, Vivien Leigh. Moreover, *Gone with the Wind* was shot in color.
76 Moses Boghossian, interview by Sarah Bishop, Los Angeles, CA, July 12, 2013, archived at the Schlesinger Library at Harvard University.
77 *Dallas*, directed by David Jacobs (CBS, 1978–91). This series global reception has been a subject for study. See Tamar Leibes and Elihu Katz, *The Export of Meaning: Cross Cultural Readings of Dallas* (New York: Oxford University Press, 1990); and Ien Ang, *Watching* Dallas: *Soap Opera and the Melodramatic Imagination* (London: Metheun, 1985).
78 Stuart Hall, "Encoding/Decoding," in *Culture, Media, Language*, eds. Stuart Hall, Dorothy Hobson, et al. (London: Routledge, 1980), 128–38.
79 For further explanation of active audiences, see John Fiske, *Television Culture* (London: Verso, 1987); John Fiske, *Understanding Popular Culture* (Boston: Unwin Hyman, 1989); Janice Radway, *Reading the Romance: Women, Patriarchy, and Popular Literature* (Chapel Hill: University of North Carolina Press, 1984); Stuart Hall, "Encoding/Decoding;" Stanley Eugene Fish, *Is There a Text in This Class?: The Authority of Interpretive Communities* (Cambridge, MA: Harvard University Press, 1980); Rico Lie, *Spaces of Intercultural Communication: An Interdisciplinary Introduction to Communication, Culture, and Globalizing/Localizing Identities* (Cresskill, NJ: Hampton Press, 2003); and Pertti Alasuutari, ed., *Rethinking the Media Audience: The New Agenda* (London: Sage, 1999).

2
REFUGEES' USE OF MEDIA IN PRE-DEPARTURE PREPARATION AND ORIENTATIONS

Abdikadir Abdiyow Barake is a sixty-seven-year-old man from Somalia who was forced to flee his country after an unknown man burst through the door of his home, demanded that Abdikadir rape his ten-year-old daughter, and cut off one of Abdikadir's testicles when he refused to follow the man's orders. Abdikadir's family fled from their home on foot until a stranger in a pickup truck offered to drive them to the Kenyan border where they could seek asylum. Sadly, when they arrived at the border, Abdikadir saw what he described as "an ocean of bodies" on the ground, and people fighting and shooting. A helicopter that he believed belonged to the United Nations appeared and dropped a ladder to help the weaponless Somalis who were being attacked. Abdikadir tried to help his family onto the ladder, but sadly, his wife and two of his children were shot and killed in the process. Abdikadir's only surviving son from Somalia, Said Abiyow, now the director of the Somali Bantu Association of America (SMAA), introduced me to his father during my visit to San Diego in November 2013. While we sat in the SMAA offices, Abdikadir told me his story and showed me the scar from where he was shot in the back as he climbed the ladder to the UN helicopter. Abdikadir does not know how long he lived in the Dadaab refugee camp in Kenya after the helicopter rescued him, but he knows that before his arrival in San Diego,

> We don't even know, like, there is a America, there is a Africa, there is a Dadaab, we just know only Somalia . . . They gave me a form that [was] about America, you know, that's the first time that I hear about America. They gave me a form that to fill it out bring it and the government said "Anything that you need, from us, let us know. But . . . you cannot stay here in this situation; We're going to take you to America. Is it okay with you?" And I said, "Everywhere you guys taking me, I'm ok with it. As long as it's not in here."[1]

After this conversation, the government officials helped Abdikadir fill out the application to the United States because he did not know how to read or write. His application was approved, and he arrived in San Diego in 2002.

Fadhail Irbrahim remembers that after she and her children fled her home in Baghdad to seek asylum in Damascus in 2007, "When we get [to] Syria, I call my brother. I said, 'I'm here.' He said, 'Ok. Go to United Nations. They can help you to bring me, to bring you, your family, to Australia.' That was my aim," Fadhail explained. "To go Australia, not to America. After four months, [the representatives from the UN] call me. They said . . . 'There's a group of interviewers, or officers. They're going to come from America and you're going to be the first one to have interview.'" As Fadhail revealed in the last chapter, she was fearful of the United States due in part to the frightening American films she had seen. Fadhail told the officers, "'I don't want to go to America; I want to go to my brother.' But they said, 'You have to go through processing,' and all of those things. And I did apply through the embassy, Australian embassy, and they reject my application."[2] Four months later, Fadhail arrived in Erie, Pennsylvania.

The first line of chapter 1 in *Welcome to the United States: A Guidebook for Refugees*, typically disseminated by the International Organization for Migration (IOM) to refugees attending pre-departure cultural orientations before their resettlement to the United States, reads, "Like many other refugees, you have made the decision to resettle and start a new life in the United States of America."[3] As is evident from the aforementioned narratives, however, refugees may have varying degrees of interest in or understanding about this "decision" to resettle in the United States. Like Abdikadir, some refugees are not aware that America exists until they apply for resettlement; others, like Fadhail, do not want to resettle in the United States and only make the decision to do so after they are rejected from other countries' resettlement programs.

In this chapter, I consider the media that refugees encounter after being approved for resettlement in the United States and before their departure dates—either in cultural orientations abroad or in refugees' individual pre-relocation preparations that occur outside of formal orientations. By providing a multisited view of overseas cultural orientations, I endeavor to situate orientation media within a broader framework of enculturation. To this end, I analyze the messages that orientation media includes and excludes in order to elucidate the techniques through which the United States government represents itself in cultural orientations as well as the efforts made by these orientations texts to normalize the refugee experience by describing repeatedly what "most people" in the United States want, have, or do. Throughout, I will work to reveal how orientation media often communicate what the implicit and explicit consequences are for refugees who fail to abide by the orientation's counsel, and several ways the illusion of choice may function within refugees' relocation processes.

Because not all preparatory media encounters occur during official cultural orientations, and because several factors may inhibit refugees from attending pre-departure orientations or from digesting the media that is provided in such contexts, I will also consider the ways refugees use media that they encounter outside of formal orientations as they make independent preparations for relocation to the United States. These independent preparations include activities such as Internet research on the United States or an increased consumption of American films or television immediately before one's resettlement. I anticipate that an appraisal of both official orientation and non-orientation media will allow a useful view into the diversity of refugees' interpretations of and access to mediated representations of the United States from multiple sources before their arrival.

The process of applying for resettlement to the United States as a refugee is complicated in large part by the activities that lead refugees to this action. Although multiple countries accept refugees, government quotas and funding limit the number of successful applications to any given destination.[4] Refugees may decide to apply for resettlement to the United States because they have family members living there or because they have seen films or other media that make the United States appear as an attractive destination.[5] Other times, as in Fadhail's case, the decision to apply to the United States may only occur after an application to another country is rejected. In other instances still, refugees may apply for U.S. resettlement as a result of some outside pressure. For example, Sitay, a Somali refugee living in San Diego, remembers,

> When we came to Nairobi, the government asked us, "You know, you guys have this kind of situation, so which place you guys want to go?" And we don't even know there is America in the world. We didn't even know there is a country named America.

Because Sitay knew that Kakuma (a refugee camp in Kenya) was the name of a place where some Somalis lived, she told the government representatives, "We want Kakuma." Hearing this answer, the representatives cursed and scoffed at her. Sitay remembers,

> They said, like, "When the government asks what place you want, why don't you say America or Europe? How come you say Kakuma?" And we don't know which one is America and which one is Europe, we just know only Africa. That's why the government—when they ask us, "What country?"—we said, "Kakuma." And you know, the government said, "No, why don't you choose another country?"[6]

Sitay obliged and applied for resettlement in the United States. Because she was married to a Kenyan man who was not eligible for relocation, she arrived, alone, in 2003 to San Diego.

The paths that lead refugees to apply for U.S. resettlement are neither simple nor straightforward. But whatever the circumstances that resulted in their resettlement application, the ways that the refugees in this project viewed and interpreted U.S. media took on new significance once they were approved for U.S. resettlement and began to prepare for departure to the other side of the world.

Pre-Departure Overseas Orientations

For many, the majority of pre-departure encounters with media that portray the United States occurred during the orientations that are mandated and funded by the U.S. Department of State's Bureau of Population, Refugees, and Migration (PRM), and conducted by the Cultural Orientation Research [COR] Center before a refugee's resettlement. The timing of pre-departure cultural orientations varies by local context; refugees may attend at any point after they have been approved for resettlement in the United States and before their departure date. This means some refugees receive their orientation several weeks—or even months—before they relocate, while others, like Sancha, attend only a few days before their departure. The timing of a cultural orientation may have a direct effect on refugees' memory of it or their ability to interpret the presented information. Sancha explained that in his own case,

> [We attended] that orientation only before coming to U.S. like, 15 days before. I say if it was done more earlier, it would be more beneficial for people. So that people, you know, they can think and they can judge—they can analyze themself and they'll have enough time to do everything before coming U.S. Like, if they are taught only 10 days early or 15 days early, already they are in a type of, you know—what to say—rush preparing for moving to U.S.[7]

Sancha's comment serves as a reminder that one should not only consider what kinds of media were made available to refugees during their orientations but also the contexts in which the orientation media were provided. The extraction of refugee encounters with pre-departure media from other lived experiences, so that media can be analyzed in isolation, can provide only a fractional perspective. For a broader view, one must follow the lead of the third wave of audience studies described by Pertti Alasuutari and consider the ways media are embedded inside and inform other complex facets of pre-departure contexts—both in and outside of official orientations.[8] As Sancha revealed in the first chapter, some of his expectations about the United States were a direct result of the multiple U.S. films he watched while living in Nepal. The information he was given during his pre-departure orientation provided him with a new layer of understanding for comparison with what he learned from the films, so that his expectations acted as dynamic, negotiated sources of knowledge about the possible characteristics of his future life in the United States. Indeed, orientation media, media outside of orientation, and the events surrounding this consumption—such as interpersonal conversation—are not altogether separate phenomena but rather interlocking parts that make up an intricate, layered process of preparation for resettlement in the United States.

Media abound in pre-departure orientations. For the majority of the narrators I interviewed, the orientation leaders had access to electricity to demonstrate—through video, audio recordings, or even functioning examples of kitchen and bathroom electrical appliances—what to expect during the first days in the United States. When electricity is not available, orientation leaders may depend more on hard copy images such as photographs and printed texts to illustrate the lessons. In Figure 2.1, a photograph from a cultural orientation in Thailand shows Burmese refugees viewing photographs and drawings of different places, people, foods, and animals found around the world, including the Eiffel Tower, the Statue of Liberty, Martin Luther King Jr., a traditional American Thanksgiving dinner, a cheeseburger, a woman in a bikini, and a bald eagle. In the upper right hand corner of the frame, a globe and a bin of papers are visible.

FIGURE 2.1 Cultural orientation in Thailand[9]

Orientations provided for individuals who are living independently, rather than in refugee camps, exhibit more variation in physical location, content, and media. For example, an Iraqi refugee living in Jordan will likely already be familiar with American-style toilets and electric kitchen appliances. Therefore, lessons that take a good deal of time in some contexts may be unnecessary in others.

In order to determine the content of the overseas cultural orientation, the COR Center liaises with PRM, overseas Resettlement Support Center Cultural Orientation programs, and national and local resettlement agencies. According to the COR Center, "The purpose of overseas CO [cultural orientation] is to help refugees develop realistic expectations about life in the United States."[10] Inherent within this single sentence, several assumptions exist; this statement insinuates that some refugees' expectations have stronger correlations to reality than others and that an orientation possesses the ability to instill in its attendees expectations that are more realistic than the ones they would have held otherwise. Moreover, at its essence, the statement implies that expectations *matter* within the relocation process. Anyone who has ever traveled to an unfamiliar location under any circumstances may testify to the effect of expectations on the experience of the traveler; but to understand the full significance of orientation media, one must ask, why would arriving refugees' expectations matter to the U.S. Department of State? In other words, what motivates the U.S. government to fund an expensive, time-consuming, multisited project aimed simply at changing refugees' minds by "develop[ing] realistic expectations?" The answer to this question is worth lingering over, as it opens up a window through which to view the relationship of media to the imagination.

Dilip Parameshwar Goankar, the director of the Center for Global Culture and Communication at Northwestern University posits,

> The entry of imagination into the logic of everyday life is given a global inflection by the twin forces of modernity: mass migration and mass mediation. Whether moving voluntarily in search of better lives or moving involuntarily as refugees and persecuted peoples, the migrants have lost the worlds into which they were born and are therefore forced to construct new imagined worlds that rarely coincide with geopolitical space or the ideologies of nation-states.[11]

Here Goankar suggests that without some manipulation, migrant's imaginations are unlikely to "coincide" with the ideologies of the new locales into which they are willingly or unwillingly placed. This perspective causes the relationship of the "twin forces" of mass migration and mass mediation to take on new significance as one considers the purpose and effects of orientation media, because it highlights not only the perceived benefits of orientation to refugees but also the benefits of orientation to the state.

From first glance, using orientation media may appear as a straightforward means of education designed for the simple task of teaching a refugee some processes that s/he may be unfamiliar with. But Michel Foucault provides one explanation of a more complex reason that a government may invest generously in the well-being of some of its (future) residents. Foucault describes how, taking on the good will of ethos, a government may begin to demonstrate a kind of Aristotelian sense of caring about its "audience"—the "increase of its wealth, longevity, health, and so on."[12] If subjects—such as the refugees in attendance at U.S. State Department-funded orientations—believe that the government is looking out for their safety, their defenses can rest in the assuredness that as long as they conform to the system and do what is asked, the State has their best interests in mind. I do not mean to suggest here that the State's intentions for refugees are necessarily malevolent or devious but rather, simply, that it has a stake in orientation media that goes beyond altruistic care for the well-being of refugees. By assessing the means through which orientation content is produced *by* the U.S. government and *for* the U.S. government, one can better determine just how this power functions in the lives of arriving refugees.

Figure 2.2, a still taken from a widely used refugee resettlement orientation video titled "Welcome to the United States," typically shown in pre-departure orientations, shows Lang Za Thang, a Burmese refugee, about to shake hands with his caseworker upon arriving at a U.S. airport.

This single still reveals several potentially useful components: Lang is carrying his IOM bag, which helps American caseworkers identify refugees when they exit the gate area and often proves especially useful for refugees who do not speak English or who are unfamiliar with navigating airports. Because Lang

FIGURE 2.2 Still taken from "Welcome to the United States"[13]

is arriving during the winter, he is shown here wearing a jacket; the next scene depicts his caseworker providing Lang with a heavy coat, a winter hat, and gloves. Lang is smiling in this still, and during the next few shots of the film, he remarks, "I felt really happy, there were so many people at the airport [to greet me]." Watching even just this single scene during pre-departure orientation, a refugee could learn about the appearance of the interior of an American airport, the importance of carrying one's assigned IOM bag during travel, the likelihood that one's arrival destination will be colder than one is used to, the proper way to greet a case manager, and the possibility of experiencing happiness upon arrival in the United States. But scenes like this one may serve conversely to confound refugees whose arrival scenarios differ from those portrayed on screen. In comparing the expectations they formed during encounters with pre-departure orientation media and their experiences after resettlement, several narrators described experiencing some combination of expected and unexpected circumstances, confirming orientation media's ability to offer helpful, yet inherently limited, instruction. While I will discuss this phenomenon in more detail in the next chapter, here, I'll provide one example that speaks directly to the themes evident in the scene from the "Welcome to the United States" orientation film.

Tek remembers learning in a refugee orientation in Nepal that "The weather in U.S. it is really fluctuating. No one can predict how it is going to the next hour," and so he was not surprised when a big snowstorm in New York delayed his arrival. Tek also learned during his orientation that refugees are supposed to wait at the airport for their case managers, but these instructions did not clarify that Tek must first exit the gate area, so that upon his arrival, Tek remembers,

> I waited there at the waiting area for about twenty or twenty-five minutes but no one was there. All the passengers they left the board. There was no one. My family, three of us, we were waiting over there. And after a while I thought, I think no one is going to come here to pick us up.[14]

Because many refugees—including Tek—had not been inside an airport before the day of their resettlement, orientation media that depict scenes such as Lang Za Thang easily finding and identifying his caseworker may not adequately prepare refugees for the chaos and expanse of typical American airports. Despite his surprise at finding no one waiting for him at the gate, eventually Tek used what little English he knew at the time to ask an airport employee for help and managed to find his case manager.

Jasmine, from Burma, remembered learning from a film screened during her orientation that took place near the end of a sixteen-year-long stay in Thailand,

> If you go to America, you're going to see snow, you're going to live [in] a house, and then I was thinking that, if I go to United States, I'm going to

have my own house, and going to see a lot of snow, but when I came here, like, everything's like, different. And then, the first day I cannot wait to go back, because my dream and [what] I faced so different.[15]

Jasmine has been living in San Diego since 2010. She has yet to see the snow she was prepared for in orientation. One explanation for Jasmine's experience may be that because the media utilized in overseas orientation is designed for dissemination to refugees who are moving to multiple parts of the United States, it inevitably conflates—visually and verbally—different geographies, cultures, and norms in order to provide a generalized view of a generic "America."

Importance of Visuality in Orientation Media

Because overseas orientation takes place before refugees arrive in the United States, and because most refugees have never visited the United States before they are relocated here, overseas cultural orientation educators use varying combinations of digital, video, and print media to help refugees envision their first few days in their new homes. It is difficult to overstate the role that visual images play for this purpose. For refugees who are illiterate or who do not speak the language in which the media is produced, pictures, drawings, and the action in orientation videos may be the only parts of orientation media that can be understood without an interpreter. Moreover, for refugees who—because of a lack of technology, interest, or governmental freedom—have not encountered any visual representation of the United States in films, television, or books prior to their orientation attendance, visual orientation media may prove especially important, and may communicate to the viewer much more than was intended by the media's author(s).

Hsit Hsa, a Burmese refugee I met in November 2013, was provided with a resettlement orientation book in her native language, Karen, while living in a refugee camp in Thailand. Hsit Hsa e-mailed me a photo of the book, published by the International Rescue Committee and titled simply *RSC*[16] *Thailand*, a few days after I interviewed her near her home in San Diego, California, where she has lived since 2011. She told me,

> We had three days American culture orientation. Because we just hear, and when they taught us, just verbally, so we don't have a chance to practice, and to see things for real. So, I think I need more. For example, they told us, when you get into the plane, what do you have to do. What things you have to notice. Everyone cannot remember, like, everything. And then the other thing is that some people, they don't—they cannot read! So, even though we had book, we don't—we cannot read. They just can listen when the translator say, but they don't have—they forget easily.[17]

Because Hsit Hsa was concerned about forgetting the information she learned during orientation, she brought the book with her to the United States, where she keeps it in her apartment. Based on the configuration of the cover of the text, in which eight small photographs appear overlain atop a large image of the United States, it seems that these photos are meant to show a variety of Burmese individuals performing different activities in the United States; for example, one of the photos shows a mother walking a boy to the door of a school bus. For individuals familiar with such cultural activities as dropping off young children at a school bus, these photos may seem typical or even mundane. But for an individual who has never encountered a school bus and, indeed, cannot read the English words "SCHOOL BUS" that appear in the image on the side of the bus, such a photograph would be less clear. Does the vehicle belong to the boy and the woman or to a resettlement agency? Is the woman going to get onto the vehicle and leave the boy behind? Is the vehicle going to take the boy and the woman to work or to see their family? Is the woman pulling the boy away from his home and his family? Without knowledge that some schools in the United States offer a busing system to transport students to and from a building that may be beyond walking distance from their homes, this picture may either lose some of its intended meaning or take on new meaning that was not intended.

The Relationship between Orientation Content and Context

For refugees originating from rural areas who are minimally educated, have never traveled by plane, and have been living for ten or even twenty years unemployed in refugee camps, a good deal of pre-departure cultural orientation will likely be consumed with simple practical instructions regarding the travel experience, such as directions for navigating an airport and using a seatbelt. In these instances, when electricity for films or computer-based media is not available to orientation leaders, they may rely on photographs, drawings, and descriptions to explain electricity, the proper use of household appliances such as microwaves and stoves; and the use and maintenance of indoor toilets. In some cases, the International Organization for Migration or another NGO may be able to provide physical examples of a few such household items for demonstration during orientation meetings. In these instances, photographs, drawings, and films may become less necessary or important.

Balaram, a Bhutanese refugee who arrived in Pittsburgh in 2010, helped me understand one reason why learning basic information about living in American homes during orientation was helpful: "Even though I studied in India—it is developed, you know—still the toilet system is different [in the United States]," Balaram explained.[18] "This kind of toilet is raised, this system is not popular there and there you don't use toilet paper at all, people use water." Fortunately, in Nepal, where Balaram attended orientation, the International Organization for

FIGURE 2.3 An instructional diagram on the door of a bathroom at a refugee camp in Nepal[19]

Migration facilitates cultural orientations at two sites[20] where refugees have an opportunity to see and interact with basic household appliances, which include a refrigerator, a microwave, and a Western toilet. In Figure 2.3, a photograph of one of the toilets at the site where Balaram attended orientation shows a diagram hanging on the door instructing refugees to sit down rather than squat on top of the toilet. No words appear on the diagram; only about 65 percent of refugees living in Nepal are literate.[21]

When the photograph in Figure 2.4 was taken in the Dadaab refugee camp in Kenya in 2009, Western toilets were not available for demonstration purposes to orientation leaders teaching Somali refugees. In the absence of the physical object, the orientation leader, Amina, shows a film that depicts a Western toilet, pausing when the toilet is in center frame to explain to the attendees the necessity of sitting instead of squatting when using the bathroom.

Orientation leaders may consider lessons such as the previous one unnecessary for more educated, technologically advanced, or well-traveled refugees, and choose instead to spend the duration of the orientation venturing into more nuanced topics, such as instructions for connecting with other members of one's religion post-arrival, gender roles in the United States, and the causes and/or stages of culture shock. The Resettlement Support Center, an agency serving refugees from Iraq, reported in a 2012 publication the kinds of topics that are unique to Iraqi refugee orientations. The report states,

> Most Iraqi refugees in the region are accustomed to modern life amenities such as satellite T.V., Internet (both at home and in commercial

FIGURE 2.4 Orientation attendees watch a film at the Dadaab camp in Kenya[22]

establishments such as coffee shops), cell phones, and computers, including high-end laptops. Refugees tend to expect that they will be provided with such items upon arrival into the U.S.A. . . . Refugees are informed that items such as computers, cell phones, Internet service, and satellite T.V. are not provided by resettlement agencies.

While in this case, it appears that the orientation content was tailored because of attendees' prior access to technology, at other times, the reasons for variations in the content of orientation are more difficult to pinpoint.

The range of topics that the narrators in this project reported learning from pre-departure orientation media—and, notably, that they can still remember in detail today—surprised me. From orientation books, different narrators remembered learning about topics ranging from the history of the United States,[23] that Washington, DC, is the center of government,[24] what it means to establish an emergency contact, how to call an ambulance, varying methods for transporting children to school,[25] and welfare assistance from the U.S. government.[26] From orientation videos, the narrators remembered learning about the necessity of visiting American doctors,[27] the travel process from one's country of asylum to the United States,[28] how to use an oven and freezer,[29] English vocabulary,[30] how to vacuum, the mix of cultures in the United States,[31] how to use eye contact and shake hands when meeting an American,[32] how to lock a door, how to shop at a grocery store and interact with a cashier,[33] how to get an ID and social security card,[34] and what an American bed looks like.[35]

Because of the pervasion of selective media within overseas cultural orientations and because of the vast diversity of content the narrators extracted from this media, it becomes necessary to ask a simple question: How does orientation media function in the lives of refugees? By approaching this question with patience for diversity within different manifestations of the answer, one may gain a greater view of the power of orientation media within the lived realities of incoming refugees to the United States.

The Power of Orientation Media

Regardless of the variations within the specificity of their content, it is clear that pre-departure cultural orientations present a partial, constructed version of reality to their attendees and that this construction is aided and reinforced by print, video and digital media. If mediated communication does indeed hold the power to create subjective truths or realities as cultural certainties, one might ask in a consideration of orientation media: *Whose truth do these media communicate? Which realities are evident, and which are concealed? Whose purpose do these realities serve?* Rather than decrying or supporting the particular constructions of reality that resettlement orientations facilitate, I wish instead to argue for a consideration that these texts may be simultaneously useful, productive, and problematic.

While some pre-departure orientation media provide pragmatic directions for resettlement travel and survival during the first weeks in the United States, there exists a notable and substantial trend of social, religious, familial, and lingual directions for refugees. As I hope to elucidate in the following sections, these cultural instructions are particularly revealing. Toby Miller, who considers how culture and citizenship are constructed, represented, and negotiated in American television, argues, "Citizenship has always been cultural."[36] Moreover, Miller asserts,

> In the United States, immigrants are crucial to the nation's foundational ethos of consent, for they represent alienation from origins and endorsement of destinations. This makes achieving and sustaining national culture all the more fraught. The memory of what has been lost, even if it is by choice [in refugees' case it is not], is strong and so is the necessity to shore up "preferences" expressed for U.S. norms.[37]

In Miller's view, because immigrants to the United States must necessarily allow the imposition of the State into their lives this transitional period provides the

U.S. government a crucial opportunity to publicize and perpetuate a particular cultural narrative.

As the refugees in this chapter demonstrate, some orientation media perpetuate this narrative by working simultaneously to construct the understanding that refugees' previous knowledge is inadequate and to assemble a new reality in which refugees will only succeed if they heed the media's instructions for their future. By providing both pragmatic travel and housing instructions as well as insights and instructions regarding American culture as a whole, orientation media support Nick Couldry's view that "Media transform the smallest details of individual actions *and* the largest spaces in which we are involved."[38] So that I do not risk overstating the role this media plays, I wish to remind the reader that any media about the United States that a refugee encounters before his or her relocation may function as one of many pieces of communication that potentially affects refugees' complex processes of forming and negotiating their expectations about life in the United States.[39]

As one explores the possibility that any piece of communication asserts limited, constructed representations of situated reality, one must also ask to whom this reality is addressed. Most of the orientation media that the narrators in this study remember were addressed to refugees generally rather than to any particular ethnicity or group. In this way, orientation texts, images, and videos construct an imagined but ambiguous readership through the messages they include and exclude. Because of this characteristic, one might view the audiences of orientation media according to Wolfgang Iser's notion of an implied reader—a term that, Iser posits, "incorporates both the prestructuring of the potential meaning by the text, and the reader's actualization of this potential through the reading process" and "refers to the active nature of this process."[40] The implicit presuppositions that appear about the implied reader in orientation media present a contradiction previously observed by Charles Briggs (drawing on Michael Warner's work) in an analysis of the Venezuelan government's attempt to teach citizens about the prevention of cholera in the early 1990s: the media "project[s] an image of reaching an actually existing public at the same time that it creates multiple publics as it circulates."[41] In order to uncover how the latter half of this statement functions, one must become familiar with a process Louis Althusser calls *interpellation*: at the moment an individual recognizes him or herself as the intended audience for some kind of message, s/he becomes subject to the power of the institution that produced the message.[42] While in Althusser's example the subject is *interpellated* when s/he chooses to turn around after a police officer calls out across a public street ("Hey, you!"), in the case of orientation media, an orientation attendee need only recognize him/herself as a member of the media authors' intended audience to become a part of an imagined public of refugees who are "other" than Americans and in need of some instruction. In light of Briggs, Warner and Althusser, one can examine the techniques through which orientation media both presuppose and invent a public. In order to unpack the ways a refugee public is convinced of their need for the information delivered during a pre-departure orientation, as well as how this constructed need is fulfilled, one must home in on some existing orientation media. Indeed, without sustained attention to concrete examples, this discussion runs the risk of slipping into the realm of conjecture.

A Closer Look at One Orientation Text

To assay the means through which orientation media affect and inform refugees' lives, one could take multiple approaches that vary from a wide-scale, comparative analysis of orientation books, films, and images, to an in-depth analysis of a single scene from an orientation film or one page from a sole text. Both macro- and micro-media analysis is fruitful in its own right, and each of these approaches offers some insights that the other does not. Though I intend to continue the trend of brief examples of orientation media that I have already begun in this chapter, in this section, I will linger over one particular piece of orientation media for the sake of more thorough, sustained analysis.

The 266 page COR-produced text *Welcome to the United States: A Guidebook for Refugees*—chosen because of its widespread use in overseas orientation and for its repeated mention by the narrators in this project—is funded by the U.S. Department of State and typically distributed by personnel affiliated with the International Organization for Migration in pre-departure refugee orientation contexts.[43] The 2013 edition of the *Guidebook* is available in seven languages and accessible free of charge in PDF format on the COR-CAL website.[44] Also available on this website is a film of the same name that sometimes accompanies the text in orientation contexts where video viewing technology is available. While the *Guidebook for Refugees* is meant to be used first and primarily in pre-departure orientation contexts, the third chapter of the *Guidebook* instructs readers to pack the text into their carry-on luggage—along with "quiet toys for children" and "snacks"—when they relocate to the United States so that it can be used throughout and after the travel process.[45] Unfortunately, because COR does not publicly disclose the number of visitors to the *Guidebook for New Refugees* website or statistics regarding the distribution patterns of the hard copies, it remains impossible to quantify or qualify the audience for this text. Indeed, aside from the narrators whom I interviewed, I do not know how many refugees have encountered the text, why the text is made available in certain situations, or in what contexts it is read in full or only in part. The COR website states that while *Welcome to the United States: A Guidebook for Refugees* is "applicable to all refugee populations, the 2012 version focuses on showing refugees from currently arriving populations, such as Bhutanese, refugees from Burma, refugees from Iraq, and Somalis."[46]

Notably, only one of the seventy-four refugees I interviewed could remember definitively the names of any of the texts they were given during pre-departure orientation. Said Abiyow recalled a pre-departure orientation text called *Refugee Resettlement Progress*, which I have not been able to confirm or locate. Even Hsit Hsa, who brought her orientation book with her to the United States where she keeps it in her apartment, had to consult the book and e-mail me after our interview to confirm its title. Though they could not remember the name of the text, many of the narrators remembered that the International Organization for Migration, which disseminates and promotes the use of *Welcome to the United States: A Guidebook for Refugees*, delivered their pre-departure orientations. The U.S. State Department reports that once they are approved for resettlement to the United States, "every refugee family receives *Welcome to the United States* [*A Guidebook for Refugees*]," although it was difficult to confirm this ubiquitous dissemination from my own interviews.[47] It is clear from my interviews that the *Guidebook* is not the only text available in overseas orientation contexts; local orientation leaders may create their own curriculum or use a combination of resources to construct a curriculum for overseas orientation. Because the *Guidebook for Refugees* is only a single orientation text, the following analysis must be understood as one example among many possible examples. In order to avoid viewing this single piece of media as an isolated, finite entity, I will consider this text situationally and contextually, considering the varieties of ways it may appear within, affect, and interact with refugees' lives. Of course, the *Guidebook* cannot guarantee its effect on the reader, and the text's meaningfulness for any given reader is likely to vary by context; a reader who only encounters the text in a pre-departure orientation is likely to use and interpret it differently than a reader who reads the text after relocating to the United States and can choose to apply or not apply its instructions immediately.

My method for analyzing the *Guidebook for Refugees* included a close reading of the text with a consideration that all included language and images are both symbolic and value laden. Throughout, this text promotes certain possibilities for refugees' lives in the United States, while simultaneously concealing others. After examining the text in detail, I identified five major themes that appear throughout: (1) the production of reader ignorance, (2) the promotion of refugee obedience, (3) the condoning of "American" normativity, (4) the invitation to multiculturalism, and (5) the foretelling of the emotions of refugees arriving in the United States. In the following sections, I will discuss each of these themes in detail, providing visual and textual examples from the text or comments from refugee narrators when they are relevant.

In an attempt to convince attendees of the orientation's importance, orientation media often work rhetorically to create a sense of ignorance in its audience. The first chapter of the *Guidebook for Refugees* asks readers,

> What have you heard about life in America? Draw or write about the things you have heard below. When you are finished with this book, come back to this page. Circle what is still true and cross off what is no longer true.[48]

In a weeklong independent observation of the Dadaab camp for Somali refugees in Kenya, Robinson Cook, the employment director at Lutheran Immigration and Refugee Services in Minnesota, took the photograph in Figure 2.5 of one refugee group's answer to the previous question during a pre-departure orientation meeting.

Though it is impossible to know how the ideas listed in Cook's photograph were formed, it is significant to note that refugees—even those from underdeveloped nations such as Somalia—may have a whole host of opinions about various aspects of professional, social, and personal life in the United States before they encounter a text such as the *Guidebook for Refugees*.

The notion that the *Guidebook* allows for interactivity is important; refugees are invited to complete several quizzes, do drawings, and create lists throughout the text. Although attendees could hypothetically respond to these invitations in a variety of ways—assuming their ability to read and write—the *Guidebook* controls refugees' participation through appendices that reveal the correct answers to all quizzes, banks of ideas for possible drawings, and instructions, such as the ones mentioned earlier, for refugees to "cross off" anything they add to the text that does not fit the *Guidebook*'s objectives. Through this repeated process of controlled interactivity, the text simultaneously promotes refugees' ignorance and

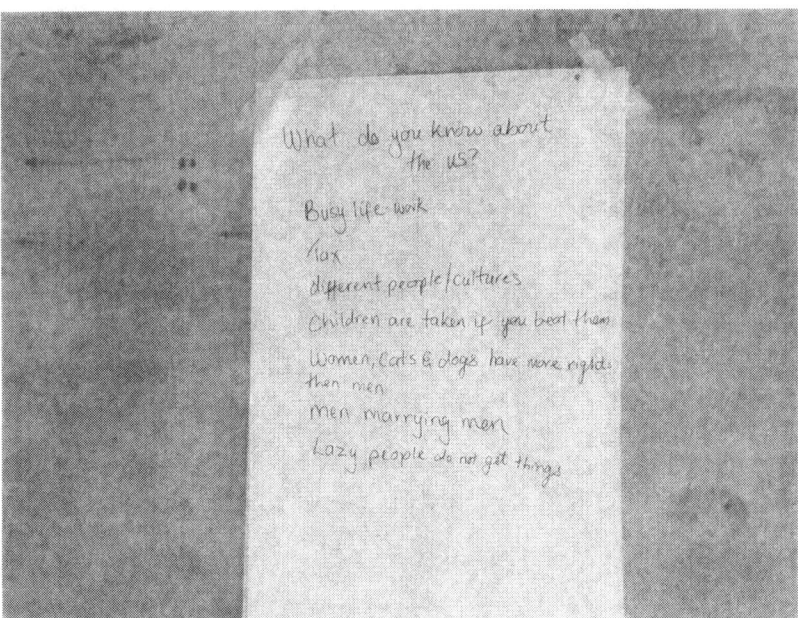

FIGURE 2.5 Refugees respond to a question during pre-departure orientation[49]

assures the reader of the text's ability to deliver the right kinds of knowledge. Indeed, Shannon Sullivan states, "Rather than oppose knowledge, ignorance often is formed by it, and vice versa."[50] In her essay, "White Ignorance and Colonial Oppression, or, Why I Know So Little about Puerto Rico," Sullivan describes the systems of education for Puerto Ricans that were instituted soon after Puerto Rico became a U.S. colony in 1898, and her narrative is directly relevant to an analysis of the *Guidebook for Refugees*.

First, Sullivan asserts that as a result of U.S. colonization, Puerto Ricans were "ambiguously designated as belonging to, but not part of, the United States."[51] In the *Guidebook for Refugees*, this same ambiguous distinction exists in language that includes statements such as, "You will be more successful in the United States if you watch what is going on around you and are open to new ways of doing things, and if you are willing to ask questions about behavior that puzzles you."[52] Here the author(s) of the *Guidebook*—who only ever identifies himself/herself/themselves according to an affiliation with COR—represents the native voice of some presence that stands at the metaphorical door of the United States and has the power to speak knowledgeably about the path to "success" in the United States. Throughout the *Guidebook*, this unspecified, authoritative voice will refer to refugee readers as "you." But no delineation appears that qualifies this "you" as belonging to a certain race, sex, ethnicity, or age. Instead, it refers to all refugees, irrespective of difference, in need of instruction.

Sullivan's work reveals how citizens of the United States' ignorance of Puerto Ricans "led them to view Puerto Ricans as ignorant and to believe that their (alleged) ignorance interfered with their ability to become true Americans."[53] As a result, educational "opportunities" that taught Puerto Ricans to behave in ways that Sullivan argues were decidedly middle-class, Protestant, Euro-American, old-fashioned, and promoted a privileged view of hard work, truthfulness, and cleanliness were made available. This educational process hinged on a pivotal acceptance: the Puerto Ricans had to recognize and accept that they were

> uncivilized, childlike, ignorant, and weak (read: feminine) people with no cultural or political history of any value who were fortunate enough to receive help correcting this problem from a benevolent democracy that had only their best interests at heart. Puerto Ricans were implicitly told that by becoming ignorant of who and what they were before 1898, they could remake themselves into true, manly Americans.[54]

While Sullivan describes a process that began more than a century ago, the same themes appear throughout the 2013 edition of the *Guidebook for Refugees*. Indeed, the text works efficiently and explicitly to establish a perception of ignorance and need in its readership and to assure the reader that the guide will "help you prepare for your first few months in the United States."⁵⁵ The possibility that a refugee may already possess the resources s/he needs for life in the United States is not addressed.

The implications of this interplay of ignorance and knowledge in the text is tied up with the belief—evident in some of the interviews I conducted—that orientation presents a kind of exhaustive standard of truth. For instance, Buddhi Rai, from Bhutan, told me that before her pre-departure orientation in Nepal, she "only knew a few things about the United State." She explained, "I knew that comparing of all the countries, this is a developed country, but I didn't imagine this." During her pre-departure orientation, Buddhi told me, "Our teacher told us everything about America."⁵⁶ Similarly, although Zahraa, an Iraqi, attended a predeparture orientation that was only three days long, she believed, "They told us everything about the life in the U.S. They told us all the details . . . So when I came here, almost I know everything about it. They explained everything."⁵⁷ Said, from Somalia, explained that in his orientation, IOM disseminated a book called *Refugee Resettlement Progress*. "That book, we just read it about how the United States does, so, that's the time that we figured it out—everything about the United States."⁵⁸ When orientation attendees come to believe for whatever reason that their orientations present a kind of instrumental truth, rather than a constructed version of reality that may exist among several alternative constructions, the orientations and their corresponding media take on a heightened degree of power.

In the narratives that are advanced within the *Guidebook for Refugees*, refugees are consistently envisaged as both lacking some imperative knowledge, and responsible for gaining that knowledge as quickly and efficiently as possible. In fact, for a group of people allegedly in need of so much education to function as normative residents, the refugees *interpellated* by the *Guidebook* are given an amazing amount of responsibility to be wholly self-reliant and obedient to American rules. Chapter 4 states, "Resettlement Agencies will help you with basic expenses and living costs for the first thirty days in the United States . . . But remember: Americans value self-reliance, so you will be expected to work and take responsibility for your own life as soon as possible."⁵⁹ Imposing such a duty on refugees after reassuring them repeatedly of their ignorance may seem contradictory, but in fact this tactic manages a kind of productive control: if, having been given all the tools a refugee should need to survive, one fails, this text ensures that no one is to blame but the refugee him or herself.

Refugees from multiple locations and circumstances consistently reported a focus during overseas cultural orientation on the importance of obeying the law and rules of the United States. Ya Wee, who was only two years old when his family was displaced from their home in Burma, remembers that the pre-arrival cultural orientation he attended in Thailand before being relocated to New York taught him the tools he would need in the United States to "follow the rules and laws, regulations."[60] Laxmi—who attended orientation during an eighteen-year stay in Nepal after fleeing Bhutan[61]—remembered,

> People [that were teaching] that orientation talk about we need to follow the rules and regulations of United State and . . . we need to adapt the ways of life of American . . . we need to follow the rules and regulations and we need to adapt according to the amendments of United State.

Likewise, when I asked Abreer, who attended a brief orientation in her birth country of Iraq before resettlement to Houston, Texas, what her orientation was like, she recalled, "You have to obey everything . . . They told that States is a country of law. So if you obey, you can survive, without law, you cannot be there."[62] Abreer's memory echoes the *Guidebook's* instructions; it states, "In the United States, you can be punished if you break the law, even if you did not know about the law you broke. The penalty for some offenses may be deportation (return) to your home country. For this reason it is very important to learn and obey the laws."[63] By promoting obedience to American rules and laws before refugees arrive in the United States, the *Guidebook* presents life in the United States as a privilege that may be revoked should refugees fail to prove themselves as law-abiding residents.

The relationship of the kind of strict obedience that the aforementioned narrators described to self-sufficiency becomes clearer when one considers that each of the four groups involved in this study come from cultures that are traditionally collective rather than individualistic. In collective cultures, William B. Gudykunst describes, individuals take a communal approach to survival, so that the goals, needs, and well-being of one's community—which may include extended family, neighbors, coworkers, and/or members of one's religion—take precedence over one's own goals, needs, or well-being.[64] The necessity of transitioning out of this collectivist view and into a more individualistic outlook in order to achieve self-sufficiency is made clear in the *Guidebook for Refugees* and was echoed in the narrators' memories. The first chapter of the *Guidebook* begins with a list of vocabulary words that "are used when discussing resettlement in the United States." Readers are asked to write a definition of, or—for those who cannot write—draw a picture that describes the following words: Courage; Determination; Goals; Independent; Journey; Resettlement; Self-Reliance. The importance of individualism is thus established through this list at the very outset of the first chapter of the text and is reinforced through fictitious vignettes about refugee individuals throughout the chapters. One such vignette reads,

> Kumar asked for advice from his case manager and the employment specialist at his resettlement agency, and learned how to look for jobs on his

own. Krishna sat at home or in the resettlement agency office and waited for staff to find a job for him. Who do you think probably got a job first? Who do you think was more successful over time?[65]

The narrators remember similar instruction regarding self-sufficiency. Iptisam, who attended a four-day cultural orientation in Jordan with her husband after fleeing Iraq and before arriving in Los Angeles in June 2013, remembered that her orientation taught her "To respect the law here . . . you have to depend on yourself when you move to U.S . . . everybody has to work to be independent."[66] Jala also fled Iraq, and attended a three-hour orientation in Jordan before his relocation to San Diego in July 2013, during which he remembers seeing "some parts of movies—short movies." He explained, "They told us about the relationships between people . . . American people, how we treat them."[67] I asked Jala to clarify what he learned about American relationships in his pre-departure orientation media. He answered,

> You know, the relationships between people here, it's not so—it's not together, they are separated—if you have neighbors, you don't dial them or don't talk with them too much because there is no connection between people too much, like in our country. In Iraq there is friendship, relationship between the neighbors; they talk with each other, they go visit each other but here, just you say "Hi" to them, to greet them.

Nanda, who grew up in Bhutan, summed up his orientation this way: "Basically the orientation stresses the proactiveness of the people, it's not like—they don't teach us dependency, they teach more independence, they think, they just try to give the idea that we should be independent in the United States."[68] This consistent stressing of self-sufficiency would understandably serve the state well; if a refugee becomes self-reliant, s/he will not need to burden the state by relying on public assistance for his/her well-being.

The necessity of self-sufficiency is reinforced in the *Guidebook* through the following fictional vignette: "After a few months in his apartment, Kyaw Oo finds cockroaches living in and around his sink. His apartment has also become dirty. Who is responsible for keeping the apartment clean? Who is responsible for getting rid of the cockroaches?"[69] Such vignettes reveal the creative rhetorical strategies orientation media may employ to ensure that refugees have the "right" kind of knowledge upon their arrival in the United States. To be clear, there is no doubt that a good deal of information in orientation media has the potential to be directly helpful for refugees attempting to secure basic necessities and stay out of unfamiliar legal trouble. Unfortunately, however, even if refugees follow orientation media's directions, as one of the narrators revealed, they may not be able to avoid this trouble.

Said Abiyow, a Somali refugee and the director of the Somali Bantu Organization of America in San Diego, told me a story he heard in the news a few years ago about a young refugee who was walking to school in the United States. When the boy noticed that police were following him, he began to run. The police chased the boy and, Said remembers, "said it's time to stop and he stopped. Then the police drop him down on the ground, and he kinda lose two teeth."[70] The boy couldn't speak English well so the police arrested and "picked on him" before finally releasing him. "Finally," Said explained, "They found out he is not the suspect, he was a student—he was innocent."

This story sounded familiar to me, and I remembered having read an almost identical narrative in the *Guidebook for Refugees*:

> Police officers are public servants who protect the public and help people. You should do what a police officer tells you to and not be afraid of them. If a police officer approaches you and asks you to stop, do so. Running away will be seen as a sign that you have done something wrong and may lead to problems for you.[71]

It is impossible to know whether the boy from Said's story ever read the *Guidebook for Refugees*, but regardless, he did exactly what the *Guidebook* recommends by stopping when a police officer requested it. But following these directions did not help the boy to avoid the "problems" the text warns about—indeed, the problems he incurred included harm to both his body and his criminal record, despite his not breaking any laws.

The content of the rules and laws mentioned in the *Guidebook for Refugees* boast an impressive scope that ranges from explanations of how to follow mundane social norms of interpersonal interaction to avoiding illegal activity to the necessity of taking up certain attitudes and values to assure one's success. In this way, the text acts as a manifestation of Toby Miller's assertion that "The U.S. Government, a putatively culture-free zone, [has] profoundly cultural qualifications for citizenship."[72] The *Guidebook* reinforces the necessity of following these cultural norms, rules, and laws by suggesting how important they are to most Americans.

Young Yun Kim, a scholar of cultural integration, asserts that a host culture's dissemination of information-rich texts may reveal useful cultural knowledge that helps migrants "change from being cultural outsiders to increasingly active and effective cultural insiders."[73] However, as I will argue in this section, the *Guidebook for Refugees* presents vague, ideal, and contradictory evidence regarding the nature of the United States.

Throughout, the *Guidebook* makes several references to what "Americans" want, have, or value.[74] However, it is never made clear exactly to whom the title of "Americans" refers. Perhaps it is the United States government, or domestically born United States citizens, or perhaps it includes refugees who have come before and been granted U.S. citizenship. In his seminal text, *Imagined Communities*, Benedict Anderson reveals how the nation is "imagined as a *community*, because, regardless of the actual inequality and exploitation that may prevail in each, the nation is always conceived as a deep, horizontal comradeship."[75] In the *Guidebook*, this comradeship is manifest in portrayals of the ways that "most people" in the United States live their lives.

The title page of chapter 2 states, "There are certain basic beliefs and ways of doing things that most Americans share."[76] Then the chapter goes on to explain multiple things Americans want, do, or value, including:

> Americans value self-reliance and hard work and respect people who ask questions.
> Most Americans value self-reliance and hard work . . . They also expect newcomers who do not speak English to learn it as quickly as possible.
> Americans respect people who ask questions.
> Americans smile a lot.
> Americans believe that being on time is very important. Americans try to be on time and expect others to be on time too.
> Americans place a high value on personal privacy.
> Americans believe that it is important to follow rules.
> Americans believe that a person is never too old or too young to learn new things.
> Most Americans view education as something people can enjoy all their lives.[77]

While these statements about the values, activities, and desires of Americans are perhaps meant to acclimate refugees to cultural practices they may encounter upon their arrival in the United States, in fact these statements do not always provide a statistically accurate representation of American life. For example, page 100 of the *Guidebook* states, "Most Americans see a doctor once a year for a checkup so that they will know about any health problems before they become serious."[78] In fact, the *Journal of the American Medical Association* estimates that only about 21 percent of Americans receive preventative health examinations yearly, and the Centers for Disease Control and Prevention suggested in a 2013 press release that Americans only access preventative health services at about half of the recommended rate.[79] Discrepancies like this one provoke the question, what is the purpose of information in the *Guidebook* that is incongruent with statistical reality?

In addition to a lack of statistical veracity, the *Guidebook* also remains unclear regarding the methods through which the author(s) gained access to the emotions and values of "most Americans." One of the multiple-choice quizzes, which conclude each chapter, asks, "How do most Americans feel or respond when they see a police officer?"[80] The possible answers include "a. They feel safe and protected," "b. They become afraid," "c. They insult the police officer," and "d. They run away." The correct answer—"a"—is available in Appendix A at the back of the text. But the appendix does not reveal exactly how the author(s) came to be familiar with the emotions of "most Americans" toward police officers.

Indeed, while the guide declares that "Each community in the United States is different," it implicitly limits this difference through the pronouncement of homogeneity in Americans' beliefs, attitudes, and actions.[81] Literary critic James Boyd White calls this type of rhetoric "constitutive," in that it "constitut[es] character, community and culture in language," constructing a group identity through symbols and narratives.[82] This constitutive rhetoric proposes implicitly to the reader that, while a refugee may have unique beliefs and practices, the most advantageous path to success includes clothing oneself in the kind of dominant "American" normativity described throughout the text.

Recent intercultural communication scholarship—especially work by Ronald Scollon, Suzanne Scollon, Rodney Jones, Krum Krumov, Knud Larsen, Chul-Byung Choi, Christine Walsh, Dave Este, Brigette Krieg, Ashley D. Paterson, and Julie Hakim-Larson—stresses the importance of and possibility for *en*culturation over *ac*culturation, and the *Guidebook* reflects this trend.[83] Enculturation differs from and complicates the idea of *ac*culturation, or the process by which one sets aside facets of a former culture while learning and accepting a new cultural context. Still, enculturation is not an unproblematic term; for example, it lacks the capacity to consider the ways culture may be negotiated collectively (by members of a collectivist culture), rather than individually. Fernando Ortiz's notion of "transculturation" may get closer to incorporating a consideration of collectivism during cultural change. Still, because Ortiz describes transculturation as "the product of a meeting between an existing culture or subculture and a migrant culture, *recently arrived* . . . ," the concept is not immediately applicable to pre-arrival contexts.[84]

Enculturation suggests that cultural learning is not one directional and that any individual may choose to accept, resist, question, or deny certain facets of a new culture while simultaneously maintaining, negotiating, or blending his or her former culture into a new context. For example, the *Guidebook* states, "Some values in the United States may be different from the values you think are very important. It will be important for you to find a balance between the two sets of values," and assures, "The United States is a nation of people from other countries who have brought with them many different cultural traditions and practices."[85] But while the guide mentions in several places this possibility for enculturation instead of acculturation, when I asked the refugee narrators in this project to describe their overseas cultural orientations, none of the individuals I interviewed mentioned learning from orientation media the possibility of the maintenance of their home cultures while living in the United States. Rather, the narrators reported being taught to conform to American culture no matter how different it is from one's former culture. For example, Jasmine, from Burma, remembers that at her cultural orientation in Thailand before her relocation to San Diego in 2010, she learned "about the American culture, it say that—the guy told me that if you go to the United States, 'You should not ask them age, like, how old are you? It's rude.' But in Thailand, it doesn't matter."[86] Sahro, from Somalia, remembers,

> They give us orientation . . . they tell us, "If you see, like, man and woman who stay in the back in our street, who are naked, and probably, or they hug and kiss . . . and if you see someone who dancing in the street, has something, don't [be] thinking that person's crazy."

Sancha remembered that while in Bhutan and Nepal it is typical for people to interact with other people's kids, his orientation taught him, "Do not touch American kids, or you could get into trouble with the law. Don't get too close to adults either; they need personal space." In these and other cases, it seems that the narrators' orientation experiences encouraged *ac*culturation rather than *en*culturation.

The discrepancy between the text and the narrators' reality is difficult to pinpoint; while it is possible that the maintenance of one's home culture while living in the United States was not presented as an option during pre-departure orientation, it is also feasible that this possibility was presented and that the refugees did not consider it noteworthy or even simply that they chose not to discuss this phenomenon during our interview. While an interviewer may take pains to assure narrators that there are no right or wrong answers to questions, Valerie Raleigh Yow reminds us that the possibility of selective exclusion is never wholly absent.[87]

The promise of the possibility of maintaining an intercultural outlook and behaviors seems to directly contradict the *Guidebook's* promise that "success" is directly related to one's ability to identify what most Americans want, have, or do as well as the text's directive for readers to "watch what is going on around you and [be] open to new ways of doing things."[88] From this critical perspective, the promise of the ability for multiculturalism in the *Guidebook for Refugees* appears lacking in candor.

In addition to promoting a view of refugees' ignorance, endorsing obedience, condoning American normativity, and promising the possibility of enculturation, the *Guidebook* clearly and repeatedly foretells the emotions that refugees in the United States will experience as a result of their relocation. Consider the following page in Figure 2.6, taken from chapter 3 of the *Guidebook*:

Here the guide gives readers the opportunity to fill in three circles with faces that express the emotions they anticipate feeling upon their arrival in the United

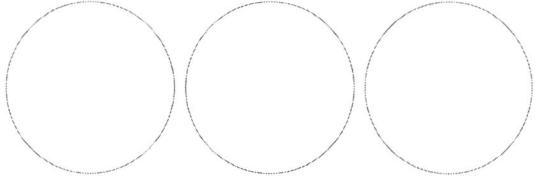

FIGURE 2.6 Page 40 of the *Guidebook for Refugees* orientation text[89]

States. However, readers are not supposed to conceive of these emotions themselves; instead, they must choose the appropriate emotions from a provided bank: "Appendix C: Faces of Emotion," is included in Figure 2.7.

As we know from scholars of affect and psychology such as Rachael Jack, facial expressions of emotion are *not* culturally universal.[90] Moreover, by providing a range of possible emotions instead of allowing readers to create the faces from their own experiences, the guide effectively limits the range of emotions a

APPENDIX C

FACES OF EMOTION

You may have trouble expressing yourself sometimes. The faces below may help you identify some of the feelings you are experiencing during the process of resettlement.

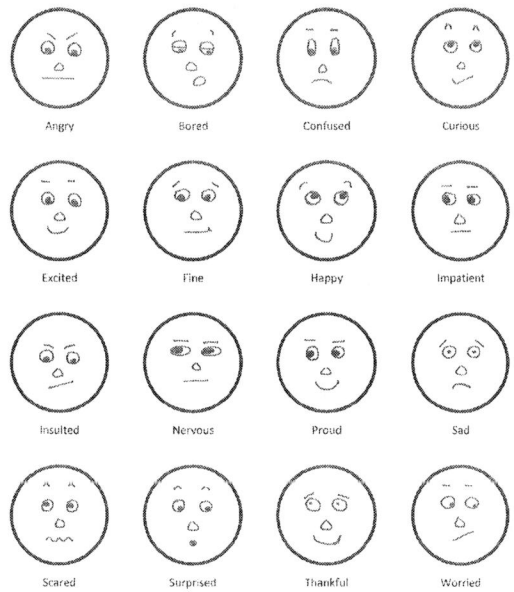

FIGURE 2.7 Page 226 of the *Guidebook for Refugees* orientation text[91]

refugee may claim to feel. While refugees may draw faces that depict emotions such as "thankful," "nervous," and "proud," they are not able to claim emotions such as "overwhelmed," "content," or "disappointed." When refugees claim to possess one of the emotions provided in Appendix C, the *Guidebook* assures the readers, "These feelings are normal," thereby implicitly denying the normalcy of emotions that are not represented by the provided list.[92]

The significance of this limited range of emotions is further underscored by the *Guidebook's* foretelling of the duration of particular emotions. As can be seen in Figure 2.6, the bottom of page 40 includes a text box that exclaims, "You may be tired after your long journey, but you'll start to feel better in a day or two!" Such predictions about the duration of particular feelings and experiences reoccur throughout the text. For example, the text states, "You will probably feel worried and frustrated as you try to adjust to your new country. These feelings are normal, and they usually go away over time."[93] Later, the text reassures readers, "Children may feel lonely at first, but as their English gets better, they make friends and feel more comfortable at school."[94] By providing a range of possible emotions and also predicting the amount of time these emotions will persist, the *Guidebook* implicitly manufactures a standard of appropriate and inappropriate emotion and ignores any refugees' emotions that do not conform to the purported normal.

This analysis has considered how the *Guidebook for Refugees* works to establish refugee ignorance, promote obedience, condone American normativity, suggest the possibility of enculturation, and foretell the emotions of refugees in the United States. But before one can fully realize the potential of this—or any—orientation media's influence, one must ask: What is at stake? In other words, what are the practical and theoretical implications of orientation media for their audiences? Orientation media often suggest that refugees have much to gain from the bounty of resources described in detail by the media; but the question remains, what do they have to lose if they reject the media's advice? In order to comprehend the extent to which a refugee's failure to accept the knowledge produced by some orientation media may lead to implicit consequences, I will remind my reader that the media that prepares refugees for life in the United States is often produced, funded, or authored by the U.S. government. For instance, the Cultural Orientation Resource Center, which published the *Guidebook for Refugees*, is funded by the U.S. Department of State, Bureau of Population, Refugees, and Migration—the same division of the government that develops application criteria, determines refugee admission ceilings, and presents eligible cases to a division of the Department of Homeland Security, which then facilitates the administration of immigration benefits and services and bears the right to institute or revoke individuals' refugee status. With this knowledge, one must complicate any view of orientation media as an altruistic resource for refugees as they transition to life in the United States.

Orientation media's implicit consequences become more readily visible in light of its frequent pronouncements of refugees' ability to choose from a variety of opportunities offered to them in the United States that are tempered by explanations of consequences should readers make the wrong choice. For brevity's sake, I will provide just one example here, from the *Guidebook for*

Refugees: Chapter 7's title page promises to teach refugees about different forms of transportation, including "Owning and driving a car." While this chapter states clearly the right of a refugee to buy a car should s/he be able to afford the payments, it repeatedly hails the benefits of using public transportation instead, as well as the problems that may occur if one chooses to buy a car. Page 86 states, "It is expensive to own and drive a car. Try to use public transportation." The harms of car ownership are reiterated through fictional vignettes, including one about a refugee man named "Henri" who was in a car accident shortly after purchasing a car in the United States: "The accident wasn't Henri's fault, but he had many problems since he was driving without a license or insurance." Henri is not the only one with problems; the *Guidebook* warns the reader that anyone who doesn't follow traffic laws "may also pay a large fine, or even spend time in jail."[95] The text then instructs readers to "Think about the differences between using public transportation and owning a car in the United States. What are the benefits to using public transportation rather than owning a car?"[96] While these instructions arguably reveal useful information regarding the costs and responsibilities associated with car ownership and avoid any explicit denial of a refugee's right to buy a car, they simultaneously attempt to control refugees' actions. By strategically framing a refugee's choices so that they appear in the form of discussion questions and hypothetical vignettes, the author(s) of the *Guidebook* maintain(s) the rhetorical right of refugees to make their own choices but implicitly and consistently guides the readers toward a more limited set of options.

This strategy is reinforced in the *Guidebook* through the foretelling of consequences that result from making wrong choices. The end of chapter 7 tells the story of "Yin Nyo." "Yin Nyo is tired of spending so much time taking the bus to and from work every day. She wants to buy a car. Is that a good idea?"[97] In view of this chapter's strategic framing of refugees' choices, the answer to the question about Yin Nyo's situation is clear.

Again, my close reading of the *Guidebook for Refugees* provides only a partial view into pre-departure orientation media. I analyzed this text in particular because COR provides it to each of the four populations involved in this study, but because all but one of my narrators could not remember the names of their pre-departure orientation texts, it is impossible for me to state with certainty whether this text was the one to which many of them referred. Moreover, in cases where this text is made available, several variables are inevitably present: attendees may be directed by orientation leaders to read it in full or in part, copies of the text may be given to refugees to keep or orientation leaders may require that the text is returned; various readers may be more or less inclined to believe the text or have more or less of a desire to follow its instructions than others; refugees may not have the ability to access the text because of a lack of language comprehension, health, or interest. In the next section, I address these possibilities in detail by considering the limitations that may prohibit certain audiences from accessing multiple kinds of orientation media.

Limited Access to and Disappointment with Orientations and Their Media

When considering the implications of orientation media, one must remember that not all refugees have the same access to mediated representations of the United States in pre-departure orientations. Indeed, while the standards, objectives, and best practices of pre-departure cultural orientations are clearly defined on the COR website, all kinds of situational factors may inhibit a refugee's ability to attend a full-length orientation, or to receive all of the intended purposes of orientation even if they do attend. Specifically, children, refugees resettled without sufficient notice, those unable to read or write in English or their native language, those who do not live in refugee camps or in communities with many other refugees, and those refugees who are anxious about their resettlement may be at a disadvantage in gaining access to and interpreting orientation-related media.

Habiba, from Somalia, explained that because she was only twelve years old when her family was relocated to the United States, "I didn't get the orientation, only my grandma did. And my sister, the older one, and the other one . . . they get orientation. [Ages] fourteen to go down, no orientation; only adults."[98] COR maintains that while "Some of the overseas programs . . . periodically conduct special classes for refugee children and youth," typically, only "refugees over the age of fifteen who have been approved for resettlement to the United States are eligible to receive CO [cultural orientation]."[99] Fadhail did not receive an orientation because her stay in a secondary country of asylum was shorter than she expected.

> After fifteen days from our stay in Damascus in Syria, I left because the lady there from UN, she told me, "You done with here. Take your children and be in secure place until I will call you." Like . . . no orientation. Nothing.[100]

I asked Fadhail if the UN had at least provided her with some paper work or literature to help her know what to expect in the United States. She replied, "No, no. Honestly, no. I have nothing." Likewise, Zau, who was born in Burma in 1974 and fled to Malaysia around 1995, did not have an opportunity to attend a pre-departure orientation because he did not live in a refugee camp like many other Burmese refugees. Instead, Zau rented a room and lived by himself in an urban area of Malaysia where he ran a restaurant for about fifteen years before being relocated to Houston, Texas. Though Zau feared the police in Malaysia and for that reason stayed very close to his business and home, he was able to procure an English dictionary, which he read diligently to learn vocabulary and American pronunciation, because, Zau revealed, "I need to be going to U.S. or Japan, when I have the ambition. That's why I am starting that. Because around the world, English is the number one."[101] Even though there was not an available orientation to attend, Zau was able to ask his customers—"Some is American, [or] stay in Canada, you know"—about life in the United States before his relocation.

In some unfortunate cases, refugee orientation becomes unavailable because of a lack of security or safety in one's country of asylum. Waleed, who fled Iraq to Syria after a threat to his life in 2005, had to return to Baghdad when the Syrian uprising intensified in 2012. Because he had previously worked with the U.S. military, Waleed was not safe after he returned to Baghdad, and his resettlement case was expedited. Before he arrived in New York on July 2, 2013, he had the opportunity to attend only one day of orientation.

Even when an individual is of the minimum age and lives in a stable situation near an available orientation site, COR explains, "Because of childcare obligations, logistical considerations, or class size, sometimes only one family member can attend CO."[102] Sometimes even those who attend orientation may not have the means or desire to ingest all that the orientation and its media offers. Dahabo, from Somalia, remembers seeing an orientation video at the refugee camp where she lived in Ethiopia until 2009. The video "showed us how to clean and vacuum in the house," Dahabo told me. "Plus they show us a lot of people, Chinese, American, Vietnam, how the cultures—they mix it in the United States." I asked Dahabo how she felt when she was watching the video. She replied, "I am happy to [watch] because I didn't have any information." Still, Dahabo revealed, "I have my mother, she in a wheelchair at that time, so I watching her and holding her, I not [give] real attention [to] anything of that movie."[103] For Dahabo, the limited digestion of orientation media was not due to a lack of resources but rather a conflicting concern.

Kalsumo also fled Somalia for Ethiopia, where she lived until early 2013. She remembers that before her arrival in the United States, "We were given a three-day orientation. I still have the form that they gave me. I don't know how to read and how to write. I just put in my bag."[104] Although she could not read it, Kalsumo told me that she thinks the form said something like, "This is how America is. This is the country, I mean, the state that you going. And this is how they are, the people, and this is how they act, and this is what you going to do." The issue of understanding the language of orientation media came up repeatedly in the interviews—especially with narrators from Bhutan and Somalia.

Bishnu Champaign, who was born in Bhutan in 1963 and fled to Nepal in 1993 where she lived for twenty years before being resettled to Pittsburgh, remembers that in her pre-departure orientation, "I received a book [in English] but I didn't understand English, but my kids used to read. I didn't really know whether it was helpful or not."[105] Similarly, Hawa, a Somali refugee, remembers that in her orientation,

> There was a video, it was a culture of America. It was English, but we just looking, and moving, and talking, but we wasn't understanding what was it. It was orientation, and everybody was supposed to look. And the only thing that they will show you is the video that you're supposed to watch no matter if you don't know English, or if you know English.

I asked Hawa what she remembers seeing in the video. She answered, "It was for long; I cannot remember anything about it." Hawa did remember that her first few days in the United States were "very hard;" "Everything was new to me." Hawa further explained:

> I don't even know how to say bathroom. I came to America; I didn't even use bathroom for three days, un[til] they show me how to use it. Because I was afraid of it, you know. And the kitchen—I wasn't even know what was it, you know. I was scared of it, to touch it, or to look it.

Hawa's experience suggests that a lack of orientation media that teaches refugees basic skills for living in the United States may lead to increased—albeit temporary—difficulty or hardship.

A consideration of the limitations and situational factors that may inhibit refugees' ability to attend full-length orientations—or to receive all of the intended purposes of orientation even if they do attend—provides a good reminder that orientation media do not always achieve their intended effects simply because they exist. All kinds of variables may cause refugees to interpret or respond to media in unique ways that are dissimilar from each other. Still, as the narrators explained, even when significant hurdles prohibit full access to orientation media, the bits and pieces of the media that orientation attendees can access have direct and meaningful effects on their relocation expectations and experiences.

Even when refugees have access to an orientation and ample time to attend it before their resettlement, they may find the orientation media frustratingly insufficient. Fadhail suggested that beyond just being forgettable, some of the information delivered in pre-departure orientations is inaccurate, so that refugees' experience upon arrival does not fit with what they have learned to expect. Fadhail clarified,

> It's not wrong, totally, but there are many mistakes through this orientation. They told people, as example, "You're going to get [an] apartment; everything's going to be new. You're going to get this amount of money, this amount of money—they will pay that much for you." People when they reach here they don't find that. It's a small decent house with decent, maybe, you know, furniture and with [a] limited amount of money [from] the government . . . people when they came here—many, actually of them—when they get in the house, they say "What the heck is this?"[107]

Fadhail, whose family was fairly wealthy before their displacement, remembers that her own children cried when they saw their new home in Erie, Pennsylvania for the first time, because their house in Baghdad had been to them much more comfortable. Notably, orientation media such as the *Guidebook for Refugees* do attempt to prepare refugees for less than perfect housing conditions. For example, the *Guidebook for Refugees* provides a vignette about a refugee named Shada and her family who "arrived in their new home and were disappointed to find that the furniture was used."[108] But because Fadhail was resettled with only a few days' notice and thus did not have an opportunity to attend a pre-departure orientation, she and her children did not have access to such preparatory information.

Meghann Perry, the director of Programs and Adult Education at Journeys End Refugee Services in Buffalo, New York, explained the frustration she experiences when working in situations where refugees were not provided with sufficient information in their pre-departure orientations: "Books that some refugees are given overseas . . . they've been very dated for a long time."[109] Meghann had an overseas orientation book in her office and began flipping through it as we talked. She observed,

> Definitely the photographs are dated. I don't know if there's anything that's necessarily wrong in here, so things like explaining where the resettlement agency is, that's accurate. Social service agencies, that's accurate. I think maybe more accurate than the fact that it's dated would be that it's very general. What's a hospital? What's a clinic? What's an emergency room? You know? What's a phone? Where will you buy food? This is very general.

Certainly, it would be impossible in a short orientation to prepare refugees exhaustively for every facet of life in the United States. From a most rudimentary standpoint, it is clear that these orientations act as opportunities for formal education regarding an unfamiliar upcoming experience. If a refugee has never seen a gas stove, it is likely that after attending this orientation, s/he will be skilled enough to turn a gas stove on and off. But as the narrators in this section reveal, all kinds of tangible and intangible obstacles may inhibit a refugee's ability to access or digest orientation media, and in cases where no obstacles exist, orientation media may still be deemed lacking.

Relocation Preparation outside of Orientation

Of course, media encounters that aid refugees during their final preparations before relocation do not only occur during orientation. Instead, refugee individuals who are in the process of preparing for resettlement to tl e United States may seek out mediated representations of the United States independently, in order to form or negotiate their expectations regarding a range of topics.

Anmar Alhasani grew up in Baghdad and was determined to stay in Iraq even after his business office was struck by a car bomb. Unfortunately, he was forced to change his mind when his two daughters' lives were put in danger by a nearby shooter when they were walking home from a Baghdad school. For a father, Anmar explained, "the daughter is everything."[110] After he faced the possibility of losing his daughters, Anmar felt he had no choice but to apply for his family's resettlement; and a short while later, his application for resettlement in the United States was approved. While he was preparing for the move, Anmar attended a "very short" orientation. "They told you a general thing about living here in U.S.," Anmar explained. But Anmar already knew everything his orientation leaders told him, because, he said,

> I read—I search every place in the Internet about this thing. I go to search about everything, about U.S., about the state, and which one is better for me and for my family. About the study in the U.S., about many things. And also about what the first things we need to do, because we are come just starting from zero. And I know if you need to do something, you need to learn anything about this thing, and you need to read everything about that. And you need to be ready for everything. It should become true about ninety percent.

Anmar's decision to use the Internet to learn about the United States before his relocation allowed him to learn about the differences between states and about U.S. education, even though he felt like he was "starting at zero." But he was not only concerned with his own knowledge of the United States. Anmar explained that because he wondered about the effect that relocation to the United States would have on his daughters, he created a "strategy" that he believed helped them prepare: Anmar would pretend as if he needed to know something about the United States and ask one of his daughters to find the answer for him on the Internet.

I put this thing—I start to put this thing in her mind, and I go to give them something to read, and to search about. Sometime I am ask them to search for me something. I know about that, but I ask her to search for me about that—make me a schedule for any market here in U.S.A., like a huge market, when it can help you to go, when we need to go to market something. Go to search, to check it. This way, I don't need to ask them about it, but I need them to know.

Anmar had his daughters go online and plan detailed schedules for visits to Disneyland and figure out what kinds of items would be available in American stores so that their Internet searches would begin to acclimate them to life in the United States. While his strategy was somewhat unique, he believes it helped his daughters form realistic expectations about life in the United States.

Though he worked as a well-respected engineer in Iraq, Anmar now works full time as a cashier in Houston, Texas, and volunteers eight hours every day at the YMCA International Services to help other refugees. His outlook on life is optimistic. Anmar told me that while his standard of living is not what it used to be, he tells his daughters, "'I lose everything, but I don't lose anything, because I still have you, and you are my future.'"

Linda Estefan also used media to help during her final preparations before relocating to Los Angeles. During her youth, as she explained in the previous chapter, Linda saw several American films. After she was approved for resettlement to the United States, she also attended a four-day cultural orientation in Syria, where she was granted asylum after fleeing Iraq. The films and the orientation depicted multiple locations in the United States rather than any one area in particular. Thus to form her expectations about Los Angeles specifically, Linda relied on a photograph that her family members, who moved to Los Angeles several years before Linda, sent to her of a new house they purchased. Linda explained that after her family sent the photograph, she thought, "I have an opinion. I have an idea about their homes and about their furniture."[111] Linda's narrative provides one example of situations in which individuals who have plenty of pre-arrival access to U.S. media may privilege a single image or text over others.

In other cases, instead of using popular or personal media as clues about what refugees may find in the United States, refugees may use these media as points of contrast from reality. Mohammed's parents had visited the United States several times before Mohammed was forced to relocate from Iraq to Pittsburgh due to three assassination attempts on his life incurred as a result of his work with the U.S. Army during the 2003 Iraq War. Before his departure, Mohammed remembers his father, who lived in the United States already, told him "'not to believe everything in the movies.'"[112] Mohammed's narrative provides a unique manifestation of the relationship of media to relocation; while most of the narrators I interviewed used media to form some expectation of life in the United States,

Mohammed's father used media as a reference point from which to contrast fiction from reality.

My purpose in this chapter was to highlight the ways unique encounters with a few or many pieces of media about the United States shape refugees' experiences and expectations in ways that allow more insight into the power of representational rhetoric, the imagination, and the government's strategic role in refugee immigration to the United States. By analyzing these media and refugees' interpretations of them closely, one can realize the reasons the U.S. government invests in pre-departure orientation media geared toward shaping expectations and why refugees may choose to accept, resist, or negotiate this media based on their previous understanding. The narrators I interviewed consistently showed themselves to be active audiences of orientation and other pre-departure media; their interpretations were unique, creative, and sometimes dissimilar from each other. Still, because refugees are compelled by the UNHCR to attend pre-departure orientations, because orientation media often provides instructions coupled with descriptions of consequences to be instituted if instructions are not followed, and because refugees often have comparatively less access to U.S. media than other kinds of immigrants, orientation and other pre-departure media may play significantly persuasive roles in refugees' lives.

As the narrators testified, pre-departure orientation media—as well as media that they read, see, or hear during their final preparations for relocation outside of orientation—affect refugees' expectations and lived realities in ways that are tangible and personal. But to comprehend the implications of these encounters, one must compare refugees' pre-departure interpretations of U.S. media to their post-arrival experiences in the United States. In the next chapter, I pick up with refugees' experiences traveling to the United States and what happened in the days immediately following their arrival. The narrators reveal how media continued to serve as an ever-present companion throughout the post-relocation process.

Notes

1 Abdikadir Abdiyow Barake, interview by Sarah Bishop, San Diego, CA, November 20, 2013, archived at the Schlesinger Library at Harvard University.
2 Fadhail Ibraheem, interview by Sarah Bishop, Erie, PA, February 7, 2013, archived at the Schlesinger Library at Harvard University.
3 United States of America, Department of State, Bureau for Population, Refugees, and Migration, Cultural Orientation Resource Center, *Welcome to the United States: A Guidebook for Refugees* 4th ed. (Washington, DC: Cultural Orientation Resource Center, Center for Applied Linguistics, 2012), 72.
4 *The State of the World's Refugees 2012: In Search of Solidarity* (Geneva, Switzerland: United Nations High Commissioner for Refugees, 2012).
5 See, for example, Linda Estefan, interview by Sarah Bishop, Los Angeles, CA, July 12, 2013, archived at the Schlesinger Library at Harvard University; Tek Rimal, interview with Sarah Bishop, Pittsburgh, PA, March 18, 2013.

6. Sitay Mbere, interview by Sarah Bishop, San Diego, CA, November 20, 2013, archived at the Schlesinger Library at Harvard University.
7. Sancha Rai, interview by Sarah Bishop, Pittsburgh, PA, February 5, 2013, archived at the Schlesinger Library at Harvard University.
8. See Pertti Alasuutari's discussion of the "third wave" of audience studies in *Rethinking the Media Audience: The New Agenda* (London: Sage, 1999).
9. © IOM/Thierry Falise 2007.
10. http://www.culturalorientation.net/providing-orientation/overseas
11. Dilip Parameshwar Gaonkar, "Toward New Imaginaries: An Introduction," *Public Culture* 4, no. 1 (2002): 13.
12. Michel Foucault, *Power/Knowledge: Selected Interviews and Other Writings, 1972–1977* (New York: Pantheon, 1976), 217.
13. Still taken from "*Welcome to the United States*," DVD (Washington, DC: Cultural Orientation Resource Center, 2012).
14. Tek Rimal, interview with Sarah Bishop, Pittsburgh, PA, March 18, 2013, archived at the Schlesinger Library at Harvard University.
15. Jasmine Seymo, interview by Sarah Bishop, San Diego, CA, November 18, 2013, archived at the Schlesinger Library at Harvard University.
16. [Resettlement Support Center].
17. Hsit Hsa, interview by Sarah Bishop, San Diego, CA, November 18, 2013, archived at the Schlesinger Library at Harvard University.
18. Balaram Gurung, interview by Sarah Bishop, Pittsburgh, PA, March 22, 2013, archived at the Schlesinger Library at Harvard University.
19. © IOM.
20. One is at a location near the three Beldangi camps and another near Sanischare camp.
21. *Bhutanese Refugee Health Profile* (Atlanta, GA: Centers for Disease Control and Prevention, 2013), http://www.cdc.gov/immigrantrefugeehealth/profiles/bhutanese/background/index.html#four.
22. © Robinson Cook. "Dadaab Cultural Orientation Mankato MN—What Do Refugees Know About The U.S. Before Coming?" Independent Observation (2009), http://www.slideshare.net/rccook/dadaab-cultural-orientation-mankato-mn-what-do-refugees-know-about-the-us-before-coming.
23. Abdi Askar, interview by Sarah Bishop, San Diego, CA, November 18, 2013, archived at the Schlesinger Library at Harvard University.
24. Abreer Bayara, interview by Sarah Bishop, Houston, TX, November 13, 2013, archived at the Schlesinger Library at Harvard University.
25. Abdirahim Mohmmed, interview by Sarah Bishop, San Diego, CA, November 21, 2013.
26. Sancha Rai, interview by Sarah Bishop, Pittsburgh, PA, February 5, 2013, archived at the Schlesinger Library at Harvard University.
27. Abdikadir Abdiyow Barake, interview by Sarah Bishop, San Diego, CA, November 20, 2013, archived at the Schlesinger Library at Harvard University.
28. Abreer Bayara, interview by Sarah Bishop, Houston, TX, November 13, 2013, archived at the Schlesinger Library at Harvard University.
29. Bal Baduj Rai, interview by Sarah Bishop, Houston, TX, November 14, 2013, archived at the Schlesinger Library at Harvard University.

30 Chan Myae, interview by Sarah Bishop, Buffalo, NY, August 7, 2013, archived at the Schlesinger Library at Harvard University.
31 Dahabo Abdulali, interview by Sarah Bishop, San Diego, CA, November 21, 2013, archived at the Schlesinger Library at Harvard University.
32 Darjee Januke, interview by Sarah Bishop, Houston, TX, November 13, 2013, archived at the Schlesinger Library at Harvard University.
33 Fatuma Aden, interview by Sarah Bishop, San Diego, CA, November 20, 2013, archived at the Schlesinger Library at Harvard University.
34 Shiraz Minasaqen, interview by Sarah Bishop, Los Angeles, CA, July 11, 2013, archived at the Schlesinger Library at Harvard University.
35 Anonymous, interview by Sarah Bishop, Los Angeles, CA, July 11, 2013.
36 Toby Miller, *Cultural Citizenship: Cosmopolitanism, Consumerism, and Television in a Neoliberal Age* (Philadelphia: Temple University Press, 2006), 52.
37 Miller, *Cultural Citizenship*, 60.
38 Nick Couldry, *Media, Society, World: Social Theory and Digital Media Practice* (Cambridge: Polity, 2012), 4, emphasis original.
39 For a look into the other types of communication that may influence migrants throughout relocation, see Sin Yi Cheung and Jenny Phillimore, "Social Networks, Social Capital and Refugee Integration," *Research Report for Nuffield Foundation* (2013); Cecile Russeau, Taher M. Said, Marie-Jose Gagne, and Gilles Bibeau, "Between Myth and Madness: The Premigration Dream of Leaving among Young Somali Refugees," *Culture, Medicine and Psychiatry* 22, no. 4 (1998): 385–411; Melissa Anne Phillips, "Re-Visualising New Arrivals in Australia: Journey Narratives of Pre-Migration and Settlement" (PhD Diss., University of Melbourne, 2012).
40 Wolfgang Iser, *The Implied Reader: Patterns of Communication in Prose Fiction From Bunyan to Beckett* (Baltimore: Johns Hopkins University Press, 1978), xii
41 Charles L. Briggs, "Why Nation-States and Journalists Can't Teach People to be Healthy: Power and Pragmatic Miscalculation in Public Discourses on Health," *Medical Anthropology Quarterly* 17, no. 3 (2003): 287.
42 See Louis Althusser, "Ideology and Ideological State Apparatuses," in his *Lenin and Philosophy and Other Essays*, trans. B. Brewster (New York: Monthly Review Press, 1971), 127–86.
43 *Guidebook for Refugees*, 18.
44 http://www.culturalorientation.net/resources-for-refugees/welcome-set. A 2007 version of the guidebook is available in twelve languages, and the COR website states, "As the guidebook and the DVD are translated into various languages, those translations will be posted here . . . Until that time, the 2007 edition remains available, and you can read this edition of the guidebook in a number of translations."
45 *Guidebook for Refugees*, 34.
46 http://www.culturalorientation.net/providing-orientation/toolkit/welcome/english-welcome-to-the-united-states-dvd.
47 United States Department of State, United State Department of Homeland Security, United States Department of Health and Human Services, *Proposed Refugee Admissions for Fiscal Year 2012: Report to the Congress* (2012), http://www.state.gov/documents/organization/181378.pdf.
48 *Guidebook for Refugees*, 8.
49 © Robinson Cook 2009.

50 Sullivan, Shannon. "White Ignorance and Colonial Oppression, or, Why I Know So Little About Puerto Rico." in Shannon Sullivan and Nancy Nuana (eds.) *Race and Epistemologies of Ignorance*, 153–72. Albany, NY: State University of New York Press.
51 Sullivan, "White Ignorance," 157.
52 *Guidebook for Refugees*, 18.
53 Sullivan, "White Ignorance," 161.
54 Ibid., 162.
55 *Guidebook for Refugees*, 3.
56 Buddhi Rai, interview by Sarah Bishop, Pittsburgh, PA, February 20, 2013, archived at the Schlesinger Library at Harvard University.
57 Zahraa Eskander, interview by Sarah Bishop, Los Angeles, CA, July 11, 2013, archived at the Schlesinger Library at Harvard University.
58 Said Abiyow, interview by Sarah Bishop, San Diego, CA, November 21, 2013, archived at the Schlesinger Library at Harvard University.
59 *Guidebook for Refugees*, 47.
60 Ya Wee, interview by Sarah Bishop, Buffalo, NY, August 6, 2013, archived at the Schlesinger Library at Harvard University.
61 Laxmi Adhi Kari, interview with Sarah Bishop, Buffalo, NY, August 6, 2013, archived at the Schlesinger Library at Harvard University. Laxmi does not remember what year he left Bhutan.
62 Abreer Bayara, interview by Sarah Bishop, Houston, TX, November 13, 2013, archived at the Schlesinger Library at Harvard University.
63 *Guidebook for Refugees*, 147.
64 See William B. Gudykunst, "Individualistic and Collectivistic Perspectives on Communication: An Introduction," *International Journal of Intercultural Relations* 22 (1998): 7–34; see also Judith N. Martin and Thomas K. Nakayama, *Intercultural Communication in Contexts* (Boston: McGraw-Hill, 2007).
65 *Guidebook for Refugees*, 10.
66 Iptisam Issa, interview by Sarah Bishop, Los Angeles, CA, July 9, 2013, archived at the Schlesinger Library at Harvard University.
67 Jala Yaqo, interview by Sarah Bishop, San Diego, CA, November 18, 2013, archived at the Schlesinger Library at Harvard University.
68 Nanda Chuwan, interview with Sarah Bishop, Erie, PA, February 7, 2013, archived at the Schlesinger Library at Harvard University.
69 *Guidebook for Refugees*, 62.
70 Said Abiyow, interview by Sarah Bishop, San Diego, CA, November 21, 2013, archived at the Schlesinger Library at Harvard University.
71 *Guidebook for Refugees*, 75.
72 Miller, *Cultural Citizenship*, 52.
73 Young Yun Kim, *Becoming Intercultural: An Integrative Theory of Communication and Cross-Cultural Adaptation* (Thousand Oaks, CA: Sage Publications, 2001), 221.
74 See *Guidebook for Refugees*, 18, 19, 20, 21, 182, 207.
75 Benedict Anderson, *Imagined Communities: Reflections on the Origin and Spread of Nationalism* (London: Verso, 1983), 7, emphasis original; see also Ronald Zboray, *A Fictive People* (New York: Oxford University Press, 1993).
76 *Guidebook for Refugees*, 14.
77 Ibid., 18, 19, 20, 21, 182, 207.

78 Ibid., 100.
79 Ateev Mehrotra, Alan M. Zaslavsky, and John Z. Ayanian, "Preventive Health Examinations and Preventive Gynecological Examinations in the United States," *Journal of the American Medical Association* 167, no. 17 (2007): 1876–83; Centers for Disease Control and Prevention, *Resources for Entertainment Education Content Developers: Preventive Health Care—What's the Problem?* (June 12, 2013), http://www.cdc.gov/healthcommunication/ToolsTemplates/EntertainmentEd/Tips/PreventiveHealth.html.
80 *Guidebook for Refugees*, 78.
81 Ibid., 16.
82 James Boyd White, *Heracles' Bow* (Madison: University of Wisconsin, 1985), 37; see also Maurice Charland, "Constitutive Rhetoric: The Case of the *Peuple Québécois*," *Quarterly Journal of Speech* 73, no. 2 (1987): 133–50.
83 Ronald Scollon, Suzanne B.K. Scollon, and Rodney H. Jones, *Intercultural Communication: A Discourse Approach* (Malden, MA: Wiley-Blackwell, 2012); Krum Krumov and Knud S. Larsen, *Cross-Cultural Psychology: Why Culture Matters* (Charlotte, NC: Information Age Publications, 2013); Chul-Byung Choi, "Local Collective Identity Enculturation within a Global Media Consumption Culture," *Asia Pacific Education Review* 3, no. 1 (2002): 1–17; Christine A. Walsh, Dave Este, and Brigette Krieg, "The Enculturation Experience of Roma Refugees: A Canadian Perspective," *British Journal of Social Work* 38, no. 5 (2008): 900–17; Ashley D. Paterson and Julie Hakim-Larson, "Arab Youth in Canada: Acculturation, Enculturation, Social support, and Life Satisfaction," *Journal of Multicultural Counseling and Development* 40, no. 4 (2012): 206–15.
84 See Fernando Ortiz, *Cuban Counterpoint: Tobacco and Sugar* (Durham, NC: Duke University Press, 1995), emphasis added.
85 *Guidebook for Refugees*, 129, 18.
86 Jasmine Seymo, interview by Sarah Bishop, San Diego, CA, November 18, 2013, archived at the Schlesinger Library at Harvard University.
87 See Valerie Raleigh Yow, *Recording Oral History: A Guide for the Humanities and Social Sciences* (Walnut Creek, CA: Altamira Press, 2005).
88 *Guidebook for Refugees*, 18.
89 From Cultural Orientation Resource Center (2012). *Welcome to the United States: A Guidebook for Refugees* 4th ed. (Washington, DC: Center for Applied Linguistics). Reproduced with permission from the Center for Applied Linguistics.
90 Rachael E. Jack, Oliver G.B. Garrod, Hui Yu, et al. "Facial Expressions of Emotion are Not Culturally Universal," *Proceedings of the National Academy of Sciences of the United States of America* 109, no. 19 (2012): 7241–44; Rachael E. Jack, Roberto Caldara, and Philippe G. Schyns, "Internal Representations Reveal Cultural Diversity in Expectations of Facial Expressions of Emotion," *Journal of Experimental Psychology-General* 141, no. 1 (2012): 18–25; Rachael E. Jack, Caroline Blais, Christoph Scheepers, et al., "Cultural Confusions Show that Facial Expressions Are Not Universal," *Current Biology* 19, no. 18 (2009): 1543–8.
91 From Cultural Orientation Resource Center, *Guidebook for Refugees*, 2012.
92 *Guidebook for Refugees*, 126.
93 Ibid., 126.
94 Ibid., 202.
95 Ibid., 87.

96 Ibid., 87.
97 Ibid., 87.
98 Habiba Jama, interview by Sarah Bishop, San Diego, November 20, 2013, archived at the Schlesinger Library at Harvard University.
99 Cultural Orientation Resource Center, Center for Applied Linguistics, *Overseas CO*, 2013, http://www.culturalorientation.net/providing-orientation/overseas#4.
100 Fadhail Ibraheem, interview by Sarah Bishop, Erie, PA, February 7, 2013, archived at the Schlesinger Library at Harvard University.
101 Zau Aung Marip, interview by Sarah Bishop, Houston, TX, November 14, 2013, archived at the Schlesinger Library at Harvard University.
102 Cultural Orientation Resource Center, Center for Applied Linguistics, *Overseas CO*, 2013, http://www.culturalorientation.net/providing-orientation/overseas#4.
103 Dahabo Abdulali, interview by Sarah Bishop, San Diego, CA, November 21, 2013, archived at the Schlesinger Library at Harvard University.
104 Kalsumo Ibrahim, interview by Sarah Bishop, San Diego, CA, November 20, 2013, archived at the Schlesinger Library at Harvard University.
105 Bishnu Maya Chapagain, interview by Sarah Bishop, Buffalo, NY, August 6, 2013, archived at the Schlesinger Library at Harvard University.
106 Hsit Hsa, interview by Sarah Bishop, San Diego, CA, November 18, 2013, archived at the Schlesinger Library at Harvard University.
107 Fadhail Ibraheem, interview by Sarah Bishop, Erie, PA, February 7, 2013, archived at the Schlesinger Library at Harvard University.
108 *Guidebook for Refugees*, 51.
109 Meghann Perry, interview by Sarah Bishop, Buffalo, NY, August 7, 2013, archived at the Schlesinger Library at Harvard University.
110 Anmar Alhasani, interview with Sarah Bishop, Houston, TX, November 14, 2013, archived at the Schlesinger Library at Harvard University.
111 Linda Estefan, interview by Sarah Bishop, Los Angeles, CA, July 12, 2013, archived at the Schlesinger Library at Harvard University.
112 Mohammed Mahmood, interview by Sarah Bishop, Pittsburgh, PA, March 4, 2013, archived at the Schlesinger Library at Harvard University.

3

VOLUNTARY AND MANDATED MEDIA ENCOUNTERS DURING REFUGEES' FIRST DAYS IN THE U.S.

Amira[1] grew up in Baghdad, Iraq, and now works as a case manager at a refugee resettlement organization in Glendale, California. When I met her in her office in July 2013, she told me, "Although I will tell you about our situation, you [can] never imagine." Amira's husband was killed in Baghdad, and she feared every day that her daughters, who were in their twenties at the time, would be kidnapped. In 2006, unable to face the uncertainty any longer, she and her daughters fled to Syria. Once she reached Damascus, Amira attempted to apply for her family's resettlement, but IOM told her that no countries were accepting Iraqi refugees, and so she waited, returning to the IOM office every six months to update her family's paper work and check on the status of their application. Finally, at the end of April 2008, IOM notified Amira that her family's case had been approved and that they had just five days to prepare to move to Glendale, California. "So imagine," she told me, "I had a furnished apartment, [and had to] sell everything, because I want money, and my daughter, she is attending university, my other daughter, she had her work, her job . . ." While uprooting their lives so suddenly was overwhelming, Amira did not want to miss the opportunity—her mother and brother were already living in the United States as citizens, and she longed to join them.

Because of all of the preparation that she and her daughters had to do in the few hurried days before their departure, Amira told me, "When we move to the United States, we are too, too tired. Just when the [airplane's] captain said, 'We are in the New York area,' I looked out the window, I saw Statue of Liberty." She began to cry at the memory. In the pause that followed, I asked Amira whether she had seen the Statue of Liberty in movies or on television before seeing it that day from the airplane window. She replied, "It's different. The Statue of Liberty just a picture in a movie, but when you saw the real statue—a huge statue standing in the river—it's so incredible." Of course, the Statue of Liberty is an especially iconic monument for immigrants, as Ellis Island was a gateway for millions of immigrants from 1892 until 1954.[2]

For Amira and countless other refugees, the experience of traveling by plane to resettle in the United States is a daunting, emotional task for which U.S. media could never fully prepare them. Of the seventy-four refugees I spoke with, only several Iraqis had experienced traveling by commercial airline before their displacement. Many of the others, however, soon realized why pre-departure orientation media have instructions that explain, as the COR *Guidebook* does for example, the perils of flying: "If you get sick on the plane and need to vomit, there are bags in the pocket in the seatback in front of you."[3] Teek, a twenty-five-year-old Bhutanese refugee I met in San Diego, told me that during her travel to the United States from Nepal with her parents on July 25, 2013, "I cried because I was afraid because the plane was slightly bumping, I was scared, I thought probably we will have our end right here! Because this was the first time we had experienced flying."[4] Fatuma Aden, a Somali refugee, remembers that when she boarded her plane to fly to the United States,

> I was afraid! That was my first time on the airplane. I was like this [Fatuma covered her eyes with her hands] and crying all day, begging God to drop me somewhere, throwing up, all that. That was my first time feeling dizzy. I saw like people reading a book, and white skin, and when we saw, we were scared, and there is soda, like Coke, Sprite—we were afraid it might explode! We were afraid.[5]

I asked Fatuma if there is something she wishes she had learned in her pre-departure orientation that would have saved her from some of this difficulty and fear. But she replied, "No . . . We saw the video, but I was wishing that I can get more experience." With these words, Fatuma alludes to a poignant question that is relevant to this study: What can be learned about an unfamiliar place by simply watching a video or reading a book about it? During this part of her narrative, Fatuma provided an answer to an ongoing and popular debate in American education scholarship regarding the differences between passive and experiential/kinesthetic education, taken up in the recent work of education scholars such as William Thomas, Ula Manzo, Anthony Manzo, Matthew Thomas, W.F. Dennison, Roger Kirk, and Eva Michael.[6] Her belief that an orientation film could not provide her with a necessary amount of "experience" to prepare for her first days in the United States holds intriguing implications. If one perceives that Amira did not receive sufficient "experience" from watching an instructional film or reading a book, what are such media capable of teaching? Moreover, if refugees arriving in the United States feel ill equipped or underprepared to navigate life after resettlement, to what degree can the authors and funders of pre-departure orientation media continue to justify the current place of privilege media occupies in these orientations?

This question of the contestable merit of "passive" versus "experiential" learning is perhaps nowhere clearer than in the work of American psychologist and educational pragmatist John Dewey.[7] Dewey argues that in order for a student to truly learn a skill, process, or idea, he or she must have an embodied, kinesthetic experience with that subject, instead of just a passive reading, listening, or viewing experience, such as the one Fatuma encountered when watching the orientation video.[8] Proponents of active rather than passive learning often lean on the almost uncontested relationship of experience to knowledge, recognizable as far back as Sophocles's tragedy *Trachiniae*, in which the character of the "Lady" proffers, "Well, one must learn by doing the thing; for though you think you know it, you will have no certainty, until you try."[9] This chapter will inquire into this realm of learning and experience through a concentration on refugees' first days in the United States. Specifically, because refugees carry impressions and memories of pre-arrival media with them into the United States, this chapter will provide instances in which the narrators compare what they learned in pre-arrival media encounters about the United States to the reality of their experiences upon resettlement so that we may consider what is possible to learn about an occurrence before it is actually experienced. Moreover, I will discuss refugees' acquisition of media technology after their arrival in the United States, and the varying degrees of importance this acquisition had for the narrators. Finally, this chapter will consider how local resettlement organizations in the United States use print and digital media in an attempt to guide refugees through their first days after relocation and how this post-arrival orientation media represent the U.S. government, act as a means of standardization, and facilitate refugee *deprivatization*, or, the imposition of governmental control into the realms of health, hygiene, and family.

Navigating "Home": Making Sense of American Living Arrangements and Media Access

Even for many of the refugees that I interviewed who attended what they considered to be a thorough pre-departure orientation, and who had experience seeing U.S. homes depicted in pre-departure orientation media, the arrival in one's U.S. home after a long journey was disorienting. For some, such as Ya Wee from Burma, this disorientation had to do with a lack of information regarding the specific place where he would resettle. "We already know prior one month [before our departure] that we will resettle to the United States, but we just don't know the state," Ya Wee explained.[10] I asked him when was it that he found out that he would be resettling in upstate New York. He replied, "On the day we left, that day they let us know that we will move to Buffalo." Ya Wee had access to a good deal of American films[11] in the Burmese refugee camp in Malaysia where he had lived since he was two years old, but without knowing where he would be placed in the United States, his ability to use this media to orient himself to a particular region or locale was somewhat limited. Even so, upon his arrival in Buffalo, Ya Wee did encounter some circumstances that he had previously seen depicted only in American films. For example, because temperatures in Malaysia tend to hover around eighty degrees Fahrenheit all year round, Ya Wee had never experienced a cold winter. "Because we watch movies, when we saw the movie, [it showed] like snow time, wintertime, so we want to come to the United States, because we appreciate the wintertime," he told me. Unfortunately, Ya Wee's appreciation of winter did not last long after he arrived in Buffalo, where temperatures are prone to drop below zero during the coldest months due to a lake-effect wind chill. He told me the winter is "a bit different" than the films made it seem. Though he expected to welcome the cold weather, Ya Wee revealed, "Actually, in winter I'm scared." Ya Wee's narrative speaks to the ever-present reality that seeing a phenomenon represented in media does not necessarily provide one with enough information to judge accurately how one will feel or respond when faced with a lived experience of the phenomenon.

Megeney, from Somalia, provided further evidence of this disjuncture between mediated images and reality. She told me that during her own relocation from the Dadaab refugee camp in Kenya to San Diego in 2004, she was ill on the plane and kept her eyes closed the entire time. Then once she was on the ground in San Diego, things changed. She recalled,

> I step in an airport. A lot of people were there. I felt like I was in heaven, you know. Everything was black and white and colors. I thought that I was in heaven. I wasn't expecting that I should be in America. It was really happy day for me.

Megeney's caseworker met her at the airport and took her to her new home, which was much different than she expected:

> I thought I was expecting, like I can build a house again. But when they gave me this house, there was a bed made. There was a—you know, it was snow[ing outside]; there was a jacket on the bed. There was a kitchen. There was food in the fridge. There was everything in the house. I was . . . like—wow! You know, all this stuff?

Afraid that there had been some mistake in the processing of her case, Megeney remembers,

> We just sleep; we didn't even eat nothing—until in the morning, the caseworker arrived. So when he arrived, he just opened the door, and he

said—we ask him, 'Whose is all this stuff?' [And he said,] "It's for you!" And then we were so happy!¹²

I was surprised to hear of Megeney's shock upon finding her house already built for her and the food provided for her family, because only a few moments earlier in our conversation she had told me in detail about all of the many things that she had learned from a film she saw during her pre-departure IOM orientation. This film, she remembered, taught her about everything from the problem of high blood pressure in America to the differences between Michigan and New York landscapes. Surely it explained housing conditions. Indeed, she remembered that the film showed an American kitchen and oven. But, Megeney revealed,

> When they show me the video in the IOM for the three days orientation [in Kenya], I thought the IOM people was joking, you know. We wasn't expecting like we can come to America. Like, they just said, "This is America. This is how you do. This is how you do." But we thought, like, it was a joke for them, they were showing us a video, all that. In my mind, was like a child. I was thinking like a child, you know.

Megeney did not take the possibility of resettlement to the United States seriously until she saw her name posted beside a scheduled flight:

> I was expecting it was a joke, but they [showed] me, like, a board that they can post your name on it. Oh, these days you [will be assigned to] a flight. When I saw my name on the board, I realized at that moment I was [going to go to] America, I was dancing. I was so happy for my life!

Before this moment, Megeney's doubts that she would ever actually have the opportunity to come to the United States prevented her from taking the information portrayed in her orientation film seriously. Consequently, her arrival in her U.S. home was both shocking and exciting. Megeney's experience affirms the notion that media is an imperfect tool for preparing refugees for life in the United States. Even when refugees have direct encounters with educational media about a particular subject, like Megeney, they may still feel underprepared when the experience that the media portrayed occurs. Unfortunately, not all of the refugees I interviewed were as pleasantly surprised as Megeney.

Nirmala, a Bhutanese refugee who was relocated from a refugee camp in Nepal to Buffalo, New York, on June 23, 2009, had also learned in orientation about American homes and resettlement agency provisions: "During the orientation, the people [told us] 'When you arrive in your destination, everything is ready for you, like food, a bed, clothes, everything from the kitchen, the bathrooms—everything is ready.'"[13] For Nirmala, however, this did not prove to be the case. "When I come here, I didn't see that," she told me.

> There is no house for us, we live in different peoples' house for ten days. When [the orientation leaders] talk about the apartment, they talk about its going to be clean, but it's not. We clean the house ourselves. Not enough food, some things are there, but some are not.

This was disappointing for Nirmala, because she specifically remembered learning in orientation that in America things are clean and tidy.

For Sahro, the difference between expectations and reality concerning her new American home were even more striking. She grew up watching American films in her home in Somalia, and had high hopes about the life she would have after her relocation to San Diego in 1994: "Oh, my goodness! I can't wait until go to America! Yay!"[14] Sahro told me,

> Somebody tell us you [just have to press a] button, and the beds come and they set up, and we sleep there, and then you touching another button, all the shoes, they go there! We, you know, we get good picture, and good dreaming things. But when we came here, we never get it![15]

She remembers that before her departure,

> We're dreaming. Oh, we [will] have maid! We have everything. We have, maybe somebody come in your house and cook and clean. Like, we didn't realize the people, they're working their self in the house. So I'm hoping, oh, you have now two, three children, and you get maybe three maid, or something like that. But when we come here, first night we come in here, we come in apartment with full of cockroach. So I couldn't sleep that night, and I cry; I cry. If that moment, somebody say, "I will give you ticket," I will go back to refugee camp, because refugee camp they didn't have cockroach. The area I come in, it's ghetto area—not fancy houses nor good street. And I say, "Oh, my goodness. The area you live is not area fancy." No hope!

Here Sahro's confusion and disappointment were a direct result of the discrepancy between the reality she encountered upon arrival in the United States and the "good picture" she had in her mind from the American films she had seen in her youth.

Ya Wee, Megeney, Nirmala, and Sahro's narratives highlight the interaction of media and the imagination. Even when an individual is not fully aware of it, popular and government-produced media may serve to etch out imagined expectations about the phenomena the media depict, and, as the narrators testify here, serious emotional discomfort may be induced when these expectations are not met. Still, Lily Alba, the director of the International Institute of Los Angeles, believes that pre-departure access to U.S. mass media cannot take all the credit for shaping refugees' pre-departure imaginings and expectations. Instead, as Lily suggests, refugees may have unrealistic expectations because of phone or e-mail exchanges with family who are already living in the United States. She explained,

> Many times what we see is there is a misconception. Sometimes we see cases where refugees have expectations, or where they hear that their friends and families [who have previously moved to the U.S.] have a really good job, or a big house, so sometimes [it is difficult] coming to this country and realizing that it will take time before they reach their American dream.[16]

The information refugees receive from family and friends and the expectations they develop by way of media encounters do not operate in separate spheres. Rather, these two sources of information about life in the United States may challenge, add to, reinforce, or contradict each other. By considering closely the varied resonances of pre-departure media encounters and how these encounters interact with other types of messages that refugees receive about the United States, one can better understand the means through which refugees make sense of their new surroundings in the days immediately following their arrival in the United States.

Some of the narrators I interviewed explained that the disorientation they felt in their new homes during their first few days after relocation was directly related to a lack of media access during this time. I asked Fahad—a twenty-two-year-old, media-savvy Iraqi who was resettled from Jordan to Los Angeles in 2012—what he did during his first week in the United States. He replied, "The first week, it was so hard. So like there is no phone, nothing, no Internet so I can't get connection at all. But after that we get used [to it] here, like we go to buy phone."[17] Nanda, from Bhutan, told me about his first day in Erie, Pennsylvania:

> That day, I was a little bit nervous, to be honest with you, so I was just thinking, what will happen next, because I don't have a telephone, or cell phone, or any communication with me, so if I have an emergency, what to do?[18]

These narrators' perspectives suggest that pre-departure orientation media may need to anticipate the likelihood that refugees may not have access to cell phones and computers during their first weeks in the United States. Indeed, instructions for preparations regarding different types of emergencies appear frequently in pre-departure orientation media, and so I was not surprised when a lack of access to the kinds of technology the orientation media suggest using in these circumstances was cause for concern among several of the narrators. Abdirahim Mohammed, from Somalia, remembers exactly where he learned to use technology in case of emergencies. He told me that while attending orientation in Kenya, IOM gave him "A book, and there is a disc in the top, and the book will show you like emergency contact, like if something happen, how you dial 9–1–1, how you call the ambulance."[19] The text Abdirahim received was likely the U.S. Department of State-funded text *Welcome to the United States: A Guidebook for Refugees* that I discussed in detail in the previous chapter; it is the only refugee orientation book I am aware of that is commonly presented with an attached DVD in overseas orientations. Four days after he was resettled from Kenya to Texas, Abdirahim became lost in downtown Dallas. "I re[membered] what they said in orientation—like if you're lost somewhere, if you have a phone, dial 9–1–1 and 9–1–1 will pick you up and bring you wherever you belong." But Abdirahim had a problem: "At that time I wasn't having any phones." Unsure of what to do, he finally found his way to a nearby hotel and used what little English he had learned to ask the desk attendant to call 9–1–1 for him.

Though most resettlement organizations do not have the funding to provide newly arriving refugees with cell phones, computers, televisions, or CD/DVD players, many refugees make acquisition of these types of technology among their top priorities during the weeks immediately following their arrival. This acquisition may be related to the concern for emergencies that Nanda and Abdirahim described earlier, but it also occurs because of other kinds of concerns and desires. Lily told me that at the International Institute of Los Angeles, it seems as though all of her clients have access to television and Internet, though the agency does not provide help for acquiring these resources. Newly arrived refugees may acquire media from other, unexpected sources. Kalsumo, a Somali refugee, for example, received a television from a neighbor:

> When we came to America, two night later, the kids [were] outside. And then one Somali woman, she came. She said that, "Oh, you live here? Oh, the kids, if they don't have a TV inside the house, it's hard for them. I will bring one TV for you." And she brought a TV. The kids, they wasn't—they didn't go to school yet. They was preparing to go to school, and they were jumping around, and all that, you know. And then she came to us, a new family. So she say, "Oh, I have two TV in my house. The kids will be quiet if they have a TV, and watching cartoon inside. I will bring something, and some cartoon movies for them." And then that thing, she brought it.[20]

Having access to a television was useful for Kalsumo's family during those first several weeks after their relocation. After they had been living in the United States for about a year, however, the television the neighbor supplied had curiously become less central to their routine. "Since that time she brought it, we still have it, and the kids still watch the cartoon, but they started school right now," Kalsumo told me. "When they started school, they decided to learn to focus their books and all that. They just watch the TV only Saturday and Sunday." When her children are not home, Kalsumo does not watch TV at all; she still does not know how to turn it on.

Kalsumo's narrative led me to consider other reasons why media may be more useful to or present in refugees' lives during their first weeks in the United States than it is later on, and if media acquisition has something to do with phenomena such as enculturation, comfort, and social status. In the next section, I discuss these considerations in detail.

Perspectives on the Importance of Post-Arrival Media Acquisition

That the consumption of any media may serve a variety of purposes is certainly not specific to refugees. Any individual may wish to watch, listen to, or read some media in order to learn a new skill, gain a sense of belonging, be entertained, engage in a social activity, or for any other number of reasons. While the refugees in this study are indeed a diverse group that uses varying amounts of media for a multitude of purposes, there are some ways in which their preferences for and ideas about media align. In this study, the importance of gaining access to media technology as soon as possible after relocation was linked to a few specific expressed ideas and needs that reoccurred with some frequency in my conversations with refugees from Bhutan, Burma, Iraq, and Somalia. Specifically, refugees repeatedly mentioned the relationship between post-arrival media acquisition and the desire to learn English, the belief that media use is central to "American" life,[21] the necessity of finding a job or participating in school work, and the longing to stay connected to remote family members and friends during a period of cultural adjustment.[22]

Multiple narrators and resettlement administrators I spoke with endorsed the ability of U.S. media—and especially television shows for children—as a means to help refugees of all ages learn English.[23] When Habiba, from Somalia, arrived in Kansas City, Missouri[24] in 2004 as a thirteen-year-old, she knew very little English. She started the sixth grade at a local middle school just two days after her arrival. "My teacher was really nice," she recalled. "She was really, like, helpful person. She was coming home and tutoring me, you know. Like, I was like her daughter. Without her, I shouldn't be like this."[25] Habiba remembered one thing this influential teacher felt particularly strongly about: "My teacher told me to watch only Disney Channel! She told me that I can learn from words." The teacher wanted Habiba to be able to communicate in public situations without an interpreter:

> She said, if the person, like, for example, you go to a market, or you go to a hospital, the doctor will ask you, "Hi, how are you doing?" And then, you just quiet. You don't know how to respond by the person. But if you watch more cartoon, or more, like, Disney, you will get more experience.

Amira, from Iraq, remembers similar instruction from her mother: "My mom said 'Okay, you want to have good English? Go and watch *Georgie*, the cartoon.'"[26] Now, Amira told me, she gives her own clients the same advice when they arrive.

Hiba, an Iraqi who moved to the United States in 2009 and who speaks fluent English, told me that she likes to listen to the news to improve her English. I told Hiba that I was not sure I understood, because during the time of our interview her English was nearly perfect. "It wasn't that good in 2009," she explained.[27]

> But the news uses good words. As I always say, the long words that I don't understand? Like, "informative," I didn't know how to say that before until two days ago—"It was very informative"—so I want to capture words that I can use to be professional in talking. I don't want to use the slang language, or the basic words to explain myself, so I want to learn those words, and with the pronunciation, so I can know how to say it.

While existing scholarship such as Doug Walker's "The Media's Role in Immigrant Adaption: How First-Year Haitians in Miami use the Media" shows how migrants may utilize media during the initial phases of post-resettlement life, Hiba's experience reveals that media may not only be useful to refugees who are at the beginning stages of learning a new language and culture but also to those who seek a higher level of competency.[28]

Pre- and post-arrival orientation texts sometimes encourage this relationship between media consumption and language learning. For example, the *Guidebook for Refugees* I analyzed in the previous chapter tells refugees that to learn English, one should "Watch English movies, television shows, or listen to English programs on the radio," and the post-relocation COR orientation text, *Making Your Way*, suggests, "There are many ways to learn English outside of a classroom, such as by talking with neighbors, listening to the radio, or watching television in English."[29] The ability of media to teach a second language is well documented in the work of scholars of education, such as Joyce Penfield, Wai Meng Chan, Stuart Webb, Mark Peterson, Anne Vize, Rebecca Oxford, Sukero Ito Young Park-Oh, and Malenna Sumrall,[30] but the ability to learn a language while simultaneously learning to use electronic media in general is less so. The narratives included here provide good testimony that refugees may engage in multiple and interactive forms of cultural learning simultaneously. For example, Jasmine, who was only three years old when her family fled from Burma to live in a refugee camp in Thailand, told me that the most difficult part of her resettlement experience was learning English. But in learning English, she also attained competency with computers. When she arrived at nineteen years old in the United States in 2010, she began to watch KPBS, a PBS member station owned by San Diego State University. "It's for kids, but I love to watch with my little sister,"[31] Jasmine explained. "They teach you, like words, and language." Soon after Jasmine started attending a local school, she began to gain more skill in English and to learn to use a computer for future professional purposes. She told me, "The typing, it's so difficult. Because in Thailand refugee camp, I never touched a computer, even I don't even see it." Jasmine's schoolwork was complicated by the necessity to learn English and technological literacy simultaneously.[32]

For some of the refugees in this study, the desire to learn English and to gain access to computers immediately after relocation to the United States was directly related to the desire to find a job. Resettlement agencies are direct and repetitive about the importance of knowing English when looking for employment, and many agencies host job search workshops as well as English classes that may be mandatory for refugees receiving any assistance. Several of the refugees I spoke with mentioned their frustration with searching for employment on the Internet. Abreer, an Iraqi living in Houston, told me:

> Everything here is systemized and using the Internet and we are not familiar about this thing back in Iraq. If you want to apply for a job [in Iraq], we will go there on that place and apply. And even sometimes we are not apply, someone gonna help us, [they will say] "Hey, this is a relative, this is someone I know, could you put him in this position?" And that's it. But here—everything! I mean, paying your bills online, applying for job online, checking your bank online, everything is online. Even volunteer!— I wanted to be volunteer with my kids at school, they [said], "Go online and apply for being volunteer."[33]

Tek, a refugee from Bhutan now living in Pittsburgh, Pennsylvania, knew that the Internet would be central to navigating U.S. life even before he arrived. Tek believes it is well known internationally that the United States "is one of the richest countries in the world," and he expected that people in the United States would be adept in using "everything, like advanced things, like the technologies, everything."[34] Gaining access to media technology shortly after one's arrival in a country that one perceives as being technologically advanced and dependent may provide refugees with a sense of belonging or fitting in, allowing one to advance toward what Toby Miller, Aihwa Ong, and Nick Stevenson call "cultural citizenship," wherein one maintains the right to communication and expressions of diversity within a larger group.[35]

In addition to facilitating the learning of English, enculturation into American culture, and the search for employment, media technology also provides refugees with a means for staying connected with friends and family who are still living in one's home country or country of asylum. This desire for connection during a period of major cultural adjustment provides another reason why gaining access to media technology soon after one's arrival in the United States may be a top priority for refugees, and the ability of media to serve as a tool for transnational connection is documented in the work of scholars such as Herman Wasserman, Patrice Kayeya-Mwepu, Raelene Wilding, and Minoo Razavi.[36] Fahad, from Iraq, who explained earlier how his first week in the United States was difficult because of not having a phone or Internet connection, also told me that after a week or so in his new home, a caseworker came to his apartment and provided information about getting these connections: "She helped us with a lot of things like she tell us where is the better company for the phones or everything."[37] After buying a phone, Fahad got "more used" to the United States. He is now able to use an application called Viber on his iPhone to call Iraq and Jordan for free and talk to his friends and family who still live there.

Lily, who had explained that the majority of her clients seem to gain quick access to television and the Internet, told me that this access does not seem to vary much by population and that because the agency cannot provide televisions or computers, the refugees' means for acquiring them are "purely individual."[38] Another refugee resettlement administrator who arrived in the United States as a refugee herself and who requested that I do not use her name, told me that the refugees she serves

> keep asking us a lot of things. They complain, when the refugees coming to the United States they're asking about the flat [screen] TV, DVD, coffee machine, we are asking them, "Where did you get this information?" We don't have that kind of service![39]

Resettlement agencies often do not have the available funding to provide refugees with media technologies. But because refugees sometimes view these technologies as imperative to their contentment or success in the United States, some post-arrival orientation texts address this issue directly. The 762 page Department of State-funded COR post-arrival orientation manual, *Making Your Way: A Reception and Placement Orientation Curriculum*, includes, for example, an image of a television with a large red "X" over it (see Figure 3.1) and instructions for orientation leaders to discuss with newly arriving refugees the scenario described beneath the image: "Your neighbor's family was given a television by a resettlement agency volunteer, but your family was not given a television." The discussion generated by this caption would presumably help refugees know how to cope should they experience something similar.

Page 715 of the same text asks resettlement administrators to have refugees respond "Yes" or "No" to several statements in order to ensure that they know what services to expect to receive from their resettlement agency. One example states, "If you do not receive a television or computer when you first arrive in the United States, you should complain to your case worker/manager about getting one from the resettlement agency."[40] The answer key reveals the "correct" response: "No." These inclusions seem to suggest a deficiency in refugee orientation texts:

Your neighbor's family was given a television by a resettlement agency volunteer, but your family was not given a television.

FIGURE 3.1 Page 145 of the *Guidebook for Refugees* orientation text[41]

While refugees often believe media technologies are imperative to their success in the United States, orientation texts address this belief only to dismiss it rather than offering direction or help to the refugee readers who may wish to procure these technologies.

While prompt media acquisition was among some of the narrators' top priorities, not all refugees were interested in or felt good about gaining access to media in the days immediately following their relocation to the United States. In fact, some of the narrators revealed that the media refugees encountered in their homes during the immediate post-relocation period could be unwelcome or could cause fear and disappointment. For example, the receiving of some types of mail—such as fliers depicting a missing child—may have become normalized for an individual who has lived in the United States all of his or her life. But this type of media caused one narrator to experience significant fear. Sahro was shocked when she first received a piece of mail at her apartment with a photograph of a missing child on it:

> When we come here, in mail we open, each, every day, we see, oh, this girl missing! This beautiful boy missing, missing, missing! So I get the fear, your children, somebody will kidnap. So get more scared than before, because when I get the mail, every day they say somebody missing—the lady missing, the man missing, children missing. So I say, "Oh, my goodness!" So every single day when I open the door, I'm scared.[42]

Similarly, common security signs may also cause apprehension. Amira told me that because of the time change and jetlag she experienced when relocating from Damascus to Los Angeles, she did not sleep well for her first few nights in the United States.

> I wake up, all my family are sleeping, so I opened the door at five o'clock when the sun rises and I just say "I will go to walk." So when I start to walk, I notice that every door was like writing "Beware of Dog! Beware of Dog!"—Oh my God! Then I turn back!⁴³

Amira had not encountered such signs before and was shocked to find threatening messages adorning the doors of otherwise benign-looking American homes.

In other cases, the narrators expressed their lack of interest or even disappointment in media in the days following their arrival in the United States. Dahabo, a Somali refugee in San Diego, told me through a translator that she does not want to have a television in her house. "When I go to the other neighbors, they have TV, but it's not any interesting, because the language, I didn't know. So I see how the [people on TV] move, but not even one word—I didn't understand."⁴⁴ Similarly, Megeney told me through a translator of her frustration with navigating U.S. media technologies. "I know how to turn on TV, and how to turn on radio, but I don't know how to turn on a computer or a cell phone, I can't even dial a number," Megeney revealed.⁴⁵ When I asked her what she watches when she turns on the TV, she told me she only sees the cartoons her children view, because she does not know how to change the channel. I asked Megeney if she enjoyed watching cartoons. She replied,

> When we come to America—they're saying, "If you watch a lot of cartoons you will learn English." So I was expecting that I would learn a lot of English. Since I came to America the only thing that I watch is cartoons and I'm not understanding anything!

Megeney's example is an intriguing one, as her disappointment seems directly related to her expectations about media's capabilities for teaching. In the next section, I will continue to explore this relationship of expectations to experiences in more detail.

Expectations Meet Reality during the First Days of Living in the United States

As I have already discussed in earlier chapters of this work, it is clear from listening to the narrators I interviewed that media encountered prior to relocation frequently and directly informs not only refugees' expectations but also their interpretations of experiences after relocation.[46] When I asked Fahad, from Iraq, what he thought about the United States before he arrived, his answer was simple: "I think it's like movies."[47] Likewise, Zanuba, from Somalia, told me,

> In America we thought—rich! In our mind, what we see, they are powerful country, rich . . . so we thought everyone is rich almost, and clean everywhere. When you see the film, you see, you see those high buildings.[48]

It is clear that media plays a central role in forming refugees' expectations, but Dylanna Jackson, the director of Resettlement at the International Institute of Erie in Pennsylvania, suggests that media itself is not always to blame when refugees' expectations are "dashed" by a lower-than-expected standard of living.[49] Instead, she believes that conversations *about* media and media technology may also contribute to disappointment:

> Each resettlement agency does things a little differently. So let's say, for example, one agency gives everybody brand new TVs, then family and friends would say "Well, why didn't you get a TV? We got a TV. You know, your resettlement agency isn't doing their job." Which—TVs are not a requirement to give, but these are the kinds of things that people talk about and share back and forth, so.

Still, Dylanna admits,

> "I think sometimes refugees—especially when they watch American movies—they have this idea that they're going to walk into wealthier American neighborhoods, and a lot of times they're resettled into poorer parts of town. So, I think that's kind of a shock for them—that America's not all like the movies."

Several of the refugee narrators I spoke to confirmed Dylanna's impression.

Bishnu, a refugee from Bhutan who now lives in Austin, Texas, told me, "We heard that you're going to be taken care [of] for six months but after coming here after two months they said 'No, we will not give you service.'"[51] I asked Bishnu where she had heard that she would be taken care of for six months, and she told me it was in the orientation class she had attended in Nepal before her relocation. Now, Bishnu told me, "I'm just thinking that these people [were] telling lies for us." The discrepancy between Bishnu's expectations and the reality she found in Texas may point back to the aforementioned issue of pre-orientation texts' failure to provide site-specific information. Because the benefits available to refugees vary by state, the information presented in an orientation text may prove dissimilar in amount or type to the reality one finds after resettlement. While some refugees from each of the four geographic groups I interviewed reported some discrepancy between their expectations and their lived experiences in the United States, for Iraqis, this discrepancy was particularly pronounced.

Several reports have noted and analyzed the mental health issues and lack of satisfaction among many Iraqi refugees living in the United States. For example, in 2007, Hikmet Jamil, Mohamed Farrag, Julie Hakim-Larson, Talib Kafaji, Husam Abdulkhaleq, and Adnan Hammad reported instances of post-traumatic stress disorder, anxiety, and depression in Iraqi refugees after their relocation.[52] Hikmet Jamil, Julie Hakim-Larson, Mohamed Farrag, Talib Kafaji, Laith H. Jamil, and Adnan Hammad examined mental disorders in Iraqi American Refugees more generally in 2005.[53] The U.S. Government Accountability Office filed a report in 2009 that strategized about ways to better address Iraqi's mental health needs after their arrival in the United States.[54] These reports sometimes attribute Iraqis' dissatisfaction and/or depression to the disparity between refugees' high standard of living in Iraq or in their secondary countries of asylum and the lower standard of living that newly arrived refugees in the United States are likely to experience. However, the Iraqi narrators and some resettlement administrators I interviewed revealed that perhaps this issue is more complicated than it appears in the existing literature. Specifically, the narrators pointed to the relevance of their extensive access to U.S. media in Iraq.

Rand, a refugee from Iraq who now works as a cultural orientation instructor in Houston, Texas, spoke with me extensively about the reasons why she and her clients struggled during the first days after their arrival in the United States. Specifically, Rand believes that the U.S. media Iraqis encounter leads them to believe that life in the United States is an exclusively beautiful and relaxing place to live:

> Well, because in the books, some of the movies—a lot of Iraqis, they used to see talk show like Oprah, Dr. Phil, yeah. So they kind of see the beautiful side of United States of America, but they don't see that people here are working so hard. They are very hard worker. They start working at age fourteen. They pay their expenses—like, they study and work at the same time. You know, so this is how hard people, how hard worker people are here in the United States of America. They don't see this part, you know. And also, it doesn't—the movies doesn't speak about the social system here in the United States of America. So they, even like the Office of Cultural Orientation will tell them that in America there is no such a thing as [indefinite social assistance] but I think they refuse to accept that. They still wish that there's something different. You know, it's going to be different. Sometimes you know it's hard and difficult; you know that, but you don't want to believe in it.[55]

In Rand's view, the issue is not that Iraqis are unaware of the style of life in the United States, or even necessarily that they are living lives of luxury in Iraq, but rather that they ascribe to the luxury they see in U.S. media—what Rand called "the thing that they want to hear"—instead of adopting more conservative expectations. The more difficult parts of U.S. life, Rand suggested to me, were obscured in media. "You know [sigh], I think the movies doesn't speak about those things. And it's not something that we interested in, you know. Maybe we are—when you live in Iraq, this is not something that you interested in, so." Rand's own experiences of coping with a lower standard of living in the United States than she expected and of walking her clients through similar processes of coping have caused her to reinterpret some aspects of American films after her arrival. For example, Rand now has a different perspective than before about why American films portray so much partying and vacationing:

> The way that I see things in the movie—I mean, people in the United States look like they enjoy their life. They love to have fun. Going for vacation, and fun, and party was essential part. So they live a luxury life. But I know it's not the kind of luxury life; it's very stressful. It's really stressful. [So that's] why people wants to go out and have fun, it's very important for them. It's pretty important for them to go for vacation, because it's so stressful, they *need* to go for a vacation.

Although Rand now has an explanation for the dichotomy between the luxury portrayed in U.S. movies and the less-than-luxurious experience of living in the United States, it has not caused an end to her discontentment. Wistfully, Rand still recalls life being more satisfying in Iraq:

> If something happen, crisis happen, you will not be alone. Financially, emotionally, you will have the family, friends. You know? This support system is very important in Iraq, and this is why I think people over there are very happy. I still think they are happy. They are happier than us—than me—living in the United States of America.

Rand's narrative reveals a complexity in refugee responses to mediated representations of the United States that needs to be addressed explicitly: Beyond deeming depictions of the United States "true" or "false" after comparing them to their own experiences, incoming migrants can, as Rand believes, come to realize that media may only reveal just a partial view of some constructed narrative, and, depending on viewers' interests and desires, this fractional perspective may have more or less influence on refugees' satisfaction with life in the United States.

Other Iraqis and resettlement administrators reaffirmed Rand's characterization of newly arriving Iraqi refugees. Meghann told me about her own Iraqi clients: "I think that would be fair to say, yes, to say that they're more—that they're disappointed. Um, I would also say, maybe, disillusioned."[56] Meghann believes the disparity of wealth refugees experience between Iraq and the United States has a direct effect:

> They're the group that did not know what they were coming into. They did not know that they were being resettled into poverty in the United States. Many of them had quite a bit of wealth in the Middle East and a very high standard of living. So the reality of an affordable apartment on public assistance in the city is just mind blowing.

However, in contradiction to Rand and Meghann's narratives, some Iraqis I spoke with believed that they knew exactly "what they were coming into" precisely *because* of the United States media they had encountered before their resettlement.

For example, Shiraz, who fled from Baghdad to Damascus in 1997 and arrived in Los Angeles in 2012, told me, "I know from the beginning, when I came here, I know from there, there is nothing easy in there. Everything is difficult. I know because I saw it from the movies."[57] I asked Shiraz whether there was one film in particular that he remembers depicting the difficulty of life in the United States. Like Sancha in chapter 1, Shiraz referenced the 2006 Hollywood blockbuster *The Pursuit of Happyness* and explained how he believes that this film describes realistically the likelihood of homelessness in the United States. "He had everything and then he lost his job and get homeless," Shiraz remembers about the film. I asked him whether he thinks *The Pursuit of Happyness* taught him anything. Shiraz replied, "I have to do everything legally. Because if I do an easy thing that is unlegal, maybe it's, maybe I will go to be a homeless or everything, you know? Maybe I lost everything." In fact, Shiraz is so sure that American films are able to prepare refugees for hardship in the United States that he is surprised and frustrated by other Iraqis who want to return to the Middle East after facing disappointment in the United States. To these individuals, Shiraz says, Okay, you know about America and you saw the movies and you, you know the type of life in there. Why you, why you came to America? I don't know. I don't understand.

Moses, who is also from Iraq and lives in Los Angeles, believes that sometimes the refugees who talk about wanting to return to Iraq are not being truthful. "Don't believe them," Moses told me with a good-natured smile.[58]

> This is my opinion. They all like it here. But when they talk, they are saying ["I want to] go back." Eh, it's only talking. So, ah, this is my opinion. The

life is here is very good. Even [if] they give me now ten million dollar to go to Baghdad, I will never go. Yep, this is my opinion. They are all lying. So now he came here they have, they have a good life, the easy life and they say "No, it's not good. It's not enough. The money they are giving us is not enough." This is why they are complaining. Eh, this is their opinion, you know.[59]

Moses believes that part of the reason that Iraqis are disappointed is because they lack access to a full array of media sources, and he suggested that this is what sets those who are less satisfied apart from him. "For me, I have a good life," he assured me. "Every, every morning I wake up, I'm living, true? I don't have to do everything, to go to the movies, to go to the restaurant every day. I don't have to [get] Internets or televisions, so. You have to organize your life so it would be enough. But if you like to go every day to the restaurant, to the theater? It will not be enough of course."

Saif, also an Iraqi refugee, asserted that the disappointment many Iraqis experience should not be attributed solely to media-related expectations. "Many Iraqis are disappointed when they come here, but not because of American movies," Saif told me.[60] Rather, he believes, "They found that life means to work hard, and they are not used to the system of the United States, to work, so that's why they are disappointed." Prudently, Saif noted, when it comes to assessing the relationship between media, expectations, migration, and disappointment, "It depends on the person."

In contrast, Waleed, an Iraqi refugee living in Buffalo, New York, was not disappointed by the difference between U.S. media and his experiences in the United States at all. Waleed was clear; he did not find that the United States was exactly like the United States media he had seen, but this discrepancy was a welcome one: "Most of the movies I ha[d] seen involve a lot of fights and a lot of gangs and shootings," Waleed explained. "But those I haven't seen here in the States. But I have already seen the buildings and the streets, the cleanliness, how tidy everything and how organized everything." Likewise, Jala, an Iraqi living in San Diego, told me, "When you see—in my country, in the media, they speak about the United States, they speak against the country. But the life is different here when I come here and see people, the life is different."[61] I asked Jala, "How is it different?" She replied, "They were talking in the media that people they don't have opinion here, but in real life, no, they have opinion." During her first couple of weeks in San Diego, Jala was pleased to find that despite the negative portrayal of the United States she had seen in Iraqi media, in fact, "There is no problems." These Iraqi narrators reveal that although Iraqi refugees may experience a disproportionate amount of disappointment in the United States, and although there does appear to be a link between media and Iraqi satisfaction, this link cannot be as easily generalized as some of the existing research suggests.

Indeed, as one can see from Rand, Shiraz, Moses, Saif, Waleed, and Jala, Iraqi refugees' experiences with U.S. media vary widely, are highly personal, and are always dependent on interpretation.

The aforementioned narrators point to another important variance in refugees' comparisons of media-related expectations to reality: Not all refugees—Iraqi or otherwise—are disappointed with the reality they find immediately after relocating to the United States. Some refugees found exactly what they had expected; others were pleasantly surprised. Fatuma, from Somalia, explained how during a two day IOM orientation in Nairobi, "They show us a video, how America is, how they act, what they been doing."[62] Upon her arrival in the United States, Fatuma found, "Whatever IOM told me and whatever video I saw—there's no judging or no religion accusing and all that—I'm seeing in here because whatever IOM was telling me, here I'm seeing it." Likewise, Khadija, also from Somalia, told me, "IOM—whatever they was giving us in training is true. Because this is what I saw in here, everything they said is here right now when we see it with our eyes."[63] I asked Zau, from Burma, what his first impressions of Texas were as he looked out the window of his arrival plane as it was landing. He told me,

> I study [Texas] in Burma. I know about Texas very well. They have the field, they have the mountains—a lot of things, I know that. So when I fly [from Malaysia to] L.A. To Houston, so I see exactly, you know. [It] look like story, yeah, I'm happy, and I opened my heart.

Even later, when Zau was surprised by some unexpected aspects of life in Texas, he remained happy. He explained,

> I'm very surprised in Texas, because the way the how it look like our country. No snow, so we can work every day. And then we can see that you people look like Mexico, and then the black people, our country don't have. So, we see them, look like I'm arrived in heaven, you know! They are also all very kind.

For Zau, a pre-arrival study of Texas provided a realistic albeit partial view.

These narratives provide good indication of the variety of ways that lived experiences may reaffirm, contradict, enhance, or provide a means for interpreting mediated portrayals of U.S. life that refugees encounter throughout their relocation. The perspectives included here reaffirm that one must resist the tendency to draw simple or universal conclusions regarding the impact of media related-expectations on refugees. Media's impact not unilinear. Moreover, the impact of media encountered before arrival and media that refugees read, watch, or hear after they arrive in the United States is not mutually exclusive; rather, one must consider how these two groups of media interact, reaffirm, or contradict each other in order to gain a contextualized view of their influence. Thus, in the next section, I will provide a consideration of the ways post-arrival orientation media attempt to curb and manage refugees' expectations in the first weeks after their arrival.

Post-Arrival Orientations and Orientation Media

Sometime during a refugee's first several weeks in the United States, the local agency that facilitated the refugee's resettlement will provide a post-arrival orientation, also called a "domestic community orientation," meant to ensure that new arrivals learn promptly how to navigate health care, transportation, and education systems; settle into their new homes; and recognize the importance of finding a job as soon as possible. Post-arrival orientations attempt to address what COR calls "refugees' unrealistic expectations about resettlement" and quell the disorientation and culture shock refugees may experience during this period.[64] The majority of post-arrival orientation media exists in printed form, but in some cases, refugees may be provided with videos or audio recordings that reinforce the resettlement agencies' goals and advice. Orientations typically take place either in a refugee's new home or at the resettlement agency. The resettlement agencies' contractual agreement with the U.S. Department of State mandates that refugees receive orientation relating to safety and housing within five business days of their arrival and orientation about other topics within thirty days of their arrival. Still, the duration, content, and structure of post-arrival orientations inevitably vary according to additional state and local mandates and because of limited funding. The Cultural Orientation Resource Center explains:

> Perhaps the single biggest challenge that U.S. CO [cultural orientation] programs face is the lack of specific funding for CO. Unlike overseas CO, CO in the United States is not specifically funded, but is part of a package of federally funded services. This lack of designated funds has led to a more informal, less standardized form of CO than what is provided overseas.

Interestingly, while the lack of funding for post-arrival orientations may limit the domestic orientation's length or content, the refugees in this study drew several similarities between the two orientations and helped me to locate instances wherein post-arrival orientation media mimics the subjects typically addressed in pre-departure orientation.

Consider, for example, the following two images. The first (Figure 3.2), taken from the pre-departure *Guidebook for Refugees* discussed in detail in chapter two, warns refugees against physically abusing their children and other family members and states the right of Child Protective Services to remove children from a home if parents are neglectful. Each of these instructions is accompanied by a visual image; the first is of a man with his hand raised to strike a woman, the second is of a woman holding and looking kindly at a young, smiling child. It is unclear in the second visual whether the woman holding the child is a member of Child Protective Services or the child's parent. If she is meant to represent the parent, the two images lack equivalence, as the first shows what one ought not to do, and the second shows what one ought to do. Regardless of who this adult is meant to represent, the description next to this image leaves some ambiguity, as it insists that children should not be left "without adult supervision," but it does not provide a clear definition of what constitutes supervision or the process by which a lack of supervision may "lead to the removal of the child by a child protection agency." The second image, in Figure 3.3, depicts page 26 of the YMCA Houston-produced text, *Reception and Placement: Community Orientation*, distributed during post-arrival orientations. This text issues similar warnings regarding child/family abuse and neglect, although in this instance,

 Physical abuse	It is illegal to physically abuse (hit or beat) your spouse or child. A child protection agency may remove from home a child who is being beaten.
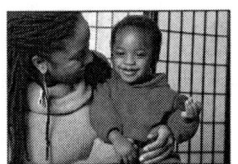 Child care	It is illegal to leave children without adult supervision. Though very few states have set a legal age that a child can be left home alone, children around the age of 12 and under should not be left alone. In some countries, older children take care of younger children, but in the United States, young children must be supervised by an adult. Leaving a child unattended is considered neglect and can lead to the removal of the child by a child protection agency.

FIGURE 3.2 Page 149 of the *Guidebook for Refugees* orientation text[65]

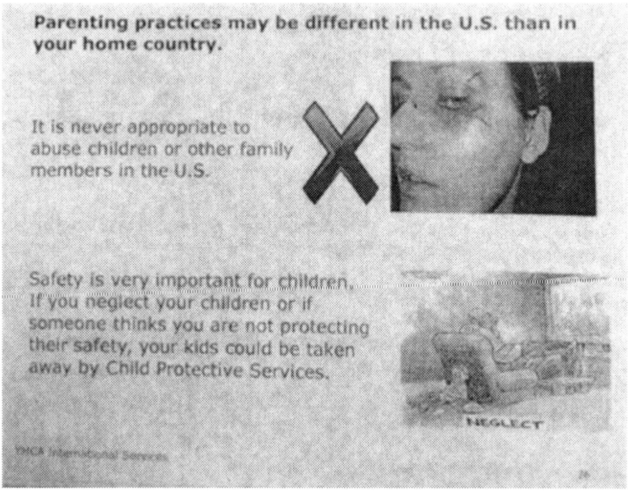

FIGURE 3.3 Page 26 of YMCA Houston's *Reception and Placement* orientation text[66]

both of the two corresponding images—the first a photograph and the second a clip-art style drawing—reinforce what one ought *not* to do.

These two pages demonstrate that the importance of visuality discussed in relation to pre-arrival orientation media carries through to post-arrival contexts. The post-arrival orientation media at each of the ten resettlement organizations I visited in New York, Pennsylvania, Texas, and California all frequently included photographs, clip art, and drawings. Amy Blose, a volunteer coordinator at the YMCA International Services in Houston and one of the authors of the YMCA-produced text, *Reception and Placement: Community Orientation*, discussed with me the importance of images in orientation texts.

> We have a very wide range of people who come here. When we were thinking of putting the pictures in there, it was much more for the people who have a lower level of literacy that may really need a visual to accompany what is put into words. 'Cause a lot of our clients—they're not literate in their own language, much less English.[67]

Amy went on to describe one problem the pictures in the *Reception and Placement* text sometimes cause. "We have more affluent refugees and then they're like, you know, 'Why are you showing this to me? These are pictures!' You know, it's just . . . lower than their level, so. But we just wanted it to work for everybody." In these instances, the cartoon-like clip art images—such as the ones depicted

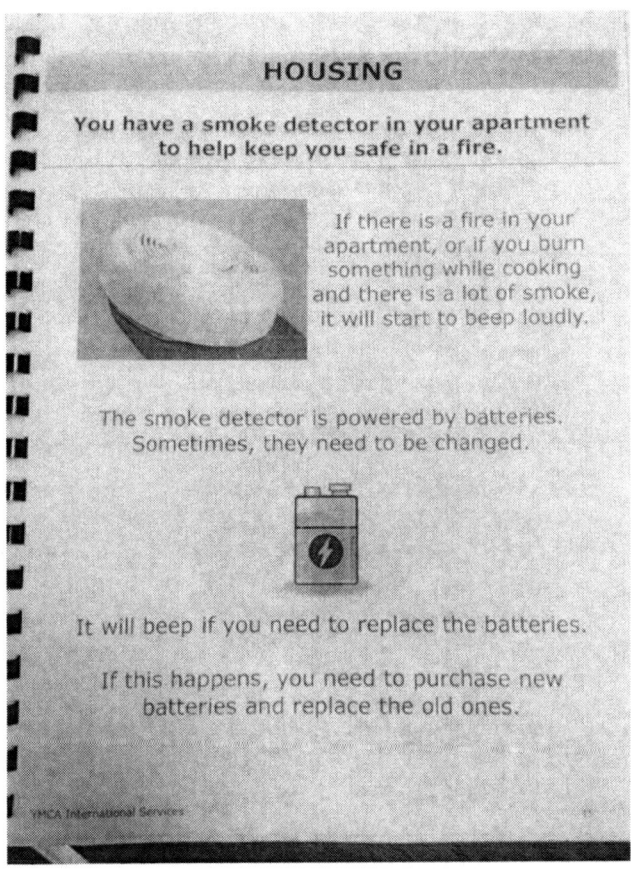

FIGURE 3.4 Page 15 of YMCA Houston's *Reception and Placement* orientation text[68]

earlier—may contribute to the affluent refugees' belief that these texts are condescending or patronizing.

Amy explained to me that she and the other contributors to the *Reception and Placement* text decided on the content of this text by considering their own experiences with refugee clients. For example, Amy's visit to one newly arrived refugee client's home motivated her to author page 15 of the text shown in Figure 3.4.

She explained,

> Sometimes we'll go and visit people and [the smoke detector] will be beeping and beeping and beeping. I went one time and somebody had covered the smoke detector with a cloth, because they didn't fully understand what

that [beeping] meant, and it was just that the battery was dying. So, just from our own experiences we just tried to put things in there that would come in handy for them.

Amy's experience provides some insight into the ways that the content of locally produced orientation texts is decided. Here, one family's lack of understanding regarding their smoke detector led to the incorporation of instructions now provided to all incoming clients, regardless of their knowledge about smoke detectors. Amy created the text in Microsoft Publisher and used the Clip Art function to find many of the photographs and drawings so that she would not need to worry about getting permission to use other types of images. The USCRI reviewed the text before it was finalized and offered Amy some suggestions for replacing images that might send a confusing message:

> There was a picture of somebody, like, giving mouth to mouth—it was like a cartoon image, like trying to show that you call 9-1-1 if someone's not breathing, right? And they had suggested, 'No, it looks like they're kissing'—to not use that. And so in some instances there were photos like that that we changed to something that would be a little more appropriate so that everybody would understand.

While it may seem obvious, one must consider that the images that appear in any orientation text may appear normal or typical to an American born individual but in fact represent ideas, practices, and/or norms that are wholly unfamiliar to refugees. This reality complicates the already difficult task of choosing images based on considerations such as fair use, representation of diversity, and, as Amy's affluent clients pointed out, for which "level" of instruction certain types of images are appropriate.

Just as chapter two pointed out that no pre-departure orientation text could fully prepare refugees for the experiences they will encounter upon their arrival in the United States, the narrators in this chapter reveal the ways post-arrival media are similarly limited. As the aforementioned examples demonstrate, the scope of topics delivered during these meetings is neither standardized nor always applicable to all orientation attendees. Though such similarities between pre- and post-arrival orientations are apparent, one particular attribute causes a distinct difference between pre- and post-arrival orientation media: post-arrival orientation media are much more likely to contain location-specific information regarding the communities into which refugees are placed.

The lack of standardization in post-arrival orientations means that resettlement personnel may provide all kinds of different media during these meetings, and the media that a refugee encounters in one locale is not necessarily similar in amount or type to the media another refugee would receive elsewhere. Rather than one widespread text, such as the *Guidebook for Refugees* I analyzed in the last chapter that is disseminated in predeparture orientations, U.S. resettlement agencies provide refugees with multiple and varied information—most often in the form of print (verbal and visual) media—that provides information specific to the assisting resettlement agency and the locale wherein the agency is located.

Meghann Perry, director of Programs and Adult Education at Journey's End Refugee Services of Buffalo, explained that compared to the overseas orientation,

> our orientation is very specific to Journey's End and Erie County and Buffalo. You know, you'll get food stamps, Medicaid, and cash assistance, all on one card. We show a picture of the benefit card. It's very specific versus "this is your settlement anywhere."[69]

While resettlement agencies sometimes provide refugees with texts produced by the Department of State or other national entities, these agencies may also provide some state government, produced texts and images—such as the photograph of the benefit card Meghann described—as well as media produced by the resettlement agency itself. For example, at Journey's End Refugee Services, refugees are given a red folder full of information upon their arrival. Journey's End caseworkers prepare the information packets and deliver them during individualized orientations, wherein a caseworker talks the refugees through some or all of the contents. The packet contains, among other print media, a brochure called "Violence in the Home" from the U.S. Committee for Refugees and Immigrants (USCRI), a booklet entitled "A People's Guide to Eating Fish Caught in Western New York" produced by the New York State Department of Health in conjunction with an organization called Buffalo Niagara Riverkeeper, a map of several Buffalo supermarkets, and a page that lists the names of all of the Journey's End caseworkers with pictures to help refugees understand the needs for which it is appropriate to solicit help from the caseworkers.[70] By using this combination of federal, state, and locally produced media, refugees will, purportedly, be able to understand which kinds of services are available to all refugees in the United States, and which services are specific to their local Buffalo resettlement agency.

In Figure 3.5, an image of one page from the YMCA Houston-produced text *Reception and Placement: Community Orientation* provides an example of the kind of location-specific information that may be included in local resettlement agency-produced texts.

This page provides refugee readers local information, including the available hours and fees for a YMCA Houston–affiliated immigration case manager who offers services to Houston refugees and therefore stand in direct contrast to predeparture orientation media, wherein the contained information must remain generic enough to be applicable to all local U.S. contexts.

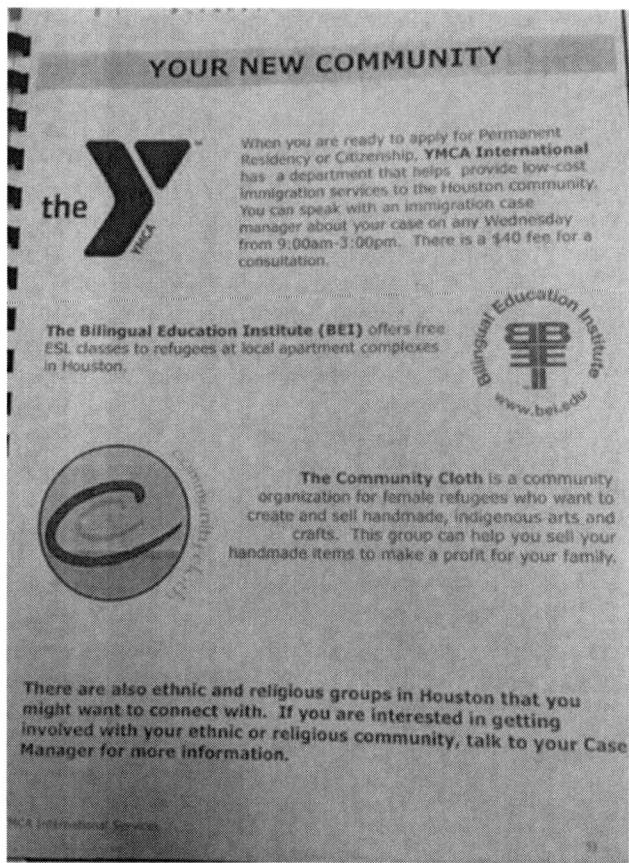

FIGURE 3.5 Page 53 of YMCA Houston's *Reception and Placement* orientation text[71]

In short, while post-arrival orientations sometimes differ from pre-arrival orientations in that they provide information specific to the American location in which refugees have arrived, the media used in these orientations often do not include information that is specific to any particular ethnicity or group. In this way, post-arrival orientation texts, images, and videos remain similar to pre-departure orientation media in that they construct an imagined but ambiguous readership through their inclusions and exclusions. Moreover, as will be made clear in the coming sections, in instances where the same media are provided to refugees from multiple groups, these orientation media act implicitly as tools for homogenization. These media encourage refugee normativity regardless of the myriad and conflicting views, beliefs, desires, values, and goals that refugees from around the world hold when they enter the United States.

While the content of post-arrival media provides some integral insight, a thorough consideration of the merits and limitations of post-arrival orientation media demands an audience-centered review. The refugees I interviewed had differing opinions regarding the efficacy of the post-arrival orientations they attended and provided some insights regarding the media they encountered during these meetings. Generally speaking, the narrators revealed that post-arrival orientations are overloaded with information and that refugees may need more individual attention than post-arrival orientations typically allow. For example, Amnar Alhasani who shared some of his story in chapter two, arrived in Houston, Texas in 2012 after fleeing his home in Baghdad and spending six years in Egypt. Though Anmar has two degrees and worked as a mechanical engineer and business owner in Iraq, when he moved to Houston, he was only able to find work as a cashier for six hours a day. In addition to this job, Anmar spends an average of eight hours a day volunteering to help other refugees affiliated with the YMCA International Services in Houston. When Anmar told me how much he volunteers, I was surprised; most of the other agencies I worked with had only part-time volunteers who contributed a few hours a week. But Anmar believes his greater presence is necessary at the YMCA because his clients require more attention than orientation sessions alone can provide:

> In the first day when they come, they give them a lot of information. And this day, you can't understand all this information in the same day. This is the problem about almost all the refugees: the information they have, they don't understand it. They need a lot of community orientation. They have here a community orientation, but also this one is not enough.[72]

Anmar's concern draws into question just how much mediated information it is possible for refugees to process and remember just after undertaking a life-changing relocation to an unfamiliar country. Moreover, Anmar believes that sometimes instead of needing more information and paper work, refugees may simply need someone to talk to: "Some of them, they don't have anyone. I know many, many family. They don't have not anyone! They need someone to talk with, because he don't have anyone to talk with." To ease this problem, Anmar spends his days helping refugees to interpret the information they received in orientation and listening to those who simply want to talk.

While Anmar's point regarding the information overload that may occur in post-arrival orientation is prudent, sometimes refugees have difficulty digesting the print and video media given to them during orientation for other reasons. For example, Abdikadir Mohammed, from Somalia, explained to me what his own domestic orientation experience was like:

> When you are in camp you get three days' orientation, then when you land in Dallas, the first time, you will sleep at night and in the morning you

> will get another orientation. When they were like giving orientation when I came to America, they show me everything, like, how to shop, how to go to school, or how to speak English, or how to ask a person as a kind word. If you put [that orientation] in your mind, you could learn more, but our people—there was a war, all that. If we see the video, we weren't putting our brain on that.[73]

I asked Abdikadir if he meant that people from Somalia could not concentrate during post-arrival orientation because they were thinking about the war in Somalia, and he confirmed this. Still, he suggested, the orientation "helped a lot." Abdikadir's narrative introduces an important consideration to the study of post-arrival orientation media: Individuals who have experienced trauma–and especially survivors of torture–may experience and interpret media in ways that are different from those who have had no such experiences. A discussion of scientific evidence of the cognitive relationship between trauma and media consumption is outside the scope of this study. However, the reality of this phenomenon is pertinent to any consideration of the media made available to refugees, as preoccupation with past violence may, as is clear in the following example, prohibit this group from fully engaging with or interpreting the media they encounter.

Like Abdikadir, Hassan is also from Somalia and also experienced a good deal of violence before his arrival in the United States. In 1994, when he was ten years old, Hassan was walking home from a market carrying a plastic bag of some food he had bought for his brothers and sisters. When he heard a gunshot, Hassan started running, and some men threw a grenade at him that hit his legs. People gathered to try to help him, but Hassan told me, "The people they try to help me, even they just get shot." Today Hassan uses crutches to walk on his one remaining leg, and still thinks about the war. I met him at the Somali Bantu Association and asked him to tell me about his first few days in San Diego. Hassan attended a post-arrival orientation and told me,

> Everything I wanted to know, is like, I get it in that class. The problem is, you have something in your mind, you cannot remember. Still we have the gunshot in our mind. It's hard to remember that stuff, cause if you start trying to remember that stuff, you gonna feel the gunshot in your mind at nighttime.[74]

I asked Hassan if he meant that he could not remember what he learned in orientation because trying to remember would cause other painful memories to arise in his mind. He confirmed. The U.S. Department of State's Deployment Stress Management Program states that the first symptom of post-traumatic stress disorder is "reliving the trauma in some way such as becoming upset when confronted with a traumatic reminder or thinking about the trauma when you are trying to do something else."[75] Hassan and Abdikadir's narratives point to this symptom directly and reveal a sad reality about the usefulness of orientation media to refugees: Sometimes, no matter how relevant or helpful the information, a haunting past keeps attendees from being able to concentrate on, remember, or apply what they have learned in those first few weeks in the United States.[76]

The Infallible Helpmate: Government Agency Self-Representation in Post-Arrival Contexts

Like pre-arrival orientation texts, discussed in the previous chapter, post-arrival orientation texts are not typically geared toward certain groups or ethnicities. In addition to a consideration of how the text portrays and conceives of its refugee reader/viewership, a thorough examination of any U.S. orientation media must also examine how the American government and government-funded resettlement agencies represent themselves through specific language and strategic framing. The first page of *Making Your Way*, the aforementioned Department of State-funded, COR orientation curriculum provides a good example for an analysis of this phenomenon. The text begins with a somewhat confusing message on page 1: "The contents of this curriculum were developed under an agreement financed by the Bureau of Population, Refugees, and Migration, United States Department of State, but do not necessarily represent the policy of that agency and should not assume endorsement by the Federal Government."[78] In the footer of each odd numbered page of *Making Your Way*, this message is repeated. Preceding and permeating the text's content with this message establishes the federal government's handle on, and authority over, refugee resettlement in the United States while maintaining a kind of ambiguity regarding the "polic[ies]" the government might endorse.

In *Making Your Way*, the trustworthiness of the U.S. government and government-funded resettlement agencies is perpetuated through a revealing of the government's role as the benefactor to multiple societal institutions that have a direct effect on refugees' well-being and through consistent—though contingent—offers for help. The author(s) encourage(s) orientation leaders to explain to newly arriving refugees that there are "services, assistance, goods, and resources available to people" and that these services "may be provided free of charge or at a very low cost by the government."[79] But later, the text states, "After a certain period of time, assistance from the resettlement agency and the U.S. government will end. When this happens, you and your family need to be ready to support yourselves."[80] Inclusions like these present clear but contingent offers to aid newly arrived refugees.

These inclusions are then reinforced with repeated direction regarding refugees' need to trust their government-funded resettlement agency to find employment so that they can become self-sufficient as soon as possible. In a section of lesson plans found on page 523, *Making Your Way* presents a "Content Objective" for one part of orientation: refugee attendees should recognize that "The philosophies of self-sufficiency and self-advocacy are central to American culture." The stated "learning indicator" for this section—included in the text to indicate to orientation leaders whether refugees understand and accept the content objective—is "Participants can acknowledge the importance of self-sufficiency."[81] Because refugees typically receive less than $1,000 of cash aid from the U.S. government, and because they must repay the government for the funds spent on their air travel to the United States, post-arrival orientation media such as *Making Your Way* state repeatedly the importance of refugees' finding immediate employment as a means toward self-sufficiency. The text instructs domestic orientation leaders to remind refugees that "A person's initial job might not be in their chosen profession" and that "Turning down any job could be used as a reason to lose benefits."[82] To emphasize this point, the text proposes an orientation activity plan that uses pages such as the one in Figure 3.6 to encourage refugee conversation about expectations for job searching and employment.

To reinforce the necessity of following resettlement personnel's instructions, a photograph of a refugee doing what he "want[s]" is crossed through with a large "X." To provide realistic expectations regarding what types of jobs might

You want to go to college, but your case worker/manager tells you that you will need to start working first.

FIGURE 3.6 Page 143 of *Making Your Way* orientation text[83]

be available to refugees, *Making Your Way* includes photographs of individuals working in different professions, such as the one in Figure 3.7.

Additionally, the text includes small vignettes about fictional hotel workers for discussion in orientation groups. One such vignette reads:

> Arjun and his wife Rupali resettled in their new community. Rupali quickly found a full-time job with benefits as a housekeeper at a hotel . . . Arjun felt uncomfortable with the situation because Rupali had never worked outside the home before, and, as the family's main source of income, she was feeling more confident . . . What could Arjun and Rupali do to deal in a positive way with the situation?[84]

Here the authors attempt to address the changes in family and gender roles that are a common consequence of refugee relocation. These changes in gender roles vary by population, are often addressed in orientation media, and have been analyzed by scholars across disciplines, including orthopsychiatry, gender studies, and sociology.[85] Chan, who fled from Burma as a teenager and now works as a caseworker at the Burmese Community Support Center in Buffalo, New York, explained to me one reason why Burmese refugees, specifically, may interpret the meaning of this text's attempt to prepare refugees for changes in gender roles in a different way altogether and may not be able to "deal in a positive way" with their caseworkers' suggestions to accept work as hotel housekeepers.

Go to work at a hotel.

FIGURE 3.7 Page 277 of *Making Your Way* orientation text[86]

They can only get like, housekeeping, cleaning, restaurant jobs for their first job, but in Burma, those kinds of jobs are very low, just the homeless people or orphan[s], or someone who is in very low stage, they just do those kinds of jobs. So, they don't want to take those kinds of jobs here, they're still thinking those jobs are very low jobs—the housekeeping women are sex workers, they just work at the hotel, so they are thinking those are very low.[87]

Because, like most orientations texts, *Making Your Way* is not geared toward any one refugee group, it is not equipped to manage culture-specific concerns, such as the correlation between sex workers and hotel housekeepers that Chan described. This text remains perfectly equipped, however, to advertise the expertise and sovereignty of the U.S. government.

Because no characteristics in these texts distinguish certain types of refugee readers from others, the text homogenizes all readers and casts them as needing the same help from the U.S. government.[88] Indeed, the *Making Your Way* curriculum sets up the U.S. government as what Bruno Latour calls an "infallible actor"—a trustworthy fail-safe of an institution that attempts to help those who do not know how to help themselves.[89] According to Latour, this kind of constructed infallibility is often strategic and begets a kind of unquestionable power that inherently works to the advantage of those who perpetuate it. If an orientation text or video can depict the government as an altruistic ally, then perhaps it can work to establish a sense of governmental trust in its readership so that the refugees who are *interpellated* by the text's call can perpetuate its power. Of course, any document produced or funded by a government is likely to paint that government in a positive light; any other approach would be counterproductive.

From start to finish, *Making Your Way* represents the U.S. government and government-funded resettlement agencies as willing and able to help throughout almost every stage of a refugee's integration process. But a closer reading of this text reveals that help is forthcoming only if a refugee is compliant, obedient, and submissive. Taking a critical view of these generous offers, one might consider that they open the doorway that leads to the U.S. government's intervention into personal and private aspects of a refugee's life. For example, *Making Your Way* states repeatedly the importance of refugees building good credit history. On page 531, the author(s) state(s), "Good credit is very important for your personal finances in the United States. Good credit shows that you make the payments that you are supposed to make, and you make them on time. Bad credit shows that you do not." But the guide does not reveal that the driving forces behind credit's importance are the complex systems of governmental regulation, rewards, and punishments that occur based on an individual's credit score. Indeed, the government not only affirms the importance of good credit but also perpetuates the existence of credit, regulates the banks that provide credit, and offers federal loans based on individuals' credit histories. By infiltrating every step of the complex realm of credit, the government can easily wield the kind of power that Foucault calls a "productive network which runs through the whole social body."[90] It is power at multiple levels of society, so colossal it is difficult to perceive its limits but perfectly camouflaged so as to appear both naturally occurring and perfectly normal. Indeed, the normative power that is perpetuated through philanthropic offers to help that appear repeatedly in *Making Your Way* allows the U.S. government to make significant progress with impressively few resources by convincing U.S. residents—refugee and otherwise—that it wishes to offer its services to the advantage of all who prove themselves worthy.

Print Media as a Means to Develop, Standardize, and Ensure Fulfillment of Post-Arrival Orientation

In post-arrival orientations, media often serves a bureaucratic function of developing, standardizing, or providing some means of ensuring completion of orientation topics. I asked Rand how her resettlement agency decides what to include in a post-arrival orientation. "Well, for the cultural orientation, we have list of topics, because we think that this is lots of the, like, general topics that the refugees need to know about the United States of America," she explained. "So there is a list of topics that we give to the client, and we explain and discuss those topics, and each topics will explain about what. And they choose from the list of topics."[91] Rand told me that the reason her agency uses this standardized list is because, "Different people need different kind[s] of cultural orientation." Certainly, a document such as the one Rand described allows for some difference between the kinds of orientation topics that are addressed with refugees from divergent backgrounds. But, as I shall discuss in this section, such a document may also limit the topics considered eligible for delivery in orientation contexts.

Richard Harper argues that documents are "crucial to organizational life" and that through documentation of organizational practices, "members of an organization can have a new means for making sense, for creating order and sharing purpose."[92] That is, when an idea of what a particular program ought to include becomes manifest in a mediated print document that is reproduced across an organization, these programs become subject to and measured according to the document, so that print media such as the list Rand described hold a good deal of power in determining a refugee's experience with his or her resettlement agency during the first few days of living in the United States.

When documents become standardized through their bureaucratic role in an organization such as a resettlement agency, and, indeed, when they reappear in caseworkers' procedures repeatedly and become a part of a daily routine, such documents may begin to take on the appearance of naturally occurring entities rather than ideologically constructed creations of some author's doing. Some documents become so familiar within the resettlement process that refugee caseworkers may not be inclined to consider that such documentation implicitly exclude some possible topics. In this way, the power of bureaucratic documentation works not only to collect and aggregate data about a specific process such as post-arrival orientation but also to limit, control, and normalize the choices that orientation may provide to refugees.

Amy Blose, the refugee volunteer coordinator in Texas who earlier in this chapter described her role in authoring the YMCA Houston–produced text, also explained why agency personnel decided this text was needed:

> We just kind of internally decided that we needed something a little more structured, cause everybody had their own style of the orientation, so there would just be like a topic, but there wasn't much control over what each case manager was saying on that topic, so we just kinda got together and pulled out things for each topic, and then I took that and started to create this book.[93]

Here Amy reveals that the impetus for the book was a direct result of the agency's desire to retain more control over and similarity between the orientations delivered to each newly arrived refugee.

In addition to playing a role in developing and standardizing orientation topics, printed orientation media may also provide a means for ensuring that caseworkers address certain orientation topics. In a document called simply "Community Orientation Form," produced by the U.S. Committee for Refugees and Immigrants [USCRI] and used by the caseworkers at the International Institute of Los Angeles, both refugee client and an instructor (usually a caseworker) are asked to sign to acknowledge and confirm that the refugee has received a community orientation that addressed all of the topics listed on the form, including items such as "Personal and household budget and finance" and "Hygiene at home." Clearly, a good deal of ambiguity remains between these federally mandated topic guidelines and the ways such topics are delivered or discussed. For example, one item on this list requires orientation leaders or caseworkers to discuss "the importance of learning English." However, further information regarding *why* learning English is important, how *soon* one should begin learning, or by what *means* one should take up this task remain unspecified. Still, by requiring that this document be signed and archived within each newly arrived refugee's file, the USCRI effectively controls what information refugees receive regarding their resettlement in the United States. Notably, this government agency requires instruction on everything from the necessity of opening windows when one is cooking to oral hygiene.

Through the creation, reproduction, and routinization of print media, post-arrival orientations may become standardized according to a fixed set of topics at the federal or local level. When these standardized topics pervade resettlement administrators' daily dealings with refugees, they may begin to appear normal and natural and thereby implicitly prohibit other topics from post-arrival orientations.

Post-Arrival Media Facilitates Deprivatization

In the last chapter, I argued that pre-departure orientation media embody a preconception that refugees do not possess the knowledge or ability to travel to or live in the United States successfully. In post-arrival orientation media, I have found that this phenomenon is manifest not only in descriptions regarding the use of public services and resources that may be unfamiliar to a newly arrived refugee but also within multiple references to the ways refugees should treat their bodies or behave in their own homes with their families. For example, in a section entitled "Parenting Practices," the aforementioned COR curriculum instructs teachers to say to refugee orientation attendees, "Try to keep an open mind during this session. If you do, you may leave the session with some good ideas to help you deal in an acceptable and effective way with the challenge of raising your children in a culture that is not your own."[94] While one might argue that choosing how to raise one's children is a personal decision not specific to relocation, this orientation curriculum reveals the belief that personal, familial guidance belongs under the government's purview by appearing with no special explanation alongside relocation-specific instruction.

The narrators I interviewed recalled several instances of this kind of personal, familial instruction during the days following their resettlement as well. For example, Kalsumo, a Somali refugee who arrived in the United States in January 2013, told me,

> I remember a lot of things that orientation tells me about, like in America, you cannot beat your kids. You can tell [them] something if they don't understand. You can say, "Don't do this. Don't do this." [But] if the kids don't understand, you just leave.[95]

Similarly, OO Meh, a Burmese refugee who was resettled to Houston, Texas in May 2012, recalled, "Cultural orientation was like about to keep clean when you're in your apartment, I mean, in your apartment in the United States, you have to like, keep clean for safety."[96] By attempting to educate refugees about the ways they should act while in their own homes as well as the practices that are best for interacting with their own children, I argue that orientation media such as this curriculum presuppose ignorance in refugees' abilities to look after their own homes and families and that this instruction sometimes supersedes the resettlement agencies' mandate to provide refugees with the tools they need to transition into a new culture.[97]

This presupposition that the State knows best how refugees should conduct their home lives is repeated in the COR orientation curriculum's chapters on housing (including "keeping a bathroom clean by U.S. standards"[98]) and health and hygiene ("There are customs and laws in the United States regarding personal and public hygiene. People who don't follow these customs and laws may offend other people in the community or at work, and may even get into trouble with the law."[99]) and reifies Charles Briggs' assertion that

> The state assume[s] the right and the duty to bring members of racialized and immigrant communities—who were seen as being ignorant of or rejecting hygiene and institutional medicine—[into compliance as] *sanitary citizens*, individuals who (1) conceive of the body, health, and disease in terms of medical epistemologies; (2) adopt hygienic practices for disciplining their own bodies and interacting with others; (3) and recognize the monopoly of the medical profession in defining modes of disease prevention and treatment.[100]

By accepting governmental advice on matters relating to health and parent-child interactions, refugees' families become subject to what Jaber Gubrium and James Holstein call *deprivatization*—the imposition of governmental control over personal or private affairs—including government-driven home inspections to ensure compliance with normative practices.[101]

Lily, the director at the International Institute of Los Angeles (IILA), explained why these home inspections are necessary:

> Our funder requires that we do an initial home visit within five days of [refugees'] arrival. So we make sure we visit them, most likely it happens [within] twenty-four or forty-eight hours, because we want to make sure that they immediately get an orientation of what services are available to them.[102]

After this visit, Lily explained, the assigned caseworker will visit a refugee (or family of refugees) several more times over the course of the next ninety days to deliver more information. Lily revealed one benefit of this in-home style of orientation and reiterated why IILA takes this approach:

> In an individual situation, they are more likely to share information that they wouldn't otherwise share in a big group. Because we're required to do a home visit, we will go to their home, and do the orientation at their home, and bring all the informational materials, let them know what the next steps, all the things that they need to do.

Without a doubt, the delivery of informational orientation materials by credentialed caseworkers has the potential to deliver useful, pertinent information that may help refugees to feel more acquainted with their new homes and to access the public services available to them. For example, OO Meh told me, "The first week, I was scared, I was worried and I was scared, so I didn't even go around my apartment, I just stay home."[103] I asked OO Meh what she was scared of. She replied,

> I didn't know anyone. I thought there were no Burmese in my apartment [building] when I arrived, and I thought like, maybe they're Spanish, and I worried if people come and talk to me, if they come to my apartment, I don't know what they saying, and I was worried, so, just stayed home.

But even in her own home, OO Meh was afraid: "The most difficult thing is when I cook and all the electric things, I'm worried about of all the electric things. I'm scared, I turn off or on, I don't even know." Much to her relief, OO Meh's caseworker soon came to her house and talked her through the aforementioned YMCA produced orientation book. This managed to alleviate some of OO Meh's fear: "In the cultural orientation I learn about the cleaners and all the tools in my apartment and how to use them and in case of emergency I have to call 9-1-1, and for fire I have to say 'Fire,' and for violence, I have to say 'Police,' and for sickness or something I have to say 'Ambulance.'" After learning the information in the book, OO Meh revealed, "After one week, I was fine, and I go around, I walk around my apartment." OO Meh provides one example of the helpful potential of government-mandated, post-arrival home visits. Still, this infiltration of orientation media into refugees' homes holds some potential beyond making refugees less fearful of their surroundings and therefore demands further consideration. If refugees are asked to abide by the kinds of governmental advice on matters relating to health and parent-child interactions found in the print media noted earlier, and if resettlement caseworkers are visiting refugees' homes to both deliver and follow up on this information, refugees may not be able to maintain the power to say "no" to State-imposed suggestions—even within the privacy of their own homes.

In the realm of refugee *deprivatization*, no territory is off limits to the State; even in cases when government-funded personnel are not physically entering refugees' homes, they manage a symbolic imposition into refugees' private lives through the State's strategic instruction about home life delivered even as early as pre-departure orientations, before refugees ever enter their new American homes.

This chapter has inquired into the realms of learning and experience through a concentration on refugees' first days in the United States. Because refugees carry impressions and memories of pre-arrival media with them into the United

States, I examined instances in which the narrators compared what they learned in pre-arrival media encounters about the United States to the reality of their experiences upon resettlement. I discussed refugees' post-arrival acquisition of media technology and the varying degrees of importance this acquisition had for the narrators. Finally, this chapter considered how local resettlement organizations in the United States use print and digital media in an attempt to guide refugees through their first days after relocation and how this post-arrival orientation media represent the U.S. government, act as a means of standardization, and facilitate the imposition of governmental control into the realms of health, hygiene, and family.

One must resist the belief that post-arrival orientation media always achieve some kind of author-intended effect. Indeed, acculturation (the learning of a new culture) and deculturation (the giving up of an old culture) do not occur in a one-way, linear progression; as an immigrant learns a new culture, s/he does not necessarily lose his/her desire for or interest in maintaining the norms and practices of an older culture. In the case of post-arrival orientation media, one must consider that readers may choose to accept a text's message not because of a willing attraction to the descriptions of a new culture, but because of a sense that their compliance is mandatory. This view supports migration scholar John Berry's suggestion for a new metaphor to describe assimilation. Berry contends, "When people choose to assimilate, the notion of the Melting Pot may be appropriate; but when forced to do so, it becomes more like a Pressure Cooker."[104] This pressure cooker metaphor suggests the necessity of a more complicated view of the relationship between acculturation and deculturation and, indeed, between refugees' needs and the post-arrival media they encounter.

Refugee resettlement is an ongoing process that does not end once refugees finish their post-arrival orientations and begin leading lives independent of their resettlement agencies. Thus, a thorough view of the relationship of media to resettlement demands a long-term view. In the next chapter, I will provide a closer look at the types of media the narrators I interviewed consume after they have finished their post-arrival orientations and after their contact with their resettlement agencies begins to wane. Specifically, by considering instances in which refugees acquire, consume, interpret, and/or utilize media in some way(s) to facilitate or resist acculturation, I will investigate the role of media in ongoing resettlement.

Notes

1 Name changed upon request of the narrator; interview with Sarah Bishop, Los Angeles, CA, July 9, 2014.
2 See Marianne Debouzy, *In the Shadow of the Statue of Liberty: Immigrants, Workers, and Citizens in the American Republic, 1880–1920* (Urbana: University of Illinois Press, 1992).

3 United States of America, Department of State, Bureau for Population, Refugees, and Migration, Cultural Orientation Resource Center, *Welcome to the United States: A Guidebook for Refugees* 4th ed. (Washington, DC: Cultural Orientation Resource Center, Center for Applied Linguistics, 2012), 38.
4 Teek Powar, interview with Sarah Bishop, San Diego, CA, November 18, 2013, archived at the Schlesinger Library at Harvard University.
5 Fatuma Mudey Aden, interview with Sarah Bishop, San Diego, CA, November 18, 2013, archived at the Schlesinger Library at Harvard University.
6 William G. Thomas, "Experiential Education: A Rationale for Creative Problem Solving," *Education and Urban Society* 7, no. 2 (1975): 1972–81; Ula Casale Manzo, Anthony V. Manzo, and Matthew M. Thomas, *Content Area Literacy: A Framework for Reading-Based Instruction* (Hoboken, NJ: John Wiley & Sons, 2009); W. F. Dennison and Roger Kirk, *Do, Review, Learn, Apply: A Simple Guide to Experiential Learning* (Oxford: Blackwell Education, 1990); Jane Fried, *Transformative Learning Through Engagement: Student Affairs Practice as Experiential Pedagogy* (Sterling, VA: Stylus Publishing, 2012); Markie L. C. Blumer, "And Action! Teaching and Learning through Film," *Journal of Feminist Family Therapy* 22, no. 3 (2010): 225–35; Eva Michel, "The Role of Individual Differences in Cognitive Skills in Children's Learning through Film," *Journal of Media Psychology* 22, no. 3 (2010): 105–13.
7 John Dewey, *Experience and Education* (West Lafayette, IN: Kappa Delta Pi, 1938).
8 Dewey, *Experience and Education*.
9 Sophocles, *The Dramas of Sophocles* (New York: E. P. Dutton, 1906), 191.
10 Ya Wee, interview by Sarah Bishop, Buffalo, NY, August 6, 2013, archived at the Schlesinger Library at Harvard University.
11 Although Ya Wee did not know the names of any of these films, he does remember that they mostly involved "fighting and shooting" and created in him a sense of admiration for American freedom. Since Ya Wee was only two when he arrived in the refugee camp in Thailand, he likely had no memory of the kind of freedom depicted in many American films.
12 Megeney Ramazani, interview by Sarah Bishop, San Diego, CA, November 20, 2013, archived at the Schlesinger Library at Harvard University.
13 Nirmala Khanal, interview by Sarah Bishop, Buffalo, CA, August 6, 2013, archived at the Schlesinger Library at Harvard University.
14 Sahro Nor, interview by Sarah Bishop, San Diego, CA, November 21, 2013, archived at the Schlesinger Library at Harvard University.
15 Ibid.
16 Lily Alba, interview by Sarah Bishop, Los Angeles, CA, July 9, 2013, archived at the Schlesinger Library at Harvard University.
17 Fahad Al Allaq, interview by Sarah Bishop, Los Angeles, CA, July 11, 2013, archived at the Schlesinger Library at Harvard University.
18 Nanda Chuwan, interview with Sarah Bishop, Erie, PA, February 7, 2013, archived at the Schlesinger Library at Harvard University.
19 Abdirahim Mohammed, interview by Sarah Bishop, San Diego, CA, November 21, 2013, archived at the Schlesinger Library at Harvard University.
20 Kalsumo Ibrahim, interview by Sarah Bishop, San Diego, CA, November 20, 2013, archived at the Schlesinger Library at Harvard University.
21 For more on the interrelationship of nationalism, media, and consumerism, see Toby Miller's notion of "cultural citizenship" in *Cultural Citizenship: Cosmopolitanism,*

Consumerism, and Television in a Neoliberal Age (Philadelphia: Temple University Press, 2006).

22 See Sandra M. Gifford and Raelene Wilding, "Digital Escapes? ICTs, Settlement and Belonging among Karen Youth in Melbourne, Australia," *Journal of Refugee Studies* 26, no. 4 (2013): 558–75; Nicolas Harney, "Precarity, Affect and Problem Solving with Mobile Phones by Asylum Seekers, Refugees and Migrants in Naples, Italy," *Journal of Refugee Studies* 26, no. 4 (2013): 541–57; and Robyn Ramsden, "'It Was the Most Beautiful Country I Have Ever Seen': The Role of Somali Narratives in Adapting to a New Country," *Journal of Refugee Studies* 26, no. 2 (2013): 226–46.

23 Several existing studies also mention the relationship of immigrant media consumption and language learning. See, for example, Don H. Sunoo, Edgar P. Trotter, and Ronald L. Aames, "Media Use and Learning of English by Immigrants," *Journalism Quarterly* 57, no. 22 (1980): 330–3; and Nelly Elias and Dafna Lemish, "Media Uses in Immigrant Families: Torn between 'Inward' and 'Outward' Paths of Integration," *International Communication Gazette* 70, no. 1 (2008): 21–40.

24 Habiba now lives near San Diego.

25 Habiba Jama, interview by Sarah Bishop, San Diego, CA, November 20, 2013, archived at the Schlesinger Library at Harvard University.

26 Name changed by request; Amira, interview by Sarah Bishop, Los Angeles, CA, July 9, 2013, archived at the Schlesinger Library at Harvard University. Interestingly, *Georgie!* is a Japanese anime series, written by Mann Izawa and illustrated by Yumiko Igarashi, which originally appeared in *Shōjo Comic* manga magazine. Adapted for television in 1982, the cartoon tells the story of a young girl named Georgie who lives in Australia. When she begins to suspect that she is adopted, Georgie travels to London to find her real parents. Though Georgie was originally produced by Tokyo Movie Shinsha in Japan, it soon was dubbed into English (as well as several other languages). While I cannot find any evidence that *Georgie!* appeared on American television, the entire television series is available online.

27 Hiba Saeed, interview by Sarah Bishop, San Diego, CA, November 18, 2013, archived at the Schlesinger Library at Harvard University.

28 Doug Walker, "The Media's Role in Immigrant Adaption: How First-Year Haitians in Miami Use the Media," *Journalism and Communication Monographs* 1, no. 3 (1999): 159–96. For more on the role of media in immigrant language learning, see Christina Slade, "Media and Citizenship: Transnational Television Cultures Reshaping Political Identities in the European Union," *Journalism* 11, no. 6 (2010): 727–33.

29 *Guidebook for Refugees*, 187; D. M. Abrams, *Making Your Way: A Reception and Placement Orientation Curriculum* (Washington, DC: Center for Applied Linguistics and the Cultural Orientation Resource Center, 2013), 367.

30 Joyce Penfield, *The Media: Catalysts for Communicative Language Learning*, (Reading, MA: Addison-Wesley, 1987); Wai Meng Chan, *Media in Foreign Language Teaching and Learning*, Vol. 5 (Boston: De Gruyter Mouton, 2011); Stuart Webb, "Pre-Learning Low-Frequency Vocabulary in Second Language Television Programmes," *Language Teaching Research* 14, no. 4 (2010): 501–15; Mark Peterson, *Computer Games and Language Learning* (New York: Palgrave Macmillan, 2013); Anne Vize, "Engaging ESL Students in Media Literacy," *Screen Education* 61 (Autumn 2011): 78–81; Rebecca Oxford, Sukero Ito Young Park-Oh, and Malenna Sumrall, "Learning a Language by Satellite Television: What Influences Student Achievement?" *System* 21, no. 1 (1993): 31–48.

31 Jasmine Seymo, interview by Sarah Bishop, San Diego, CA, November 18, 2013, archived at the Schlesinger Library at Harvard University.
32 Some existing studies from outside of the United States consider the relationship of refugees' employment and language acquisition. See, for example, Feng Hou and Morton Beiser, "Learning the Language of a New Country: A Ten-Year Study of English Acquisition by South-East Asian Refugees in Canada," *International Migration* 44, no. 1 (2006): 135–65; Jill Brown, Jenny Miller, and Jane Mitchell, "Interrupted Schooling and the Acquisition of Literacy: Experiences of Sudanese Refugees in Victorian Secondary Schools," *Australian Journal of Language and Literacy* 29, no. 2 (2006): 150–62; Feng Hou and Morton Beiser, "Language Acquisition, Unemployment and Depressive Disorder among Southeast Asian Refugees: A 10-Year Study," *Social Science & Medicine* 53, no. 10 (2001): 1321–34; and Mike Baynham, "Agency and Contingency in the Language Learning of Refugees and Asylum Seekers," *Linguistics and Education* 17, no. 1 (2006): 24–39.
33 Abreer Bayara, interview by Sarah Bishop, Houston, TX, November 13, 2013, archived at the Schlesinger Library at Harvard University. For more on the impact of media on relationships between refugee parents and children, see Lynn Schofield Clark and Lynn Sywyj, "Mobile Intimacies in the U.S.A. Among Refugee and Recent Immigrant Teens and Their Parents," *Feminist Media Studies* 12, no. 4 (2012): 485–95.
34 Tek Rimal, interview with Sarah Bishop, Pittsburgh, PA, March 18, 2013, archived at the Schlesinger Library at Harvard University
35 See Toby Miller, *Cultural Citizenship*, 2007; Aihwa Ong et al. "Cultural Citizenship as Subject-Making: Immigrants Negotiate Racial and Cultural Boundaries in the United States," *Current Anthropology* 37, no. 55 (1996): 737–62; and Nick Stevenson, *Cultural Citizenship: Cosmopolitan Questions* (Maidenhead, UK: Open University Press Maidenhead, 2003).
36 See Herman Wasserman and Patrice Kayeya-Mwepu, "Creating Connections: Exploring the Intermediary Use of ICTs by Congolese Refugees at Tertiary Educational Institutions in Cape Town," *African Journal of Information and Communication* 6 (2005): 94–103; Raelene Wilding, "'Virtual' Intimacies? Families Communicating Across Transnational Contexts," *Global Networks* 6, no. 2 (2006): 125–42; and Minoo Razavi, "Navigating New National Identity Online: On Immigrant Children, Identity, and the Internet," MA Thesis, Georgetown University, 2013.
37 Fahad Al Allaq, interview by Sarah Bishop, Los Angeles, CA, July 11, 2013.
38 Lily Alba, interview by Sarah Bishop, Los Angeles, CA, July 12, 2013, archived at the Schlesinger Library at Harvard University.
39 Anonymous, interview by Sarah Bishop, Los Angeles, CA, July 11, 2013.
40 From Cultural Orientation Resource Center (2012). *Welcome to the United States: A Guidebook for Refugees* 4th ed. (Washington, DC: Center for Applied Linguistics). Reproduced with permission from the Center for Applied Linguistics.
41 *Making Your Way*, 715.
42 Sahro Nor, interview by Sarah Bishop, San Diego, CA, November 21, 2013, archived at the Schlesinger Library at Harvard University. For information regarding the history of printed missing children notices in the United States from a communication perspective, see Perry Howell, "Got Worry? Missing Children Notices on Milk Cartons in the United States," *Interactions: Studies in Communication & Culture* 2, no. 1 (2012): 35–46. For more on the relationship of television to the fear of crime, see Daniel Romer, Kathleen Hall Jamieson, and Sean Aday, "Television News and the Cultivation of Fear of Crime," *Journal of Communication* 53, no. 1 (2003): 88–104.

43 "Amira" (name changed at the request of the narrator), interview by Sarah Bishop, Los Angeles, CA, July 12, 2013, archived at the Schlesinger Library at Harvard University.
44 Dahabo Abdulali, interview by Sarah Bishop, San Diego, CA, November 21, 2013, archived at the Schlesinger Library at Harvard University.
45 Megeney Ramazani, interview by Sarah Bishop, San Diego, CA, November 20, 2013, archived at the Schlesinger Library at Harvard University.
46 For more on refugees' expectations, see Art Hansen and Anthony Oliver-Smith, eds. *Involuntary Migration and Resettlement: The Problems and Responses of Dislocated People* (Boulder: Westview Press, 1982); Iris E. Dumenden, "The Soft Bigotry of Low Expectations: The Refugee Student and Mainstream Schooling," *British Journal of Sociology of Education* 35, no. 3 (2014): 484–86; Kristian Svenberg , Carola Skott, and Margret Lepp "Ambiguous Expectations and Reduced Confidence: Experience of Somali Refugees," *Journal of Refugee Studies* 24, no. 4 (2011): 690–705; Valentina C. Iversen, John E. Berg, and Arne E. Vaaler, "Expectations of the Future: Immigrant, Asylum Seeker, Or Refugee—Does it Matter?" *Journal of Psychiatric Intensive Care* 6, no. 1 (2010): 23–30; Alan B. Henkin and Carole A. Singleton, "Looking Forward: Indochinese Refugee Expectations for Post-Resettlement Change," *International Review of Modern Sociology* 22, no. 2 (1992): 45–56; and Vance Geiger, "Refugee Cognitive Expectations and Sociocultural Change Theory," *Selected Papers on Refugee Issues* 2 (1993): 67–80.
47 Fahad Al Allaq, interview by Sarah Bishop, Los Angeles, CA, July 11, 2013, archived at the Schlesinger Library at Harvard University.
48 Name changed by request; "Zanuba," interview by Sarah Bishop, San Diego, CA, November 21, 2013, archived at the Schlesinger Library at Harvard University.
49 Dylanna Jackson, interview by Sarah Bishop, Erie, PA, February 7, 2013, archived at the Schlesinger Library at Harvard University.
50 Esther (last name not included at the request of the narrator), interview by Sarah Bishop, Buffalo, NY, August 6, 2013, archived at the Schlesinger Library at Harvard University.
51 Bishnu Gurung, interview by Sarah Bishop, Austin, TX, November 15, 2013, archived at the Schlesinger Library at Harvard University.
52 Hikmet Jamil, Mohamed Farrag, Julie Hakim-Larson, Talib Kafaji, Husam Abdulkhaleq, and Adnan Hammad, "Mental Health Symptoms in Iraqi Refugees: Posttraumatic Stress Disorder, Anxiety, and Depression," *Journal of Cultural Diversity* 14, no. 1 (2007): 19.
53 Hikmet Jamil, Julie Hakim-Larson, Mohamed Farrag, Talib Kafaji, Laith H. Jamil, and Adnan Hammad, "Medical Complaints among Iraqi American Refugees with Mental Disorders," *Journal of Immigrant Health* 7, no. 3 (2005): 145–52.
54 United States Government Accountability Office, *Iraqi Refugee Assistance: Improvements Needed in Measuring Progress, Assessing Needs, Tracking Funds, and Developing an International Strategic Plan: Report to Congressional Committees* (Washington, DC: U.S. Govt. Accountability Office, 2009).
55 Rand (last name removed by narrator's request), interview by Sarah Bishop, Houston, TX, November 14, 2013, archived at the Schlesinger Library at Harvard University.
56 Meghann Perry, interview by Sarah Bishop, Buffalo, NY, August 7, 2013, archived at the Schlesinger Library at Harvard University.
57 Shiraz Minasaqen, interview by Sarah Bishop, Los Angeles, CA, July 11, 2013, archived at the Schlesinger Library at Harvard University.

58 Moses Boghossian, interview by Sarah Bishop, Los Angeles, CA, July 12, 2013, archived at the Schlesinger Library at Harvard University.
59 There is some history of refugees returning or "repatriating" to their countries of origin. See Megan Bradley, *Refugee Repatriation: Justice, Responsibility and Redress* (Cambridge: Cambridge University Press, 2013); Richard Black and Khalid Koser, *The End of the Refugee Cycle?: Refugee Repatriation and Reconstruction*, Vol. 4 (New York: Berghahn Books, 1998); Robert Gorman, "Refugee Repatriation in Africa," *The World Today* 40, no. 10 (1984): 436–43; and Gaim Kibreab, "Citizenship Rights and Repatriation of Refugees," *International Migration Review* 37, no. 1 (2003): 24–73.
60 Saif Alhadithi, interview by Sarah Bishop, San Diego, CA, November 18, 2013, archived at the Schlesinger Library at Harvard University.
61 Jala Yaqo, interview by Sarah Bishop, San Diego, CA, November 18, 2013, archived at the Schlesinger Library at Harvard University.
62 Fatuma Aden, interview by Sarah Bishop, San Diego, CA, November 20, 2013, archived at the Schlesinger Library at Harvard University.
63 Khadija Osmani, interview by Sarah Bishop, San Diego, CA, November 20, 2013, archived at the Schlesinger Library at Harvard University.
64 http://www.culturalorientation.net/providing-orientation/domestic/delivery.
65 From Cultural Orientation Resource Center (2012). *Welcome to the United States: A Guidebook for Refugees* 4th ed. (Washington, DC: Center for Applied Linguistics). Reproduced with permission from the Center for Applied Linguistics.
66 *Reception and Placement: Community Orientation*, (Houston, TX: YMCA International Services, no date), 26.
67 Amy Blose, interview by Sarah Bishop, Houston, TX, November 13, 2013, archived at the Schlesinger Library at Harvard University.
68 YMCA International Services, *Reception and Placement*, 15.
69 Meghann Perry, interview by Sarah Bishop, Buffalo, NY, August 7, 2013, archived at the Schlesinger Library at Harvard University. In some states, refugees must gain access to governmental assistance through a series of identification cards and paper coupons. In the state of New York, however, food stamps, access to Medicaid services, and cash aid are all available via a single Electronic Benefits Transfer or "EBT" card. See http://otda.ny.gov/programs/ebt/.
70 Meghann asked that I not include images of the media produced by Journey's End, as it is only applicable to local contexts and should not be appropriated for use elsewhere.
71 YMCA International Services, *Reception and Placement*, 53.
72 Anmar Alhasani, interview by Sarah Bishop, Houston, TX, November 14, 2013, archived at the Schlesinger Library at Harvard University.
73 Abdikadir Abdiyow Barake, interview by Sarah Bishop, San Diego, CA, November 20, 2013, archived at the Schlesinger Library at Harvard University.
74 Hassan Sheighei, interview by Sarah Bishop, San Diego, CA, November 21, 2013, archived at the Schlesinger Library at Harvard University.
75 U.S. Department of State, *Posttraumatic Stress Disorder*, http://www.state.gov/m/med/dsmp/c44953.htm.
76 For more on refugees and posttraumatic stress, see Robert Schweitzer, Fritha Melville, Zachary Steel, and Philippe Lacherez, "Trauma, Post-Migration Living Difficulties, and Social Support as Predictors of Psychological Adjustment in Resettled Sudanese Refugees," *Australian and New Zealand Journal of Psychiatry* 40, no. 2 (2006): 179–87; Theodore W. McDonald and Jaime N. Sand, *Post-Traumatic Stress Disorder in Refugee*

Communities: The Importance of Culturally Sensitive Screening, Diagnosis, and Treatment (New York: Nova Science, 2010); Klevest Gjini, et al., "Evoked Potential Correlates of Post-Traumatic Stress Disorder in Refugees with History of Exposure to Torture," *Journal of Psychiatric Research* 47, no. 10 (2013): 1492–8; and Niall Crumlish and Killian O'Rourke, "A Systematic Review of Treatments for Post-Traumatic Stress Disorder among Refugees and Asylum-Seekers," *Journal of Nervous and Mental Disease* 198, no. 4 (2010): 237–51.

77 Wolfgang Iser, *The Implied Reader: Patterns of Communication in Prose Fiction from Bunyan to Beckett* (Baltimore: Johns Hopkins University Press, 1978), xii.
78 *Making Your Way*, 1.
79 Ibid., 37.
80 Ibid., 525.
81 Ibid., 523.
82 Ibid., 299.
83 Ibid., 143.
84 Ibid., 598.
85 See Beverley H. Ellis, Helen Z. MacDonald, Julie Klunk-Gillis, Alisa Lincoln, Lee Strunin, and Howard J. Cabral, "Discrimination and Mental Health among Somali Refugee Adolescents: The Role of Acculturation and Gender," *American Journal of Orthopsychiatry* 80, no. 4 (2010): 564–75; Colleen Fisher, "Changed and Changing Gender and Family Roles and Domestic Violence in African Refugee Background Communities Post-Settlement in Perth, Australia," *Violence Against Women* 19, no. 7 (2013): 833–47; Goli Amin Bellinger, "Negotiation of Gender Responsibilities in Resettled Refugee Populations through Relationship Enhancement Training," *Transcultural Psychiatry* 50, no. 3 (2013): 455–71; Monica Boyd, "Gender, Refugee Status and Permanent Settlement," *Gender Issues* 17, no. 1 (2010): 5–25; and Stephanie J. Nawyn, "Institutional Structures of Opportunity in Refugee Resettlement: Gender, Race/Ethnicity, and Refugee NGOs," *Journal of Sociology & Social Welfare* 37, no. 1 (2010): 149–67.
86 Ibid., 277.
87 Chan Myae, interview by Sarah Bishop, Buffalo, NY, August 7, 2013, archived at the Schlesinger Library at Harvard University.
88 See Iser, *Implied Reader*, 1978.
89 Bruno Latour, *The Pasteurization of France* (Cambridge, MA: Harvard University Press, 1993), 53.
90 "Truth and Power: An Interview with Michel Foucault." *Critique of Anthropology* 4, no. 13–14 (Summer 1979): 131–137. Translated by Felicity Edholm.
91 Rand (last name removed by narrator's request), interview by Sarah Bishop, Houston, TX, November 14, 2013, archived at the Schlesinger Library at Harvard University.
92 Richard Harper, *Inside the IMF: An Ethnography of Documents, Technology, and Organisational Action* (San Diego: Academic Press, 1998), 29. For more on documents' role in power, see David R. Olson, *The World on Paper: The Conceptual and Cognitive Implications of Writing and Reading* (Cambridge, UK: Cambridge University Press, 1994); Sean Hawkins, *Writing and Colonialism in Northern Ghana: The Encounter Between the Lodagaa and the 'World on Paper,'* (Toronto: University of Toronto Press, 2002); and Annelise Riles, *Documents: Artifacts of Modern Knowledge* (Ann Arbor: University of Michigan Press, 2006).

93 Amy Blose, interview by Sarah Bishop, Houston, TX, November 13, 2013, archived at the Schlesinger Library at Harvard University.
94 *Making Your Way*, 605.
95 Kalsumo Ibrahim, interview by Sarah Bishop, San Diego, CA, November 20, 2013, archived at the Schlesinger Library at Harvard University.
96 OO Meh, interview by Sarah Bishop, Houston, TX, November 14, 2013, archived at the Schlesinger Library at Harvard University.
97 For an official list of post-arrival orientation objectives, see Cultural Orientation Working Group and U.S. Department of State Bureau of Population, Refugees, and Migration, *U.S. Refugee Admissions Program Reception and Placement Orientation Objectives and Indicators* (2012), available at http://www.culturalorientation.net/providing-orientation/domestic/reception-and-placement-orientation-o-i.
98 *Making Your Way*, 19.
99 Ibid., 437.
100 Charles L. Briggs, "Why Nation-States and Journalists Can't Teach People to Be Healthy: Power and Pragmatic Miscalculation in Public Discourses on Health," *Medical Anthropology Quarterly* 17, no. 3 (2003): 288.
101 Jaber Gubrium and James Holstein, "Qualitative Inquiry and Deprivatization of Experience," *Qualitative Inquiry* 1 (1995): 204–22. For more on immigrants in the United States and deprivatization, see Jane Addams and the Chicago School's work with immigrants in Chicago in Mary Jo Deegan, *Jane Addams and the Men of the Chicago School 1892–1918* (New Brunswick, NJ: Transaction Publishers, 2005).
102 Lily Alba, interview by Sarah Bishop, Los Angeles, CA, July 9, 2013, archived at the Schlesinger Library at Harvard University.
103 OO Meh, interview by Sarah Bishop, Houston, TX, November 14, 2013, archived at the Schlesinger Library at Harvard University.
104 John W. Berry, "Immigration, Acculturation, and Adaptation," *Applied Psychology: An International Review* 46, no. 1 (1997): 10.

4
MEDIA AND REFUGEES' ONGOING RESETTLEMENT

In a popular shopping area on the west side of Buffalo, New York, a long white sign affixed to the front of a small storefront marks in both English and Karen the entrance of the Burmese Community Support Center (BCSC).[1] The BCSC is not a refugee resettlement agency, and the founders are clear, "it's not for the newly arrived."[2] Instead, the center aims to "promote and enhance the quality of life" for the approximately eight thousand refugees from Burma who have been living in Buffalo for three months or more, after they have completed their post-arrival orientations and after the frequency of general contact with their respective resettlement agencies begins to decrease.[3] To advertise their services, the founders of the BCSC operate a Facebook page that includes announcements regarding the hours of operation and available appointment times, a link to a video of one of the cofounders recording an interview for a local radio station, photos of the grand opening, and promotion of upcoming events such as a meeting entitled, "You and [the] American School System." The page publicly thanks the Buffalo and Erie County Public Libraries for donating some children's books to the center and provides a link to a local NPR news story about the BCSC's programs.

I spoke with Chan Thu, one of the cofounders of the BCSC, at the International Institute of Buffalo on August 1, 2013, about one month before the center opened. Chan is from Burma herself and is active with the Burmese community in Buffalo. To stay in touch with each other, Chan and some other members of the Burmese community in Buffalo meet every Saturday night at a monastery for prayers and a meal. By nature of its venue, Chan explained, this meeting is "mostly for Buddhists," and therefore excludes some of the local Burmese population. The BCSC, by contrast, seeks to serve any Burmese refugees—regardless of their religion—and their Facebook page promotes this message of inclusivity with welcoming posts like "Join BCSC this Saturday at 10am as we celebrate the grand opening of our center! We will have a ribbon cutting ceremony, speakers from the community, local politicians, blessings from various religious groups and light refreshments!"[4] In this way, the BCSC Facebook page is able to reach beyond more traditional, in-person meetings available to subcultures within larger communities who wish to stay connected, and avoid the religion-specific nature of face-to-face meetings at the monastery. Still, the BCSC Facebook page has its own limitations; while it is intended to supersede boundaries within the community and welcome all Burmese refugees who have been in Buffalo for three months or more, in fact, it serves as a source of information and connection only for those who know English, are literate, and have access to Facebook.

The Burmese Community Support Center's Facebook page provides one example of the nuances present in the kinds of media created for or available to refugees after they have completed their post-arrival cultural orientations in the United States. As refugees begin to detach from their resettlement agencies and gain increased independence and familiarity with their new locales, their media habits begin to change. Nevertheless, even after refugees achieve the governmental definition of self-sufficiency,[5] many still do not speak English fluently and may not be able to access certain types of media due to a skill deficiency, issues related to language comprehension or literacy, disinterest, or a lack of funds or other necessary resources.

While much research about refugee resettlement deals with a time frame that encompasses refugees' experiences immediately before, during, or immediately after their resettlement, I argue that a detailed view of refugee resettlement necessitates a long-term view that surpasses the weeks and months immediately following resettlement. Christie Sherstha, writing for the United Nations High Commissioner for Refugees (UNHCR), argues, "Resettlement is an on-going process that does not end with refugees' arrival to the host country." Instead, Sherstha reveals that the complex processes of resettlement subsist long after refugees settle into their new homes and include dynamic ongoing acculturation to the social, political, economic, and cultural facets of their new locales.[6] The Burmese Community Support Center's Facebook page provides just one of a multitude of examples of the ways that media may continue to inform and interact with processes of ongoing resettlement long after refugees have arrived in their new homes and completed their post-arrival orientations.

In view of the reality that resettlement is a long-term process without a clear end, this chapter will explore, from multiple angles, the interaction of media and refugees' ongoing resettlement. I will consider how refugees may use U.S. media as well as media from or about their home countries or secondary countries of asylum once they have completed their post-arrival orientations and settled into their new U.S. homes. First, the chapter will address the ways that refugees are portrayed in U.S. media and how they interpret or respond to these portrayals. Next, I explore the interaction of media, language, and religion and demonstrate the ways that these three phenomena are inextricably linked in refugees' lives. Finally, the chapter turns to address the role of media in maintaining or negotiating connections between refugees' families and friends.

Of course, once refugees become familiarized with the culture and norms of U.S. life, many of the ways they encounter and use media are indistinguishable from the ways that U.S.-born individuals might. Still, there are some notable cases in which refugees' media use remains unique. Specifically, by considering instances in which media is acquired, consumed, interpreted, and/or utilized in some way(s) to facilitate or resist acculturation, one can gain insight into how media may work as a tool or obstacle for refugees who are continually negotiating their places within the cultural landscapes of their new locales. Throughout, this chapter remains primarily concerned with media's role in ongoing resettlement, and the mediated resources available to forced migrants who may or may not wish to conform to the cultural norms of the communities into which they have been placed.

Media about Refugees in the United States

A discussion of media's role in ongoing refugee resettlement would not be complete without a thorough consideration of the ways that refugees are portrayed in U.S. media and how refugees interpret or respond to these media. This consideration proves necessary for two primary reasons. First, the interviews I completed in New York, California, Pennsylvania, and Texas revealed that many refugees are keenly aware of the ways U.S. media portray their communities and that these portrayals often have direct implications for refugees' livelihoods. Second, because of the geographical dispersion of refugees in the U.S., combined with the relatively small ratio of refugee to American-born nationals (approximately 1 to 5,100), many Americans' only information about refugees comes from various media—a telling glimpse into how individuals form opinions when lacking direct interaction with a particular group.[7] Indeed, Vibert Cambridge argues that the ways American entertainment programming and news present ethnic diversity in general "has significant consequences, because it may be the only contact that some Americans have with this diversity."[8] Mediated portrayals of refugees possess the ability to alter the lived experiences of Americans and refugees alike. Scholars Joachim Trebbe and Philomen Schoenhagen reveal in their work that the ways refugees are portrayed in media may affect everything from a refugee's ability to find a job to his or her acceptance in a social group.[9] Because media about refugees may affect Americans' opinions about the federal tax funds spent on refugee resettlement, opinions about the likelihood that refugees would make good friends or neighbors, or even opinions about the status of immigration to the United States in general, one should not underestimate the significance of mediated portrayals of refugees in U.S. media.

An exhaustive view of the ways refugees are portrayed in all genres of U.S. media would be impossible to provide in the limited space of this chapter. For this reason, I will focus my efforts only on the genre that was—by far—most discussed by both the refugees and resettlement administrators I interviewed: local newspaper articles. The eight cities I visited for this project house some of the largest communities of refugees in the United States, and, as a result, the local newspapers in these cities include articles about them. In each city I visited, I asked the narrators I interviewed about what kinds of media—if any—they had encountered about refugees in the United States. Any time the narrators mentioned local newspapers, I took note of it. After the interviewing took place, I visited the largest local newspaper's website containing their digital archives and searched the term "refugees." Because the newspapers also included stories about refugees living outside the United States, I narrowed my search to only the "Local" sections of each. My findings were surprising, upsetting, and heartening, and in the following pages, I intend to describe both the ways refugees are portrayed in U.S. news journalism and the ways that refugees respond to these portrayals.

Refugees in U.S. News

First, I should note, academic analysis of portrayals of immigrants in news journalism is not uncharted territory. Youna Kim, Myria Georgiou, Regina Branton, Johannah Dunaway, Jonathan Ong, Christine Du Bois, Rita Simon, and Athanasia Batziou have each produced enlightening studies on this topic.[10] But because refugees comprise a unique, specific group of immigrants in the United States, not all of the existing research is applicable to the current study. Though several studies regarding the portrayal of refugees and other forced migrants in news media exist internationally,[11] this area has received very little attention in U.S. scholarship. One notable exception is Melinda B. Robins's 2003 study. Robins analyzed daily local newspaper portrayals of the cities in which the "Lost Boys"—a group of five hundred Sudanese refugees who arrived in the United States in early 2001—had been settled. In these newspapers, Robins discovered the consistent "use of the word 'boys' to describe young black men," the suggestion that Americans must "tame and civilize" the refugees as though they were wild animals in need of domestication, and references to the refugees' homeland that described it as a "dark nullity that barely existed before westerners turned their gaze upon it."[12] Such tropes serve to paint rhetorical pictures of refugees for readers and viewers, and, again, these pictures are made significant in part because of the ways they may stand in for interpersonal interaction between refugees and American-born citizens.

Certainly, more research such as Robins's is needed to sort out the impact of mediated representations of refugees in the United States. Still, within the existing scholarship that examines U.S. news portrayals of immigrants generally, some telling tropes emerge that helped me identify the breadth and boundaries of the power of media to represent a group of others in ways that have direct consequences for those populations. For instance, several studies have noted the prevalent use of a few, recurrent metaphors to describe voluntary immigrants in U.S. news. Otto Santa Ana's study of articles from the *Los Angeles Times* between 1992 and 1994 revealed that immigrants in America were consistently portrayed as burdens, diseases, dangerous waters, and/or weeds.[13] Similarly, a ten-year study of the *Forum*, a community newspaper from Fargo, North Dakota, found three main metaphors in articles describing immigrants in America: "the burden, the flood, and the uprooted of the world."[14] In an analysis of reports on immigration from CNN and Fox News from September to December of 2005, J. David Cisneros reported, "in addition to being conceived as a crime wave or invasion, immigration is framed metaphorically as a dangerous pollutant."[15] These three studies in particular indicate the necessity of analyzing not only overt descriptions and assertions about refugees in U.S. media but also the ways that acceptance, fear, or prejudice may be couched and embedded within the stylistic elements of a journalistic account. As these authors found, deploying metaphors is a rhetorical strategy adopted by American news journalists to communicate the offensiveness of immigration without having to explicitly decry immigration's supposed harms.

In my interviews, I found that refugee resettlement administrators in particular are acutely attuned to the ways refugees are portrayed in U.S. news. By nature of their profession, resettlement administrators are likely to both seek out news about refugees and to converse with refugees who have encountered and/or have questions about such news. Several of the resettlement administrators I interviewed mentioned a recent phenomenon in online local news articles about refugees. While many of these articles show support for or talk favorably about refugees, they are often accompanied by fearful or hateful comments from readers about refugee resettlement in the United States in general. My analysis of digital comments about refugees, when added to the existing studies of online articles about refugees, will provide heightened understanding of the ways audiences interact with online news journalism. In ways similar to the articles analyzed by the aforementioned scholars, I found that such comments advance a series of metaphors that implicitly describe the perceived harms of migration to the United States. But, unlike the existing studies of articles, my own analysis reveals that these comments also include overt and explicit criticism of refugees in addition to these metaphors.[16]

Meghann Perry, director of Education at Journey's End, a resettlement agency in Buffalo, New York, explained bluntly her own frustrating experience in reading these posts:

> If you Google any newspaper article about refugees, and you look at the comments on the bottom, you'll see people's comments about, you know, "These people shouldn't come here and use taxpayer dollars"—a conservative, Republican, "Our money shouldn't go to foreigners" attitude.

To follow up on Meghann's assertion, I searched the *Buffalo News*[17] website for any digital stories about local refugees and found that, in fact, most had no visible comments. The comments that did follow a few articles about local refugees ranged from wholly positive to incendiary and revanchist. For example, after a February 2014 article titled "Multivenue Show in Allentown Highlights Faces of Buffalo Refugees," the nine available comments include three that seem to show support for refugees in the area, three that are ambiguous, and three that demonstrate overt aversion to refugees. Perhaps the most positive response to this article reads, "The refugee community is a big part of the West Side Revival still underway. Kudos to the artists for bringing them center stage!" But at the opposite end of the range, another commenter posted, "Keep the immigrants out, am I right?"[18] Likewise, the twelve comments following a December 2013 *Buffalo News* article called "Refugees Turn Hard Work into Better Future through Programs Here" are divided between those who show support of refugees and others who suggest some detriments or disadvantages to refugee resettlement in the United States.[19] One comment reads, "People who've lived in war-torn countries sometimes have trouble assimilating into Western culture. A perfect example is the Somali immigrant who punched an infant in the face in Buffalo," to which another commenter responded,

> And what about all the Americans who punch kids in the face? . . . we can NOT make a generalization that refugees = punching infants in the face or other forms of violence. Violence is everywhere and not contained to one group.[20]

The dichotomous nature of these comments suggests a divide in the Buffalo community's perspectives of refugees.

The most commented upon recent article about refugees in the *Buffalo News*, titled "Refugees Get First Taste of Thanksgiving Traditions," currently displays twenty-five comments.[21] Five of these comments show overt support of refugees in the area, including one that begins, "Great article. Immigrants bring new life to cities." Two comments (both from the same commenter) are ambiguous in their support of refugees, and the eighteen remaining comments speak negatively about refugees in Buffalo, though the same commenter, identified as "aldonco," posted ten of these eighteen comments. None of the comments following this article appears to be written from a refugee perspective. Instead, the commenters frequently use pronouns such as "we" and "us" to represent Americans, and "they" to discuss refugees. Aldonco, for example, writes

> The only problem is everyone of those refugees have a benefit cards [sic] on them and we are paying for them . . . I believe in charity but you have to deserve it. America can't keeping [sic] giving the store away we are broke. Get you [sic] head out of your backside and think of our people first.

Aldonco's repeated use of the inclusive pronouns "we" and "our" allows for a rhetorical fashioning of an "in-group" of Americans for whom s/he acts as the spokesperson. Moreover, within these comments, aldonco characterizes all refugees in Buffalo according to some traits both explicit and metaphorical: they are "free loaders" who are "a drain on the whole population" and who believe it is "easier spending other people's money" than supporting themselves. Aldonco does not reveal how this knowledge of refugees was acquired; rather, the source of this knowledge remains rhetorically invisible and therefore implicitly presumed. Throughout these responses, the use of inclusive pronouns testifies to Gerard Hauser's notion that "Social actors are able to construct shared social realities . . . because they share a language of common meaning and a common reference world."[22] This sharing of "common meaning" becomes clear when viewing instances of ideological group self-identification alongside instances in which respondents identify an "other," or a group that does not belong.

By addressing each other as members of an ideologically constructed in-group to take a collective stance against local refugees, the members of the aforementioned comment forums do not speak to refugees or invite refugee perspectives and opinions but instead create a rhetorical divide between who belongs and does not belong in the United States. Majid KhosraviNik has found that this imagined comradeship manifests widely in discourses of immigrants, in which "the in-group is predicated as being the people who are concerned about community relations and the out-group—immigrants—are implicitly referred to as the threat to that."[23] Likewise, Joachim Trebbe and Philomen Schoenhagen argue, "perception of the other [always] includes the perception of one's own group and the feeling of being a part of this group."[24] In an article that considers both voluntary and forced migrants in the United States, Tatyana S. Thweatt revealed that deleterious descriptions of immigrants and refugees are often accompanied by positive, ideological statements about America.[25] Indeed, when news journalism constructs a negative view of incoming migrants, the nation into which the migrants are arriving may be simultaneously esteemed and reified. The available comments to articles in the *Buffalo News* about refugees reveal that digital media may foster both optimistic and hateful discourse about refugees in the United States.

Despite the pervasive negative "attitude" Meghann reported encountering in local Buffalo news, she remains optimistic about her community's acceptance of refugees. Meghann's face-to-face encounters with Buffalo residents have been largely positive, leading her to believe that the xenophobia found in some of the incendiary newspaper comment forums "doesn't really reflect the population" in Buffalo as a whole.[26] She explained, "Overall you hear much more positive things about the refugee population. I hear all the time, you know—'These streets would be abandoned. These storefronts would be empty'—how good refugees are." Indeed, one of the five comments that demonstrates support of refugees after the aforementioned Rey article reads, "Immigrants bring new life to cities . . . they revitalize broken-down neighborhoods." I asked Meghann, "Why do you think there's that disconnect between the comments that are on the digital news stories and what you encounter?" She replied,

> I think—and it's my personal opinion, really—but I really think that the people making those comments, they're pretty ignorant about the situations. They don't really know a lot about what's going on, and it's easy. It's anonymous. You can post whatever you want on the Internet. You don't have to back it up. But, come in my office and make your argument. Let's see how it goes. I think that's a lot harder, you know.

Meghann's suggestion that posting "ignorant" comments online is easier than talking face-to-face about one's feelings toward refugees raises several pertinent questions. Are comment forums providing an outlet for opinions that are not discussed in face-to-face interactions? Does anonymity afford commenters more boldness, or does having to identify oneself online have no effect upon which comments appear and which are withheld? Finally, do people who are more knowledgeable about refugees demonstrate more acceptance toward them, as Meghann suggests? To address these questions, one must gain a broader perspective of viewpoints on digital comment forums about refugees in the United States.

After talking with Meghann, I began to ask other resettlement administrators in other areas whether they, too, had encountered some negative responses to articles about refugees in local news. I soon learned that this widespread phenomenon is quite familiar to resettlement agencies across the United States and that—like Meghann—many of the resettlement administrators attribute the comments' negativity to a lack of knowledge about who refugees are and why they are arriving in U.S. communities.

Kheir Mugwaneza, the director of Community Assistance and Refugee Resettlement at a resettlement agency in Pittsburgh, told me he believes negative comments following news about refugees are a direct result of the Pittsburgh community's ignorance about refugees. People living in the area have a tendency to place all incoming migrants in the "same basket—illegal, legal, [international] students," Kheir explained, and this generalization perpetuates an indiscriminate prejudice. He lamented, "There are just some people who will never get it, no matter how hard you try." Lily Alba, the director of the International Institute of Los Angeles (IILA), echoed Kheir's opinion. Though Lily believes that the Los Angeles community is, in general, welcoming to refugees, "There's always that opposition from people—ignorance," Lily explained. Early on in her career with IILA, Lily realized that "people didn't know why refugees were coming." Since then, she told me, "I feel like we've seen a positive change and more education." Lily is confident that more education about refugees leads to more community acceptance, and for this purpose, the IILA website includes thorough descriptions of all of the institute's refugee programs as well as multiple color photographs of refugees, including some that depict refugees arriving in the United States, sitting in classes, playing with their children at a park, sharing a meal around a table, and performing music.[27] Back in Buffalo, I asked Meghann if she too believes that a positive correlation exists between knowledge and acceptance of refugees. She answered,

> I hope so. I don't know if I know that factually. I mean, it seems absolutely logical, and that's the assumption that we want to go—you know, that we work with. We have all kinds of awareness raising events. That's how we do things. [But] how would I know if that's actually true or not? I don't know.

If knowledge about refugees does indeed lead to more acceptance, the expense of community awareness-raising events may be well worth it, but if not, the end goal of such events becomes more convoluted.

As a whole, the resettlement administrators I interviewed seemed hopeful that when members of the local communities do understand why refugees have resettled nearby, they are more likely to take a positive stance toward refugees in general. But resettlement administrators believe that the type of knowledge required for such a stance is, unfortunately, too often lacking, and that even the kinds of descriptive websites and awareness-raising events that Lily and Meghann described are not enough. Working now as a caseworker for the refugee resettlement agency that helped him relocate from Nepal to Pittsburgh, Sancha is frustrated by negative portrayals of refugees in U.S. media. When he spoke to me in February 2013, he remembered,

> Around a month ago . . . we were on news, refugee people were on news, because people, local people at that place, they were not happy with the activities of refugees, because they had no idea, you know, from where refugee are coming, [or] who are the contact person[s] in the refugee community.

Some of the negativity in the comment forums following news about refugees could be prevented, Sancha believes, if Americans were more aware of other outlets where they could voice their concerns. He explained if individuals who complain about the "activities of refugees . . . before going to news media, they could have come to us"—meaning the staff at Jewish Family and Children's Services—"you know, if they had idea that we are in the community. But they had no idea who is the contact person in that community, so they had no other solution than going to press."

While Sancha's reflection may seem generous, his response is similar to the other administrators who agree that, generally, the more local individuals know about refugees, the more accepting and tolerant they will become in both words and action. Still, the question of the relationship of knowledge and acceptance is a tricky one, confounded by the ironic reality that in the instances explored here, the production of positive local news stories about refugees is the exact action that creates the public digital space in which intolerant comments about refugees exist and perpetuate. It is such phenomena that led Radha Hegde to observe, "As people cross borders, cultures are reinvented and mix on the street, but the language of assimilation and obligation to the mythos of national community ironically gains momentum."[28] Likewise, Edward Said does not ascribe to the positive correlation between knowledge of others and acceptance and instead argues that, "Knowledge of subject races or Orientals is what makes their management easy and profitable; knowledge gives power, more power requires more knowledge, and so on in an increasingly profitable dialectic of information and control."[29] Indeed, the resettlement administers' opinions I noted earlier point to salient questions in local refugee contexts: Is a community more likely to respond favorably toward refugees if they have more knowledge of the types of situations that lead to refugee displacement? If so, how can one explain the trend of local U.S. newspaper articles about refugees generating revanchist, incendiary comments about these populations? Moreover, if knowledge about refugees in the United States does indeed lead to more local acceptance, how can such a relationship be measured or tracked? In the next section, I will attempt to address these questions by providing examples of instances where refugees and Americans respond to portrayals of members of their communities in U.S. news journalism.

Refugees and Americans Respond to News about Refugees in the United States

The ways U.S. media portrays refugees holds little significance without an understanding of the nature of refugees' encounters with and responses to these portrayals or recognition of the ways this discourse may affect the lived experiences of both refugees and American-born individuals. One British study by Ivan

Leudar, Jacqueline Hayes, Jiri Nekvapil, and Johanna Turner Baker found that refugees negotiated their identities in response to themes of hostility that existed within UK media.[30] Teun A. Van Dijk observed that through representations of ethnic minorities in newspapers and television, a dominant group that controls the production of popular media is able to influence directly how less powerful groups are perceived by the public.[31] Indeed, representation in media is directly related to enculturation and integration of refugees, as it holds the power to influence the beliefs and behavior of individuals from both the majority and minority groups.[32] Unfortunately, even false accusations in media representations about refugees may have tangible negative implications. Much is at stake, especially in instances where mediated discourse stands in for any firsthand contact with a represented group, as is likely to be the case for refugees who make up such a small percentage of the United States population. In addition to false or hyperbolic knowledge production regarding, for example, the number of refugees in a community or the influx's effect, xenophobic narratives about refugees may cause American readers to be less likely to provide the community support that many local nonprofit agencies depend on for the successful integration of refugees into a community. Moreover, as Leudar, Hayes, Nekvapil, and Turner Baker have proven in their work, refugees may negotiate their identities based on public opinion, such as is found in the comments following articles about refugees. Or they may presuppose that the incendiary comments available in such comment forums represent the overall feelings of the community at large, even when this is not the case.[33] Media critic Teun A. van Dijk asserts, "Media discourse is the main source of people's knowledge, attitudes, and ideologies."[34] To assess the process by which this sourcing occurs, however, one must consider carefully what media says about particular groups and what the portrayed groups themselves think, feel, and/or do about these portrayals. It is precisely because of the real-world implications of media about refugees that further examination of refugee-related discourse is necessary.

That positive articles about refugees in local news are often followed by revanchist, hateful comments in online forums was of particular concern to the refugee narrators I interviewed and contests the notion that intercultural contact through media and acceptance of difference are always positively correlated. In fact, I suggest instead that the exposure of refugee-related activities in local news might in some cases perpetuate the hate and prejudice refugees in America encounter. The breadth of this phenomenon necessitates an examination both broad in scope and detailed in its analysis of the style and context of the portrayals themselves. For breadth I will look to the interviews I completed in eight cities across the United States, as well as some scholarship on the public sphere that will shed light on this related area of inquiry. For detail and specificity, I will draw to the fore a few examples of articles about refugees with comments—brought to my attention by the narrators I interviewed—so that the reader can gain insight into the typical content of such media and so that I can provide an analysis of the ways that the language, format, style, and composition of these texts reveal and conceal particular ideologies and perspectives. Not all articles about refugees in the United States are the same, and I will not attempt to describe the portrayal of refugees in U.S. news as a whole. Instead, my main concern has to do with the relevance of these texts for the refugees I interviewed. Thus, in this section, I utilize a mixed-methods approach to analyze some of the portrayals of refugees in news in more detail. The narrators demonstrate how these articles and comments affect their sense of belonging and/or their understanding of Americans' perceptions of refugees.

Refugee narrators I interviewed in Los Angeles, San Diego, Pittsburgh, Erie, and Houston all reported encountering stories about members of their own populations in local U.S. media and explained that because these encounters do not occur frequently, these stories stand out as notable. These stories are often shared on community blogs or by way of a listserv specific to a certain immigrant population. Several of the refugees I interviewed in these cities were aware of the trend of strongly worded reader comments posted on news websites under corresponding articles about refugees. Digital media critic Jaime Loke suggests that online comment forums following news articles involving cultural difference cause a blurring of the previously mutually exclusive spheres of public and private space. Loke's work applies here directly, as she argues that the recent push for political correctness in the United States "may have taken away public expressions of bigotry, but the advent of this new space [for online responses to news] is allowing the public's genuine emotions to be amplified publicly without fear of repercussions."[35] By carefully considering instances of these public expressions of emotion, one can better understand their nature, purpose, and implications.

One such instance that left a deep impression on a few of the narrators I interviewed in Pittsburgh occurred shortly after Diana Nelson Jones's 2012 article was published on the *Pittsburgh Post-Gazette's* website. Pittsburgh is a post-industrial city with a long history of working class immigration and of labor conflict. The end of the booming steel industry in the area in the early 1980s spelled the end of the relatively high blue-collar wage locally and led to a rise in unemployment. Jones's article, entitled, "Carrick Home for Ethnic Nepali Refugees," focuses on the ways Carrick, a neighborhood in Pittsburgh that was the site of former steel mills and is still suffering from the mills' closures, has "attracted the largest population of ethnic Nepali refugees from Bhutan of any in the city," and includes some positive quotes from community members who are living alongside the refugees.[36] For instance, Matthew Onega, a teacher at the Greater Pittsburgh Literacy Council, believes the refugees have proven to be "hard-working, interested and committed" to their jobs. Later in the article, local councilwoman Natalia Rudiak observes, "Who's to say that one of these Nepali kids might not be a future councilperson?" The author quotes an owner of a local shoe repair business in Carrick, saying, "They [the refugees] seem to be great family people." While this positive exposure in the largest local newspaper in Pittsburgh may appear to be a broader testament to that community's overall acceptance of refugees who have settled in the area, it took only a brief glance at the comment section below the article for me to see why the narrators had found this piece of media so memorable. As of July 1, 2013, the responses following this article numbered 122. Notably, while a few commenters speak in defense of the Nepali refugees living in Carrick, only one of the 122 comments speaks from a first-person Nepali perspective. Phuyel Bhanu, whose comment appears second to last in the string of comments to Jones's article, stands out. First, while all of the previous 120 comments were posted over the four days immediately following the digital publication of Jones's article in September 2012, Bhanu's comment was posted about five months later, on February 12, 2013. Moreover, whereas some of the other comments received as many as thirteen replies from other commenters, Bhanu's comment received no replies. His comment reads,

> good things come from good mind and bad things come from bad mind. depends on your eyes, how you see. you can explain in any ways you want. But the reality matters. Carrick has been a good place for us. people are very helpful and they love us. those who understand us love us.[37]

This inclusion of only a single refugee voice in the 122 comments following Jones's article points to a unique rhetorical aspect of this public: Though both the article and the comments speak *about* refugees, they never speak *to* or *invite* refugee perspectives. In fact, through the use of exclusive, ideological pronouns that manufacture a rhetorical divide between "us" and "them," as well as displays of patriotism, the responses accomplish the opposite.

Sara McKinnon explains that in cases of refugees seeking asylum in the United States, public discourse often constructs America as a "home" in which refugees are "guests."[38] In this view, "guests are made coherent in their relation to global capital along lines of productivity and the threat of reproductivity"—or, the propagation and spreading of some unwanted groups, cultures, or ideas.[39] That is, a "productive" guest presents his or her efforts for self-sufficiency or entrepreneurship in the midst of hardship as a "gift" to the "home," which offsets his or her status as a burden. Refugees, however, by nature of their need for asylum, McKinnon explains, arrive without gifts and, moreover, produce the threat of reproductivity. *Post-Gazette* commenters on the Jones article, such as Ramona Klien, speak to this threat explicitly. Klien is clear that the source of her knowledge comes from firsthand experience and is seemingly sure that this firsthand experience provides her with the confidence to speak about the characteristics of "all" of the refugees in Carrick. She writes, "I have had the opportunity to see the culture that moved in and yes they are all on welfare and have lots of children and having more by the minute." The *Post-Gazette* commenters relate the threat of reproduction with the fear of a home that is overtaken by outsiders and transformed as a result. This fear manifests in additional comments that describe how "these people" "take over" Pittsburgh neighborhoods and appear "everywhere."[40] For example, Daniel Trzeciak posted,

> I work very hard for the money that I earn and happily pay those taxes. I'm sorry, but I want that money to go to our own citizens. The ones who deserve it and need it. Not the leaches that milk the system or the agencies that create that possibility for others. Call that racist if you want. I call it Patriotism. . . . These apartment buildings look like refugee camps, not a new beginning in America.

Here Trzeciak implies not only knowledge of the appearance of refugee camps but also a preconceived impression of what a new beginning in America *should* look like. John Sayenga, too, defends a nostalgic memory of an uncorrupted home. He posted, "It was a great place for a long time. . . . Those days are gone and never to return." Radha Hegde suggests that this type of "appealing through abstractions to a lost homogeneity" is a common strategy in xenophobic narratives,[41] and these comments speak to Gerard Hauser's suggestion that "Cultural narratives [are] used for more than inspiration; they [are] a vernacular source of models for the type of society to which [a community] wishe[s] to belong."[42] Through wistful descriptions of an uncorrupted home, *Post-Gazette* commenters pay homage to an ideological cultural narrative of an America that existed before an influx of migrants.

While a few commenters decry other commenters' negativity (i.e., Jonathan Chappel posted, "These comments are ridiculous. Trace your lineage and you will find out that your family were struggling immigrants too."), the majority of the responses assert a negative, fearful, or hateful view of refugees, and several commenters declare an unwillingness to cohabitate the neighborhood of Carrick alongside the current refugee population.

Daniel Trzeciak wrote,

> This article makes it sound like a great thing, but it's not. These people are an eyesore and are making Carrick look even worse than it already is. They are crammed into apartment buildings to a disgusting level. And I'm sorry, but to say that these people are not on welfare is a bunch of BS. I see them in the grocery store using their Access cards all the time. I don't mind that they look different, dress different and I can tolerate the fact that they don't speak english, but they do not enhance the

community in any way at all. You can drive on Brownsville road and see many of them wondering [sic] the streets or standing on the sidewalk all day long, every day.

Another commenter, Candi Richards, posted,

> The foreigners who cant speak english and dont even try, can live on welfare and get everything handed to them including our american children's school slots. It is so frustrating. I understand this is the land of foreigners but when my great grandparents cam [sic] over here from ireland, they weren't handed anything. [. . .] It really disgusts me seeing how they live in those apartment building because I can see that they all just sit around in the grass all day long, none of them working or trying to make a living in any way whatsoever . . . but good hardworking people like my husband cant get help for anything because basically, we are white americans. if we were foreigner we would get the world handed to us and our children . . . we are american born and raised . . . PROUD AMERICANS, so we shouldn't be outcasted or forced to pay more because of it.

Commenter Jim Ernst wrote, "We must fix what is broken NOW, before it gets worse," to which Michelle Soski Gregory responded, "Amen Jim!!!!!!!!!!!!! Close down the borders!" Notably, even this small sample reveals staunch implicit assumptions regarding a number of cultural issues, including race, number of persons per household, public assistance, loitering, language, unequal access to education, and judgments regarding normative work hours and an implicit conclusion about who belongs in "America." Benedict Anderson suggests that in order to grasp what goes on in any invoking of "the idea of America," one must recognize that the process of constructing a national consciousness is far from neutral in its ideology. Rather, boundary drawing and nationalism are the results of strategic webs of political desire, religious history, and intricate, socially constructed networks of domination and subordination.[43] While these networks may be manifest institutionally or politically, they might also appear in individuals' narratives and imaginations, as the earlier comments suggest.

A link to the *Post-Gazette's* commenting policy appears under each digital article to which readers are invited to respond.[44] It begins:

> We invite you to add your comments, and we encourage a thoughtful, open and lively exchange of ideas and information at post-gazette.com. Some content and comments will generate heated discussions, but we expect—and require—that the tone of the commentary be civil and respectful. Your comments will not be screened or edited before they appear on our website. We will, however, monitor and review your postings.

> We reserve the right to remove any comment that the community reports as abusive or the staff at post-gazette.com determines is inappropriate or offensive.

After reviewing this policy, I corresponded by e-mail with the article's author who confirmed that none of the comments following this article had been deleted by staff at the *Post-Gazette*. That the *Post-Gazette* pledges to "monitor and review" all comments could theoretically speak to an important notion of surveillance in this group. However, it is clear from the direct discrepancy between the policy—which forbids "personal attacks, obscenity, vulgarity, profanity or ethnic or racial slurs"—and the comments to Jones's article—including one which states, "I also pray [. . .] that apartment building burns to the ground and you didn't get there in time to save the leaches of the system that you and Obama support"—that the promise for surveillance in this case is not facilitating a successful panopticon.

A few positive responses to this article defended the refugees from hateful comments; Robyn Juergen Perhach simply posted, "Your ancestors were immigrants too." Jennifer England added, "It is our duty as human beings to help them. This is your chance to step up and be a good, compassionate person reflecting the ideals that we often purport to hold." Still, it is clear that the xenophobic comments were particularly impactful for the narrators I interviewed. Kheir was the first to make me aware of the Jones article, and he remembered that shortly after it was published, some of the refugee caseworkers at his resettlement agency came to him and asked whether they should respond. Kheir advised against it, suggesting instead that they focus their efforts on other outlets for positive community education about refugees.

After my conversation with Kheir, I had the opportunity to speak with Tek, who also lives in Pittsburgh and who had been featured in three local Pittsburgh news articles, including one in the *Post-Gazette* called "Pittsburgh's New Immigrants Equal Brain Gain." In it, author Christine O'Toole praises Tek and his family for their hard work and determination.[45] Tek observed that following these articles,

> There are mixed comments. Some people, maybe they didn't know maybe how the refugees get here, and how they are benefited through the federal government . . . some people they have really good idea [and] some people they are curious to meet the refugees and learn about their culture.

Even so, Tek is troubled by the consistency of negative comments about refugees that appear in online forums. He told me, "People have the freedom to like spe[ak] or express [their opinions] but if they want to make it public comment, [it would be] better if they, like, try to understand the situation before making a comment. That would be better." Notably, while Tek is keenly aware of the ways members of his own community are stereotyped, he refuses to respond in kind. "I don't blame everyone," he told me, "but some people I think that that they have a kind of like racial hate or something like that. So those kind of people they make those kind of comment I think. But it is not everyone, so I don't blame everyone." I encountered what turned out to be a revealing theme among the participants when I asked Tek if he ever responded when he encountered negative comments in these forums. He answered,

> I don't write back. I don't want to write back immediately, because I want to see what people think of me, and what correction I have to make and if it is possible, I will try to correct myself, and if not, then let it go because I cannot change those people who already have negative impression about foreigners. If I try to, like, write back to them, maybe the situation will get more worse.

Tek's desire to "see" and potentially correct the ways Americans see him and/or other refugees by interpreting the comments found in this media speaks to the ways media encounters such as these directly inform refugees' evolving understanding of their position in U.S. society, as well as the means through which they may attempt to negotiate that position. I asked Tek why he agreed to be interviewed for the three articles that featured him. He replied,

> Just to let the people know who refugees are and how they got here and what every decent qualities they have [and] what they can do. Just to publicize all the refugees. I mean it was done by my wish. I was not [obligated] or anything like that.

When I followed up with the question, "What do you think will happen if people know more about refugees?" Tek answered, "Maybe somewhat they may change positively, like they may have positive impact, and they will learn also. So if like different companies knows about refugees then they hire more refugees so that that will be helpful for the refugees." While Tek expressed wariness about responding to the negative comments presented earlier, here, his views echo those espoused by the resettlement narrators that I discussed earlier who have faith that knowledge about refugees will lead to more local acceptance.

Balaram, a Bhutanese refugee living in Pittsburgh, had been made aware of the aforementioned Jones article by way of a Bhutanese community listserv on Google Groups that often circulates local articles featuring or regarding the local Bhutanese community.

We have a Google Groups that is shared between all the Bhutanese in the Unites States," Balaram explained. "So if we find an article about a Bhutanese that is written in any newspaper, we'll just copy that link and, you know, send it, share it, so that everybody reads that one. Balaram told me he receives e-mails from this group with links to news about refugees at least once a week and that they range in subject from "success stories" to articles reporting tragic accidents involving refugees. The articles that Balaram receives are usually accompanied by comments, which he always reads. He told me,

> The comments we have been reading are good comments, except for the last two articles we have gone through that was posted in some local online news. There had pretty bad comments on refugees—Bhutanese refugees, you know, so that was—the comments are all negative, so.

I asked Balaram if he could remember what some of the comments said. He responded,

> Some of the things that we are of course remembering are like, "Refugees are the one that—these people are the one that brought bedbugs and roaches to Pittsburgh" . . . some of the comments were the other comments were like, they were saying, in the Carrick area, that the area had been degraded, the standard of the place had been degraded, it has become dirtier.

Like Tek, Balaram feared that responding to negative digital comments about his community would have an adverse effect. Referencing the aforementioned *Post-Gazette* article by Jones, Balaram told me that he knew that of all the comments, only one was posted by an individual from Bhutan who lived in another state.[46] I asked him why he thought Bhutanese people were not commenting back or defending themselves. "I would not comment, because, I didn't want to," he explained.

> If I comment, then they are going to, again, put on other comments, so that way it's gonna grow . . . If you don't defend, then it will stop, but if you comment, then it goes on and on, so that is why we don't comment, or like to comment, that's why our friends say "Don't comment."

This refugee community's collective decision to refrain from commenting because of increased adverse repercussions is somewhat perplexing considering the belief—evident in my interviews with both refugees and administrators as I showed earlier—that increased community knowledge about refugees leads to more acceptance. One may assume that faith in the positive correlation between knowledge and acceptance would lead refugees to respond frequently to digital negativity about refugees, but the Bhutanese community in Pittsburgh has taken the opposite approach. The absence of refugee voices in comment forums following articles about refugees may be explained in part by some lack of Internet access or technological skill for responding online. But as the narrators reveal, refugees may also refrain from participation because they anticipate additional negative backlash.

In Houston, Texas, Rand told me about her own involvement with the local newspaper:

> I remember in 2009, I was interviewed as a refugee from Iraq, in [the] *Houston Chronicle* . . . about how hard life is here in United States of America, because the assistance is for the limited time, and you know, the competition in the job is very high.

The 2009 article, titled "Refugees Struggle to Find Work as Houston Economy Slows," features a close-up photograph of Rand in profile, clasped hands holding a tissue to her face, and a tear rolling down her cheek.[47] The author of the article, Susan Carroll, reflects on the effects of the 2008 financial downturn on refugees and explains how Rand and her husband, both of whom have doctorates in political science, became discouraged when they were denied work after applying for jobs at a local Houston Wal-Mart and Target. Because Rand's insights about this article are revealing, I will quote from the transcript of our conversation at some length:

SARAH: Do you remember, did [the *Houston Chronicle*] post that article online, on their website?
RAND: Yeah; I read it.
SARAH: You read it online?
RAND: Mm-hm.
SARAH: And did anyone comment on the article?
RAND: The comment was so harsh.
SARAH: What do you mean?
RAND: Hostile. They said, "Well, if you don't like it, you can go back." I mean, one person said, "We are like generous to offer a shelter for you, so if you don't like it, you don't have to stay here. You can go back."[48]
SARAH: Did you respond?
RAND: No.
SARAH: Why not?
RAND: Well, I think I don't have the English ability to respond in a proper way. [Pause]

SARAH: Is that the only reason?

RAND: Yeah, I think so.

SARAH: We have had some of the same problem in Pittsburgh. There are positive stories about refugees in the local newspaper, but the comments are bad; they're negative. Why do you think those comments happen?

RAND: Well, because people [sigh]—now I understand that, now after being in America for five years. People doesn't know what's happening in Iraq. So [Americans], they be thinking they've been generous to offer, like, shelter . . . They d[on]'t know why we left our country, and they—it's not, the refugees don't leave their countries because they want to, [it is] because this is the only option. They're *forced* to leave their countries, you know. And violence was used by American governments to solve the problem in Iraq, and we've been the victim of that, so we've been victimized. You know, we think that there is other peaceful ways to help solve the problem, in order to avoid the massive civilian victims in Iraq, because of the violence. And the people, like civil[ian] people, doesn't deserve that . . . So it's also not our fault, you know . . . The situation was harsh, brutal, and a lot of people get killed, and a lot of innocent people get killed, because of the way they used the force, the military. And also, I think some of them, they believe that people, when they come as refugees, they don't—they don't want to be independent. So they are not willing to work. They only want to live on public assistance, like public housing, food stamps, Medicaid. And [Americans] are paying for that from their tax, you know. So, I mean, it's not fair for them. They are paying the tax. But at the same time, it's not our fault. It's the position that United States of America took, to invade Iraq. We lost our resources. We are from rich country who has a lot of oil, and a lot of money, and I would love to go back and work there! We don't need to come to the United States of America, and make the American people pay for us, you know. But it's happening.

Rand's reflections on the way she was portrayed in the 2009 *Houston Chronicle* article and its corresponding comments reveal a broader thoughtfulness regarding U.S.-Iraq relations, discontent regarding the place of Iraqi refugees in the United States in general, and nostalgia for her former home.

I am unsure of what to make of Rand's suggestion that she did not have the "English ability to respond in a proper way" to the negative comments that followed the article about her. Earlier in our conversation, Rand had told me that when she was growing up, her father took her on frequent trips to Europe. She also told me, "My families are very educated, so they like to read book and see movies, and interact with other people. And most of them are bilingual, so they speak English and Arabic." She explained how she wants her son to be fluent in English, because "this is very important in our family. I mean, family, you have to know how to speak English, and understand, and read books." Though I cannot say with confidence that Rand's English was excellent when she was featured in this article—four years before I met her—I believe, based on the descriptions she gave of her background, family, and doctoral education in Baghdad, that she would have been able to respond to the *Houston Chronicle* comments in English with little trouble. Regardless of her reason for refraining from a response, Rand's description of the reasons why Americans post such "harsh" comments adds a new layer of insight regarding the impetus for and implications of portrayals of refugees in U.S. media. Rand speaks directly to the reality that refugees may view negative comments from U.S.-born individuals as a small manifestation of a larger ignorance or lack of knowledge about refugees that may seem impossible to address wholly in a forum created for brief comments on single articles.

When readers of an article about refugees in the United States encounter comments that include no ostensible refugee perspectives, they may assume it is because refugees are not aware of the article, do not have access to the Internet, are not affected by negative comments, or do not care what their local communities think about refugees in the United States. But the aforementioned narratives reveal that such is not the case. In fact, as seen in the last chapter, acquisition of and competence in digital media are among many refugees' top priorities upon their arrival in the United States, and, as is clear from the narrators mentioned earlier, many refugees care very much about how they are perceived within their communities.

Some of the other Iraqi refugees I interviewed in Los Angeles and San Diego echoed Rand's frustration with Americans' ignorance about the nature of the United States' involvement in Iraq or knowledge of Iraq in general. Saif told me that many Americans he encounters "thought that most of the Iraqis are not educated, but there are many of the of Iraqi people that are educated, and that have higher degrees."[49] Zahraa noted a more general lack of awareness: "There are some people, they're asking where I'm from," she told me. "When I told them I'm from Iraq, they don't know what is Iraq. So I was surprised. [laughs] Some people know about the war. And that's all they know. And some—and the most, they don't know anything."[50]

Moses equated the lack of knowledge in the United States about Iraq with a failure of the American educational system, but he was careful to qualify that he cannot speak about Americans' knowledge as a whole. He explained,

> Here the people—I'm talking couple of the people, you know—the people they don't know the Iraqi; they don't study here. In Baghdad, in Iraq, we studied the American people. Especially when you got to the school.

They teach us about the America, the life in America. Here, they don't know about the Iraqi. They thought about the Iraqis, they are savages.[51]

The United States' ignorance about Iraq seemed especially insulting to some of the Iraqis I interviewed, precisely because of what they believed to be skewed U.S. media representations of the country as a whole that occur because of the United States' involvement in the war in Iraq. Indeed, the Iraqi refugees I interviewed do encounter more U.S. media representations of their home country than do refugees from Bhutan, Burma, or Somalia. But these portrayals lack consistency with the lives many of the Iraqi narrators lived in Iraq. For example, Fahad believes that Americans think there are no computers in Iraq and that Iraqis don't have television or movies. "But that's wrong," Fahad emphasized. "Like all people there is very good at news like, very professional. There's very intelligent people there."[52] I asked Fahad to hypothesize about why Americans may have this faulty impression of Iraq. He answered quickly, "Maybe because of the war, like, every movie [shows] the war. You see, like, there is nothing . . . it seems everything is desert, everything is war I think, yeah, like it's a war tour, you know." Amira agreed that emphasis on the war in Iraq in U.S. media produces a distorted view of Iraq for Americans. She assured me that as an Iraqi living in Los Angeles she does not usually experience prejudice from Americans. But she does encounter some uninformed curiosity. She explained,

> When they know I am from Iraq, they start to talk—"How is Iraq? How is the country?"—especially they mention Sadaam Hussein. I said, "Okay, not everybody is [like him], it's so nice country and everybody is, they are courteous." Because, you know the media, when I watch media about Iraq, just shows that political side, the war, the destroys things, but no, [Iraq] is so nice . . . so nice.[53]

Amira is glad to have the chance to clear up misconceptions about her home country and is patient with Americans who ask her about it. But because U.S. media depictions of Iraq are so consistent in their portrayals of a dangerous, war-torn, derelict country, these conversations are often frustrating. Other Iraqis also described their frustration with U.S. mediated portrayals of Iraq that they believed to be not only skewed but also sometimes mendacious. Hiba told me,

> the other day I was watching Dick Cheney, and he was talking about Iraq—it was the tenth year anniversary [of the start of the war]. Whatever he was saying, it wasn't—whatever Dick Cheney was saying, it wasn't like—how to do I say this, there were some things that I didn't believe cause it wasn't real, cause I *know* what was going on back home.[54]

The war-centric portrayals of Iraq in U.S. media disturbs these narrators, as this media seem to ignore altogether the beautiful, peaceful country that many Iraqis fondly recall from their childhoods. These narrators are well familiar with media's tendency to reveal only partial perspectives. Before their arrival in the United States, many Iraqis depended on U.S. films, television, or music to form some expectations about life in the United States. As I discussed in the last chapter, this group has reported disappointment—disproportionate to the other groups I interviewed—with the discrepancy between these media and their lived experiences in the United States. Now their experiences with U.S. media's portrayal of Iraq confirm for these narrators once more the lack of totality that is a constant presence in any mediated communication.

At the beginning of this section, I suggested that the ways U.S. media portray refugees and their homelands holds little significance without an understanding of the nature of refugees encounters with and responses to these portrayals. As the narrators in the preceding pages have shown, these portrayals remain a salient part of refugees' resettlement long after their arrival in the United States and serve to both inform and frustrate their refugee audiences.

Media, Language, and Religion

Of course, refugees do not only consume media that is specifically *for* or overtly *about* them or their home countries; they may seek out, consume, and interpret all kinds of different media produced for indiscriminate mass audiences. While sorting out the ways refugees use mass entertainment media for purposes related to ongoing resettlement may prove more difficult or complex, it is important not to overlook this phenomenon.

For many of the refugees I interviewed, media is key for both the improvement of English-language skills and the maintenance of former languages. This latter function seemed especially important for refugees with children. While the previous chapter provided narratives of the relationship of media to English-language learning, this section will include insights from narrators who reveal instances where certain types of media are sought out and consumed for the purposes of learning or maintaining one's ethnic language and preserving one's culture, religion, or ties to a former home.

I was intrigued to learn that for some of the refugee narrators, the desire to retain their first language is directly related to the preservation and maintenance of their religion. The interconnectedness of language and religion is well documented in the fields of linguistics and sociology.[55] Sipra Mukerjee, for example, asserts that because religion is communicated through narratives such as songs, prayers, holy texts, and parables, "it is through the various forms of language that the living vitality of a community's religious beliefs is passed down from generation to generation."[56] The narrators provide support for Mukerjee's perspective by pointing to the importance of certain kinds of media in facilitating connection to language and religion.

On a November afternoon in 2013, I interviewed Abreer, an Iraqi refugee living in Houston, Texas. Abreer is a Christian, and she arrived in Houston with her husband and three children in 2012 after a bomb explosion in a Christian church near their home in Baghdad caused them to feel unsafe. Upon her arrival in the United States, Abreer continued to feel some trepidation about her surroundings. "It was scary cause of the ambiguity," she explained.[57] When she told me that she was afraid to put her children in school in Houston, I asked Abreer if she could identify where her fear about the United States came from or why she felt nervous during her first days in the United States. She explained that because Iraq is a Muslim country, "even though I am a Christian, we have some rules, some cultural thing . . . that girls and boys they must not contact with each other [or] have affairs." These rules gave Abreer some measure of comfort in knowing that her children would not be allowed to engage in such activities in Iraq. In the United States, though, these rules were not enforced. Abreer had heard that there were some kids getting pregnant. In Iraq, she explained,

> This thing, it's illegal—I mean, not illegal—I'm telling you, we call it *haram*, it's like a sin in our community, so I was scared of this . . . I was afraid my kids see this. Like male and female sharing one apartment without getting married—this is sin in our community.

At this point in our conversation, Abreer's case manager, Wijdan, who is also from Iraq and who was interpreting for Abreer and me, jumped in. Wijdan suggested that Abreer's expectations about public displays of *haram* in the United States may have been formed from U.S. films Abreer had seen in Iraq that exaggerated this likelihood. Wijdan said, "I told her that, 'Don't worry. [It's] not what you see in films, Houston is—they call it a family state.'" I did not intend to interview Wijdan along with Abreer, but this pairing turned out to be serendipitous, as the two had some insights to offer regarding their understanding of the differences between their two religions. Wijdan is Muslim, and because she is not familiar with Christianity, she asked Abreer whether the *haram* caused her cultural or religious concern. But Abreer dismissed the question, explaining that *haram* is "a cultural thing *and* a religious thing;" the two cannot be separated. I was intrigued by Abreer and Wijdan's discussion of the interrelatedness of culture and religion and began asking both of them how the differences in their two religions may have affected their relocation process or their current use of media.

As the three of us were talking about television, I asked Abreer whether she watched any American shows. She answered that though she has a television, she does not watch American programs. After interpreting Abreer's answer, Wijdan asked if she could share her own opinion.

> Can I tell you something? We, as Arabs, we prefer to put [on] Arabic channels. You know why? Cause we want our kids not forget Arabic language. Because they will learn English [in] school. We want them to keep Arabic language, so she [Abreer] is the same way—all the community, I'm telling you. We have like, channels—we buy package so that we can receive Arabic channels.

I asked Abreer and Wijdan if they could explain why it is so important to them that their children do not forget Arabic. Wijdan answered first:

> My reason may be different from [Abreer's]. If you don't mind, I can just explain it to you. Because I am Muslim—we have Qur'an, Qur'an is in Arabic. Doing the prayer—the *salat*—is in Arabic. So they have to keep Arabic language to do the prayer, to read the Qur'an. So if they forget the Arabic language, how could they be, I mean, worshipping God—being close to God?

Wijdan's answer provides much insight into the tensions of multigenerational enculturation. Often, because of factors related to public education and children's increased cognitive capacity for language learning,[58] immigrant children in the United States learn and/or begin to prefer to use English before their parents.[59] Moreover, refugees are repeatedly encouraged by the U.S. government and resettlement agencies to learn English as soon as possible, and resettlement agencies often make free or low-cost ESL classes available to refugees for long after the other aspects of refugees' involvement with their resettlement agencies has concluded. The U.S. Committee for Refugees and Immigrants promotes long-term English-language learning for refugees because, they assert, "Learning English is an essential step to becoming self-sufficient."[60] But Wijdan's explanation of the inextricable nature of language and religion highlights why it is necessary to consider some refugees' motivations for resisting speaking English at home. It also shows how refugees ensure that their children maintain fluency in their first language(s) with the help of transnational media.

After Wijdan explained the necessity of language to her religion, Abreer provided her own perspective. While Abreer does not need to speak or read Arabic in order to practice Christianity, she too watches primarily Arabic television because she does not want her children to forget the language: "So they will not lose their *roots*, their Arabic roots. They are Arab; they have to be Arab to the end, even if they live in America, they have to keep their mother language." Abreer spends about one hour a day watching Arabic news and serials on television, and, like Wijdan, she purchased a package of more than twenty Arabic channels for her television after her arrival in Houston. This particular package cost $400 the first year and $200 each subsequent year—a significant amount for refugees who may arrive with little money or who, like Abreer, have not been able to find jobs. It is clear based on my conversation with Wijdan and Abreer, however, that this program package's value exceeds its monetary worth. It provides an invaluable connection to one's "roots" by giving Iraqi refugees in Houston a link to their language, culture, and/or religion.

To provide context for the ways media ties into refugees' religion and language use in the United States, I should note that not all refugees want to preserve the religion they held in their former countries when they arrive in the United States. Studies by Nancy J. Smith-Hefner, Cornelia A. Kammerer, Timothy Dunnigan, Glenn L. Hendricks, Bruce T. Downing, Amos S. Deinard, Milton M. Gordon, and George M. Scott Jr. have addressed a markedly high conversion rate of various refugee groups to Christianity or Judaism upon their arrival in the United States.[61] Mon Maya, a Bhutanese refugee I interviewed in Houston, Texas, helped me to understand the complexity of refugee religious conversion. She told me, "In Nepal I was in Hindu religion, but in America I became a Christian."[62] I asked Mon Maya why she decided to become a Christian after she arrived in the United States. She answered, "All the people who are American are a Christian and [laughing] I also follow that religion." I wasn't sure whether Mon Maya was trying to communicate that she really believed all Americans are Christian, so I responded, "But there are Hindus in America too." Mon Maya explained quickly, "I liked Christian[ity] in Nepal, but my family was not Christian." In light of the insights I gained from the narrators, I believe religious conversion among refugees is complicated by at least four key factors. First, religion is often a salient factor in refugees' displacement. As Abreer described earlier, a refugee's religion might make him/her more at risk for persecution. For example, Bhim "John" Monger" a Bhutanese Christian refugee I met in Austin, Texas, was arrested by undercover Bhutanese police when he was found with a group of people in the woods participating in a religious celebration of Christmas. John remembers,

> Because of practicing our Christianity in Bhutan, they took us to a dark room and beat us, they torture us, and then finally they ask us to leave the country or to deny our faith in Christ—to denounce the name of Jesus. And finally I said "I will *not*."[63]

The 1951 Refugee Convention—which provides the controlling definition that determines who may claim refugee status—provides that religious persecution may be the documented reason that an individual may be forced to flee his/her country of origin. The second complexity of religion and refugee resettlement has to do with the reality that the majority of local voluntary organizations that provide resettlement services to refugees in the United States are faith-based organizations, such as Jewish Family and Children's Services and Catholic Charities.[64] Third, federally funded cultural orientation texts explicitly direct refugees to seek out faith-based organizations for needed assistance. For example, in a section entitled "Community Resources," *Welcome to the United States*, the orientation text discussed in chapter 2, refugees are informed that "Churches, mosques, synagogues, and other religious groups may . . . offer various services. Some have ESL classes for adults and some give away used clothing and furniture."[65] While the text reassures readers that "no one who uses these services has to participate in the group's religious activities," there is no widespread system in place to assure that such faith-based assistance providers are not encouraging refugees to participate in religious meetings, ceremonies, prayers, or conversations.[66] In their research, Aihwa Ong and Stephanie J. Nawyn have documented instances of refugees participating in obligatory religious practices in order to receive faith-based organizations' assistance.[67] Finally, while most of the refugees I interviewed—and most of the refugees arriving in the United States in general—are Muslim, Hindu, or Buddhist, the majority of the faith-based voluntary resettlement agencies in the United States are Christian, Catholic, or Jewish.[68] The presence of these four factors necessitates sustained attention that is outside of the purview of this project. Still, I include this mention for the sake of contextualization and also to recognize the possible relationships that refugees' religion and religious conversions may have with media.

When I asked Indra, a Bhutanese refugee living in Austin, Texas, if he practiced any religion, he responded matter-of-factly: "I was Hindu in Nepal but here I am Christian."[69] Indra explained that his media intake mostly consists of watching Christian movies and listening to worship songs. I wondered if he could tell me the name of any of the movies he enjoys and he mentioned *Mukti*, a Nepali Christian film.[70] Likewise, Sahro told me,

> When [I] open the internet, usually when I'm want to go see something like my culture, my religion; I go there, and I see. And also I listen my music, and back home, all of our singers over there. So I choose one of them, and then while I wash the dishes, I listen that song. And I wash the dishes, or I clean the floor, something like that.[71]

The songs, films, and websites that the narrators describe here may fulfill multiple functions at once; in addition to providing entertainment while one is relaxing or cleaning, they provide a familiar link to one's language or religion.

The relationship between media, language, and religion is a complex one, and, I believe, a thorough consideration of any one of these necessitates some attention to the other two. Indeed, as the narrators describe here, media may provide a direct connection to a refugee's language or religion, or it may threaten to sever existing ties to tradition through the introduction of new perspectives and ways of life. The narrators whose perspectives appear here provide insight into the reasons why refugees may actively resist the U.S. government's insistence that they learn English as soon as possible and the reasons why refugees may spend what may appear to be a superfluous amount of money on media technologies and packages, even when living on relatively small incomes. The centrality of media to refugees' language and religion reveals that while technologies such as televisions and computers usually come with a sizeable price tag, refugees may perceive what these media offer in return as priceless.

Media, Friends, and Family

Beyond using media to keep connected to one's language or religion, several of the refugees I interviewed revealed the means by which they take advantage of the increasing availability of media in international contexts in order to stay in touch with friends, family, or other members of their ethnic communities who are living in the refugees' home countries, countries of asylum, or even in other parts of the United States. In these instances, media may provide connections that allow one to simply keep in touch with old friends, to plan visits and reunions, to announce life changes such as marriages or the birth of children, or even, as one narrator describes in this section, to cope with the sometimes overwhelming sense of isolation refugees may experience after their frequent contact with their resettlement agencies begins to wane.

Many refugees grew up in collectivist communities or lived in close quarters with extended family members in refugee camps before they were resettled to the United States. Because countries and cities that accept refugees restrict the numbers of incoming refugees due to a limited availability of resources, sometimes extended families are separated because members are resettled into different cities or countries or because some members are granted resettlement years before others. As Julie Keown-Bomar has shown in her work, because of the ways that traditional family structures are disrupted and reconfigured in instances of forced relocation, refugees may develop "kinship networks" that extend beyond familial ties.[72] These networks could be described as close friendships, though they resemble familial relationships in all ways except those that are biological.

While a few refugees mentioned connecting with friends and family from their home countries by phone, many more reported using Internet-based avenues for this purpose. Fahad, a refugee from Iraq who sought asylum in Jordan before arriving in Los Angeles, reaches his friends who still live in Jordan by using Viber—a free call, text, and picture-sharing application—on his iPhone.[73] Saif, from Iraq, stays in contact with his family, who are seeking asylum in Dubai, by

Facebook,[74] and Indra, from Bhutan, also uses this method.[75] Buddhi, a Bhutanese refugee living in Pittsburgh, told me she misses her family in Nepal but talks with them "on the computer, [and] sometimes phone."[76] Other refugees maintain contact with members of their ethnic communities by watching and commenting on YouTube videos about their cultures. For example, living in San Diego with her children, Sahro Nor regularly watches short films about Somalis in America on YouTube that she finds by Googling "Sheeko Gaaban"—Somali for "short story." Many of these films are produced by a company called Hagio Studio Production, range in duration from around eight to forty-five minutes, and depict Somali families living in the United States and the kinds of cultural challenges that this population sometimes faces.

Sahro told me that the *Sheeko Gaaban* films help her cope with the disappointment and depression she has experienced since moving to the United States. She explained, "I listen their story, because some of stories are similar, like [my own] feeling. So I listen to them."[77] She remembers one episode of *Sheeko Gaaban* in particular that addressed the tension between refugee parents and children. Since the film is in Somali, Sahro provided me with a synopsis:

> [Some] children and [their] mother, they didn't understand each other, so sometimes you can see the [mother], she say, "Do you pray, guys?" And the [children] say, "No, it's 2014. We don't carry that stuff. It's the old time. We don't—I'm listening to music. I'm listening to rap," or something like that. And she get the broom, and she say, "Why you didn't pray? Do you know how many times we pray in the morning?" They say, "Mm, two or three," but really, they messing with her head. But they know, but they messing with her head. So I watch that kind of episode.

Sahro helped me understand why this episode of *Sheeko Gaaban* is so relevant for some Somali families in the United States. Shaking her head, she explained,

> Like before, always the children, they obey their parents. Mama say, Mama say, Mama say "Stay in the house." Mama say "Cooking." Mama say this. But no more Mama say! No more Daddy say! They do whatever they want. All that thing, that bridge is broken.

Sahro knows this problem is a complex one, made more complicated by differences in language comprehension between parents and children as well as perceived differences about what it even means to be a family. She described the nuance of this disconnect at length:

> Sometimes you thinking, oh, these children . . . like—we didn't we have any connection. The children speak English first, growing, and the mother

and daddy, they didn't speak English. Then, the children, they take the culture in here, adapt. And mama still remember her culture, how she grow, how she took care her parents, how she took care her sister and sibling. But here—nothing. Even when you tell the children, "Hey, if you see one of my family, my sister or my sister children, how you treat?" [But the children say,] "We don't know, and we don't care." And so when they say like that, you really sad. Sometimes I say, "I want to send my family money." And then [the children] say, "Why you send all that money? I need fancy shoes. I need fancy car. I want a fancy something." I say, "Hey, this is—you have good life now. You safe. I have family who doesn't live safe area, who doesn't have food, or fancy clothes. So I went to send them money." So, it's really conflicted. Culturally, the children and parent is not [in the] same shoes; it's different.

Watching *Sheeko Gaaban* gives Sahro an opportunity to see iterations of the trials she experiences with her own family reflected on screen in scenarios to which she can easily relate. In her discussion of these films, she reveals several of the community-related challenges refugee parents and children face in the United States. In addition to disparities in English-language comprehension (discussed in more detail in the last section), Sahro believes Somali children in the United States become enculturated more quickly than their parents—and perhaps too quickly—because they have fewer memories of life in Somalia and Kenya and less of an appreciation for their responsibility to their families. Moreover, many refugees experience constant tension regarding the amount of remittances they should send back to their countries of origin. As I discussed in the first chapter, because of increasing exposure to films, television shows, magazines, and other media, refugees in other parts of the world may assume that individuals living in the United States have more wealth than they could possibly need. Though many refugees struggle to make ends meet after they arrive in the United States, friends and family members back home may begin to expect sizeable remittances because of these media-related assumptions.[78] As Sahro reveals through her discussion of *Sheeko Gaaban*, the decision of how much money to send back to one's country of origin may be complicated by children who can no longer understand why such a process is necessary after they are enculturated into an individualistic local community where one's immediate family takes precedence over extended familial ties.

Because Sahro wants her children to understand why these kinds of experiences and decisions are difficult for her, she shows her children the *Sheeko Gaaban* films, which often depict Somali refugee children undermining their parents' authority. Sahro asks her children, "Did you want to become like that kind of family? That family is broken." In this way, the films become a point of comparison for Sahro's family to negotiate their place between their old and new cultures. She explained, "So always, we show—that reason I show them, to compare, you know." The comparisons that *Sheeko Gaaban* makes possible allow Sahro and her family to address their understanding of post-resettlement family relationships.

Even in cases where media does not lead directly to the kinds of explicit conversations Sahro describes, refugees may rely on films, television, music, books, or other media to negotiate their understanding of family during processes of ongoing resettlement in the United States. For example, Sancha, from Bhutan, told me that while he does not watch much U.S. television, he occasionally watches U.S. news and a show he believes to be called "*All America Fun* or something."[79] Sancha explained, "There are some channels regarding family issues. Sometimes [children have] different father[s] or, you know, about divorce, [that] type of thing. To learn the society of U.S., I see those channels."[80] Though the writers and producers of the television shows Sancha watches likely did not create their programs with the intention of teaching forced migrants about U.S. society, Sancha's shrewd viewing practices allow him to simultaneously enjoy the television he watches and to use particular shows as a means through which to learn about U.S. family structures.

Comparing Sahro and Sancha's experiences allows insight into several facets of the relationship of media to family and community connections. Sahro reveals how media that is explicitly *about* refugee relationships in the United States may be used to negotiate one's understanding and experience of family connections and structures in the United States. But Sancha's narrative shows that even media that just happens to include some depictions of family relationships in the United States as it addresses other subjects may be just as likely to be applied for this purpose. Taken together, these narratives provide some answers to David Morley's question of

> how particular people, in particular contexts, perceive the relevance (or irrelevance) of specific media technologies for their lives, and how they then choose to use those technologies—or ignore them, or indeed 'bend' them in some way, to a purpose for which they were not intended.[81]

Refugees who participate in this "bending" reveal themselves as savvy, active audiences, and demonstrate the range of concerns and desires that media may be used to address.

This chapter has examined the ways that refugees are portrayed in U.S. media, primarily the news, and how they interpret or respond to these portrayals. I explored the interaction of media, language, and religion and demonstrated the ways that these three phenomena are inextricably linked in refugees' lives. Finally, the narrators' revealed the importance of media in maintaining or negotiating connections between their families and friends. Clearly, media remains a relevant resource for refugees to negotiate their sense of place in the United States several months and even years after their physical relocation, during the long process of ongoing resettlement.

A view of resettlement as ongoing and long-term allows one to gain insight into the ways media may continue to serve refugees as a resource for enculturation or a means for connection with their language, religion, or community. In the preceding pages, the narrators described how media connects them to both past and present, home and homeland. This ability to transcend time and place through media is one manifestation of the perpetual state of hybridity that refugees experience during life after displacement. Their having to exist between two or more worlds as a result of forced displacement is fraught with challenges. After living in the United States for eight years, Rand described it this way: "We try to create balance inside ourselves, because it's not easy. Are we belong—are we Iraqis now, or Americans? I don't know. Actually, I don't know. I'm not Iraqi [any]more. I'm not. But I don't feel like I'm American."[82] As refugees navigate their perpetual in-between-ness, media may serve as either obstacle or guide.

Notes

1 The language of the Karen ethnic group, one of the largest ethnic groups displaced from Burma as refugees.
2 Chan Myae Thu, interview by Sarah Bishop, Buffalo, NY, August 7, 2013, archived at the Schlesinger Library at Harvard University.
3 "Community Led Non-Profit to Assist Buffalo's Burmese Population," Ashley Hirtzel, WSKG, last modified September 6, 2013, http://www.wskg.org/wskg_news/community-led-non-profit-assist-buffalos-burmese-population.
4 https://www.facebook.com/pages/Burmese-Community-Support-Center/162466873944623.
5 Peggy Halpern, *Refugee Economic Self-Sufficiency: An Exploratory Study of Approaches Used in Office of Refugee Resettlement Program*, U.S. Department of Health and Human Services (2008), http://aspe.hhs.gov/hsp/08/RefugeeSelfSuff/.
6 Christie Shrestha, *Power and Politics in Resettlement: A Case Study of Bhutanese Refugees in the U.S.A.*, Policy Development and Evaluation Service, United Nations High Commissioner for Refugees, May 2011, 2.
7 Given that they compose a low percentage of the population, refugees' portrayal in media is disproportionately high; for further explanation, see David Haines, *Safe Haven?: A History of Refugees in American* (Sterling: Stylus Publishing, 2010), 1; United States Committee for Refugees and Immigrants, "Resettlement by Country," *World Refugee Survey 2009*, 29.
8 Vibert C. Cambridge, *Immigration, Diversity, and Broadcasting in the United States, 1990–2001* (Athens: Ohio University Press, 2005), 51.
9 Joachim Trebbe and Philomen Schoenhagen, "Ethnic Minorities in the Mass Media: Always the Same and Always Negative" (paper presented at the annual meeting for the International Communication Association, Montreal, May 21, 2008).

10 See Youna Kim, *Transnational Migration, Media and Identity of Asian Women: Diasporic Daughters* (New York: Routledge, 2011); Myria Georgiou, "Media and the City: Making Sense of Place," *International Journal of Media and Cultural Politics* 6, no. 3 (2011): 343–50; Regina Branton and Johanna Dunaway, "English- and Spanish-Language Media Coverage of Immigration: A Comparative Analysis," *Social Science Quarterly* 89, no. 4 (2008): 1006–22; Jonathan Corpus Ong, "Watching the Nation, Singing the Nation: London-Based Filipino Migrants' Identity Constructions in News and Karaoke Practices," *Communication, Culture & Critique* 2, no. 2 (2009): 160–81; Christine M. Du Bois, *Images of West Indian Immigrants in Mass Media: The Struggle for a Positive Ethnic Reputation* (New York: LFB Scholarly Publishing, 2004); Rita J. Simon, *Public Opinion and the Immigrant: Print Media Coverage, 1880–1980* (Lexington, MA: Lexington Books, 1985); and Athanasia Batziou, *Picturing Immigration: Photojournalistic Representation of Immigrants in Greek and Spanish Press* (Bristol, UK: Intellect, 2011).

11 See Ivan Leudar, Jacqueline Hayes, Jiri Nekvapil, and Johanna Turner Baker, "Hostility Themes in Media, Community and Refugee Narratives," *Discourse & Society* 19, no. 2 (2008): 187–221; Ashley Bradimore and Harald Bauder, "Mystery Ships and Risky Boat People: Tamil Refugee Migration in the Newsprint Media," *Canadian Journal Of Communication* 36, no. 4 (2011): 637–61; Majid KhosraviNik, "The Representation of Refugees, Asylum Seekers and Immigrants In British Newspapers: A Critical Discourse Analysis," *Journal of Language And Politics* 9, no. 1 (2010): 1–28; Cheryl R. Sulaiman-Hill, Sandra C. Thompson, Rita Afsar, and Toshi L. Hodliffe, "Changing Images of Refugees: A Comparative Analysis of Australian and New Zealand Print Media 1998−2008," *Journal of Immigrant & Refugee Studies* 9, no. 4 (2011): 345–66; Fiona H. McKay, Samantha L. Thomas, Kate Holland, R. Warwick Blood, and Susan Kneebone, "'AIDS Assassins': Australian Media's Portrayal of HIV-Positive Refugees Who Deliberately Infect Others," *Journal of Immigrant & Refugee Studies* 9, no. 1 (2011): 20–37; Jane Mummery and Debbie Rodan, "Discursive Australia: Refugees, Australianness, and the Australian Public Sphere," *Continuum: Journal of Media & Cultural Studies* 21, no. 3 (2007): 347–60; Costas Gabrielatos and Paul Baker, "Fleeing, Sneaking, Flooding," *Journal of English Linguistics* 36, no. 1 (2008): 5–38; and Leen d'Haenens and Marielle de Lange, "Framing of Asylum Seekers in Dutch Regional Newspapers," *Media, Culture & Society* 23, no. 6 (2001): 847–60.

12 Melinda B. Robins, "'Lost Boys' and the Promised Land: U.S. Newspaper Coverage of Sudanese Refugees," *Journalism* 4, no. 1 (2003): 31, 34, 37.

13 Otto Santa Ana, "'Like an Animal I Was Treated': Anti-Immigrant Metaphor in U.S. Public Discourse," *Discourse and Society* 10, no. 2 (1999): 191–224.

14 Tatyana S. Thweatt, "Attitudes Towards New Americans in the Local Press: A Critical Discourse Analysis," *North Dakota Journal of Speech and Theatre* 18 (2005): 32.

15 J. David Cisneros, "Contaminated Communities: The Metaphor of 'Immigrant as Pollutant' in Media Representations of Immigration," *Rhetoric and Public Affairs* 11, no. 4 (2008): 578.

16 Though not related to forced migration, some recent studies have examined online audience participation in comment forums. See, for example, Marisa Torres da Silva, "Online Forums, Audience Participation and Modes of Political Discussion: Readers' Comments on the Brazilian Presidential Election as a Case Study," *Comunicación Y Sociedad* 26, no. 4 (October 2013): 175–93; Cho Sooyoungand and Hong Youngshin, "Netizens' Evaluations of Corporate Social Responsibility: Content Analysis of CSR

News Stories and Online Readers' Comments," (paper presented at the annual meeting of the National Communication Association, Chicago, November 15–18, 2007); Aziz Douai and Hala K. Nofal, "Commenting in the Online Arab Public Sphere: Debating the Swiss Minaret Ban and the 'Ground Zero Mosque' Online," *Journal Of Computer-Mediated Communication* 17, no. 3 (April 2012): 266–82; and Michael McCluskey and Jay Hmielowski, "Opinion Expression During Social Conflict: Comparing Online Reader Comments and Letters to the Editor," *Journalism* 13, no. 3 (April 2012): 303–19.
17 The largest local newspaper in Buffalo.
18 Mike Ingram and Guest comment on Colin Dabkowski, "Multivenue Show in Allentown Highlights Faces of Buffalo Refugees," *The Gusto Blog*, February 20, 2014, http://www.buffalonews.com/gusto/art-previews/multivenue-show-in-allentown-highlights-faces-of-buffalo-refugees-20140220.
19 Mark Sommer, "Refugees Turn Hard Work into Better Future through Programs Here," *Buffalo News*, December 2, 2013, http://www.buffalonews.com/business/refugees-turn-hard-work-into-better-future-through-programs-here-20131202#comment-1148818119.
20 Charles Knarley and amethyst 1985, comments on Mark Sommer, "Refugees Turn Hard Work Into Better Future Through Programs Here," *Buffalo News*, December 2, 2013, http://www.buffalonews.com/business/refugees-turn-hard-work-into-better-future-through-programs-here-20131202#comment-1148818119.
21 Jay Rey, "Refugees Get First Taste of Thanksgiving Traditions," *Buffalo News*, November 23, 2013, http://www.buffalonews.com/city-region/refugees-get-first-taste-of-thanksgiving-traditions-20131123.
22 Gerard A. Hauser, *Vernacular Voices: The Rhetoric of Publics and Public Spheres* (Columbia: University of South Carolina Press, 1999), 109.
23 Majid KhosraviNik, "The Representation of Refugees, Asylum Seekers and Immigrants in British Newspapers during the Balkan Conflict (1999) and the British General Election (2005)," *Discourse and Society* 20, no. 4 (2009): 490.
24 Joachim Trebbe and Philomen Schoenhagen, "Ethnic Minorities in the Mass Media: Always the Same and Always Negative," (paper presented at the annual meeting for the International Communication Association, Montreal, Quebec, Canada, May 21, 2008).
25 Tatyana S. Thweatt, "Attitudes Towards New Americans in the Local Press: A Critical Discourse Analysis," *North Dakota Journal of Speech And Theatre* 18 (2005): 25–43. Several other scholars have also noted the prevalence of positive in-group representation contrasted with negative out-group presentation in mediated discourse about immigrants and ethnic minorities. See, for example, Sara McKinnon, "(In)Hospitable Publics: Theorizing Modalities of Access to U.S. Publics," in *Public Modalities*, eds. R. Asen and D.C. Brouwer (Tuscaloosa: University Of Alabama Press, 2010), 132–53; Ruth Wodak, "The Genesis of Racist Discourse in Austria since 1989," in *Texts and Practices: Readings on Discourse Analysis*, eds. C.R. Caldas-Coulthard and M. Coulthard (London: Routledge, 1996), 107–28; Hakimeh Saghaye-Biria, "American Muslims as Radicals? A Critical Discourse Analysis of the U.S. Congressional Hearing on 'The Extent of Radicalization in the American Muslim Community and That Community's Response,'" *Discourse & Society* 25, no. 5 (2012): 508–24; Kent A. Ono and Vincent N. Pham, *Asian Americans and the Media* (Cambridge: Polity, 2009); and

Kent A. Ono and John M. Sloop, *Shifting Borders: Rhetoric, Immigration, and California's Proposition 187* (Philadelphia: Temple University Press, 2002).
26. Meghann Perry, interview by Sarah Bishop, Buffalo, NY, August 7, 2013, archived at the Schlesinger Library at Harvard University.
27. http://www.iilosangeles.org/about/gallery/.
28. Radha S. Hegde, "Eyeing New Publics: Veiling and the Performance of Civic Visibility," in *Public Modalities: Rhetoric, Culture, Media, and the Shape of Public Life*, eds. Daniel C. Brouwer and Robert Asen (Tuscaloosa: University of Alabama Press, 2010), 161.
29. Edward W. Said, *Orientalism* (London: Penguin, 2003), 36. See also Kwame Anthony Appiah, *Cosmopolitanism: Ethics in a World of Strangers* (New York: Norton, 2007).
30. Ivan Leudar, Jacqueline Hayes, Jiri Nekvapil, and Johanna Turner Baker, "Hostility Themes in Media, Community and Refugee Narratives," *Discourse & Society* 19, no. 2 (2008): 187–221.
31. Teun A. Van Dijk, "New(s) Racism: A Discourse Analytic Approach," *Ethnic Minorities and the Media*, ed. Simon Cottle (Buckingham: Open University Press, 2000), 33–49.
32. For further evidence of this claim, see Joachim Trebbe and Philomen Schoenhagen, "Ethnic Minorities in the Mass Media: Always the Same and Always Negative" (paper presented at the annual meeting for the International Communication Association, Montreal, May 21, 2008).
33. Ivan Leudar et al., "Hostility Themes."
34. Ibid., 39.
35. Jaime Loke, "Readers' Debate A Local Murder Trial: 'Race' in the Online Public Sphere," *Communication, Culture, and Critique* 6, no. 1 (2013): 183.
36. Diana Nelson Jones, "Carrick Home for Ethnic Nepali Refugees," *Pittsburgh Post-Gazette*, September 3, 2012, http://www.post-gazette.com/local/south/2012/09/03/Carrick-home-for-ethnic-Nepali-refugees/stories/201209030122.
37. In October 2013, the *Post-Gazette* transitioned to a new content management system that was not able to accommodate comments to articles that had been published before the transition. Mila Sanina, assistant managing editor at the *Post-Gazette*, confirmed to me by e-mail (January 30, 2014) that this was the reason why the reader comments following Jones's article are no longer accessible.
38. Sara McKinnon, "(In)Hospitable Publics," 133.
39. Ibid., 133.
40. Daniel Trzeciak and Bill Antantis, [respective] comments on Diana Nelson Jones, "Carrick Home for Ethnic Nepali Refugees," *Pittsburgh Post-Gazette*, September 3, 2012, http://www.post-gazette.com/local/south/2012/09/03/Carrick-home-for-ethnic-Nepali-refugees/stories/201209030122.
41. Radha S. Hegde, "Eyeing New Publics: Veiling and the Performance of Civic Visibility," in Brouwer and Asen, *Public Modalities*, 160.
42. Gerard A. Hauser, *Vernacular Voices*, 157.
43. Benedict Anderson, *Imagined Communities* (London: Verso, 1983), 66.
44. http://www.post-gazette.com/ae/2012/03/02/Commenting-policies/stories/201203020210.
45. Christine O'Toole, "Pittsburgh's New Immigrants Equal Brain Gain," *Pittsburgh Post Gazette*, May 27, 2012, http://www.post-gazette.com/local/region/2012/05/27/Pittsburgh-s-new-immigrants-equal-brain-gain/stories/201205270140.

46 Phuyel Bhanu, whose comment appears on an earlier page in this chapter.
47 Susan Carroll, "Refugees Struggle to Find Work as Houston Economy Slows," *Houston Chronicle*, February 25, 2009, http://www.chron.com/default/article/Refugees-struggle-to-find-work-as-Houston-economy-1745961.php#photo-1296743.
48 The comments that Rand remembers following this article no longer appear on the article's webpage, and so I was unable to confirm the comments' content.
49 Saif Alhadithi, interview by Sarah Bishop, San Diego, CA, November 18, 2013, archived at the Schlesinger Library at Harvard University.
50 Zahraa Eskander, interview by Sarah Bishop, Los Angeles, CA, July 11, 2013, archived at the Schlesinger Library at Harvard University.
51 Moses Boghossian, interview by Sarah Bishop, Los Angeles, CA, July 12, 2013, archived at the Schlesinger Library at Harvard University.
52 Fahad Al Allaq, interview by Sarah Bishop, Los Angeles, CA, July 11, 2013, archived at the Schlesinger Library at Harvard University.
53 "Amira" (name changed at the request of the narrator), interview by Sarah Bishop, Los Angeles, CA, July 12, 2013, archived at the Schlesinger Library at Harvard University.
54 Hiba Saeed, interview by Sarah Bishop, San Diego, CA, November 18, 2013, archived at the Schlesinger Library at Harvard University.
55 Terence J. German, *Hamann on Language and Religion* (Oxford: Oxford University Press, 1981); David Crystal, *Linguistics, Language, and Religion*, vol. 126 (New York: Hawthorn Books, 1965); Sipra Mukherjee, "Reading Language and Religion Together," *International Journal of the Sociology of Language* 2013, no. 220 (2013): 1–6; William Downes, *Language and Religion: A Journey into the Human Mind* (Cambridge: Cambridge University Press, 2011); Tope Omoniyi, *The Sociology of Language and Religion: Change, Conflict and Accommodation* (Basingstoke, UK: Palgrave Macmillan, 2010); Tope Omoniyi and Joshua A. Fishman, *Explorations in the Sociology of Language and Religion*, vol. 20 (Philadelphia: John Benjamin's Publishing Company, 2006); James Turner, *Language, Religion, Knowledge: Past and Present* (Notre Dame, IN: University of Notre Dame Press, 2003); Peter C. Rollins, *Benjamin Lee Whorf: Lost Generation Theories of Mind, Language, and Religion* (Ann Arbor, MI: University Microfilms International, 1980).
56 Mukherjee, "Reading Language and Religion Together," 1.
57 Abreer Bayara, interview by Sarah Bishop, Houston, TX, November 13, 2013, archived at the Schlesinger Library at Harvard University.
58 Richard J. Hamilton and Dennis Moore, *Educational Interventions for Refugee Children: Theoretical Perspectives and Implementing Best Practice* (New York: Routledge, 2004); David P. Ausubel, "Adults Versus Children in Second-Language Learning: Psychological Considerations," *Modern Language Journal* 48, no. 7 (1964): 420–4; Karen Melissa Lichtman, "Child-Adult Differences in Implicit and Explicit Second Language Learning" (PhD diss., University of Illinois, 2012); Annamaria Pinter, *Children Learning Second Languages.* (New York: Palgrave Macmillan, 2011).
59 Florence E. McCarthy and Margaret H. Vickers, *Refugee and Immigrant Students: Achieving Equity in Education* (Charlotte, NC: Information Age Publications, 2012); Rosemary C. Salomone, *True American: Language, Identity, and the Education of Immigrant Children* (Cambridge, MA: Harvard University Press, 2010); Ismail Hakkı Mirici, Rebecca Galleano, and Kelly Torres, "Immigrant Parent vs. Immigrant Children: Attitudes Toward Language Learning in the U.S.," *Novitas-Royal* 7, no. 2 (2013):

137–46; Leena del Carpio, "Bridging the Gap: Immigrant Children as Language and Culture Brokers" (PhD diss, Ryerson University, 2007); Yew Liang Lee and Barry R. Chiswick, "Parents and Children Talk: English Language Proficiency within Immigrant Families," *Review of Economics of the Household* 3, no. 3 (2005): 243–68.
60 "Frequently Asked Questions," U.S. Committee for Refugees and Immigrants, last modified 2011, http://www.refugees.org/about-us/faqs.html.
61 Nancy J. Smith-Hefner, "Ethnicity and the Force of Faith: Christian Conversion Among Khmer Refugees," *Anthropological Quarterly* 67, no. 1 (1994): 24–38; Cornelia A. Kammerer, "Customs and Christian Conversion Among Akha Highlanders of Burma and Thailand," *American Ethnologist* 17, no. 2 (1990): 277–91; Timothy Dunnigan, "Processes of Identity Maintenance in Hmong Society," in *The Hmong in Transition*, eds. Glenn L. Hendricks, Bruce T. Downing, and Amos S. Deinard (New York: Center for Migration Studies, 1986); Milton M. Gordon, *Assimilation in American Life: The Role of Race, Religion, and National Origins* (New York: Oxford University Press, 1964); George M. Scott Jr., "The Lao Hmong Refugees in San Diego: Their Religious Transformation and its Implications for Geertz's Thesis," *Ethnic Studies Report* 5 (1987): 32–46.
62 Mon Maya, interview by Sarah Bishop, Houston, TX, November 13, 2013, archived at the Schlesinger Library at Harvard University.
63 Bhim "John" Monger, interview by Sarah Bishop, Austin, TX, November 15, 2013, archived at the Schlesinger Library at Harvard University.
64 For more on faith-based resettlement agencies, see Stephanie J. Nawyn, *Faithfully Providing Refuge: The Role of Religious Organizations in Refugee Assistance and Advocacy* (San Diego: University of California Center for Comparative Immigration Studies, April 2005); Sara L. McKinnon, "'Bringing New Hope and New Life': The Rhetoric of Faith-Based Refugee Resettlement Agencies," *Howard Journal of Communications* 20, no. 4 (2009): 313–32.
65 United States of America, Department of State, Bureau for Population, Refugees, and Migration, Cultural Orientation Resource Center, *Welcome to the United States: A Guidebook for Refugees* 4th ed. (Washington, DC: Cultural Orientation Resource Center, Center for Applied Linguistics, 2012), 72.
66 Ibid., 72.
67 Aihwa Ong, *Buddha is Hiding: Refugees, Citizenship, the New America* (Berkeley: University of California Press, 2003); Stephanie J. Nawyn, *Faithfully Providing Refuge: The Role of Religious Organizations in Refugee Assistance and Advocacy* (San Diego: University of California, The Center for Comparative Immigration Studies, 2005); Stephanie J. Nawyn, "Faith, Ethnicity, and Culture in Refugee Resettlement," *American Behavioral Scientist* 49, no. 11 (2006): 1509–27.
68 Nawyn, "Faith, Ethnicity, and Culture."
69 Indra Pradhan, interview by Sarah Bishop, Austin, TX, November 15, 2013, archived at the Schlesinger Library at Harvard University.
70 *Mukti*, directed by Kishor Subba, produced by Jenita Movie Makers P. Ltd., jointly made by Southern Ilam Christian Society and Gospel for Asia Publications (n.d.). Not to be confused with the 1977 Hindi-language Indian film by the same name. A representative from the production company informed me by e-mail correspondence that a version of *Mukti* exists that has English subtitles. As of yet, I have not been able to locate this version.

71 Sahro Nor, interview by Sarah Bishop, San Diego, CA, November 21, 2013, archived at the Schlesinger Library at Harvard University.

72 Julie Keown-Bomar, *Kinship Networks Among Hmong-American Refugees* (New York: LFB Scholarly Publications, 2004).

73 Fahad Al Allaq, interview by Sarah Bishop, Los Angeles, CA, July 11, 2013, archived at the Schlesinger Library at Harvard University.

74 Saif Alhadithi, interview by Sarah Bishop, San Diego, CA, November 18, 2013, archived at the Schlesinger Library at Harvard University.

75 Indra Pradhan, interview by Sarah Bishop, Austin, TX, November 15, 2013, archived at the Schlesinger Library at Harvard University.

76 Buddhi Rai, interview by Sarah Bishop, Pittsburgh, PA, February 20, 2013, archived at the Schlesinger Library at Harvard University. For more on the ways refugees and other kinds of immigrants stay in touch with family members or friends from their home country or country of asylum, see Linda Leung, Cath Finney Lamb, and Liz Emrys, *Technology's Refuge: The Use of Technology by Asylum Seekers and Refugees* (Sydney: University of Technology Sydney Press, 2009); Jenna Burrell and Ken Anderson, "'I Have Great Desires to Look Beyond my World': Trajectories of Information and Communication Technology use among Ghanaians Living Abroad," *New Media and Society* 10, no. 2 (2008): 203–24; Nelly Elias and Dafna Lemish, "Between Three Worlds: Host, Homeland, and Global Media in the Lives of Russian Immigrant Families in Israel and Germany," *Journal of Family Issues* 32, no. 9 (2011): 1245–74; and Hamid Naficy, *Home, Exile, Homeland: Film, Media, and the Politics of Place* (New York: Routledge, 1999).

77 Sahro Nor, interview by Sarah Bishop, San Diego, CA, November 21, 2013, archived at the Schlesinger Library at Harvard University.

78 For more on refugees and remittances, see Anna Lindley, *The Early Morning Phone Call: Somali Refugees' Remittances* (New York: Berghahn Books, 2010); Xu Zhimei and Ratha Dilip, *Migration and Remittances Factbook 2008* (Washington, DC: World Bank Publications, 2008); Amanda Poole, "Ransoms, Remittances, and Refugees: The Gatekeeper State in Eritrea," *Africa Today* 60, no. 2 (2013): 67–82; and Cindy Horst and Nick Van Hear, "Counting the Cost: Refugees, Remittances and the 'War Against Terrorism,'" *Forced Migration Review* 14 (2002): 32–4.

79 While no show on U.S. television is called "All America Fun," Sancha may be referring to *America's Funniest Home Videos*, a program by ABC Productions that showcases short humorous amateur videos created by individuals or families that compete for a grand prize in front of a live audience.

80 Sancha Rai, interview by Sarah Bishop, Pittsburgh, PA, February 5, 2013, archived at the Schlesinger Library at Harvard University.

81 Huimin Jin, "British Cultural Studies, Active Audiences and the Status of Cultural Theory: An Interview with David Morley," *Theory, Culture, and Society* 28, no. 4 (2011): 128.

82 Rand (last name removed at the narrator's request), interview by Sarah Bishop, Houston, TX, November 13, 2013, archived at the Schlesinger Library at Harvard University.

CONCLUSION

This book highlights media's role throughout refugee resettlement in the United States. The narrators have demonstrated that the influence of media on relocation is far more wide reaching than is currently reflected in the fields of media and resettlement studies. I have worked to show how examining refugees' interpretation and negotiation of media can advance an understanding of media's power and limitations in transnational contexts.

I began this book by interviewing a few resettlement administrators, who, when asked about refugees' expectations upon their arrival in the U.S., pointed quickly to media's role in creating in refugees' minds a picture of an America that would later, in one sense or another, disappoint them. It was not until I spoke with refugees from Bhutan, Burma, Iraq, and Somalia that I learned that the phenomenon the resettlement administrators described is only one small example among many that establishes the multifaceted and sustained roles media play throughout forced transnational relocation. Though these roles vary depending on the narrators' desires, skill, and interest, they all have tangible implications that should not be overlooked.

I have attempted to demonstrate that resettlement is an enduring, perpetual process; it does not begin when individuals board a plane, nor does it end when they arrive in a new home. Accordingly, I organized this book chronologically to demonstrate the roles media plays throughout the different phases of resettlement. The lingering memories of media encountered during a refugee's youth may follow him or her across an ocean and well into adulthood. I began by investigating the ways refugees interpret U.S. media that they encounter long before their arrival in the United States and how they may interpret these media as representations or distortions of the reality of life in the United States or use them to gain clues about the cultures and norms of U.S. life. The first chapter also explained how U.S. media may affect refugees' decisions to apply for resettlement to the United States and cause some apprehension or excitement in potential migrants about their future destinations. In chapter 2, the narrators discussed the types of digital, print, and video media they were given in United Nations' mandated pre-departure cultural orientations and/or in personal preparations for resettlement during the weeks leading up to their relocation. I provided a detailed analysis of the most widely used pre-departure orientation text, *Welcome to the United States: A Guidebook for Refugees*, so that the reader could consider with me, the implications of such a text for its intended audience. In chapter 3, I concentrated on refugees' first days in the United States and provided instances where the narrators compared what they learned about the United States in pre-arrival media encounters to the reality of their lived experiences upon resettlement. This chapter revealed the belief, made evident by many of the narrators, that some newly arrived refugees see the acquisition of media technology as integral to their success or well-being in the U.S., even though resettlement agencies rarely are able to provide such technology to refugees. Chapter 3 also chronicled how post-arrival orientation media represent the U.S. government, act as a means of standardization, and foster refugee deprivatization. The last chapter highlighted narrators' explanations of how they used media in processes of ongoing resettlement, interpreted instances where members of refugee communities have been portrayed in U.S. media, and considered how these portrayals affect their sense of belonging or understandings of Americans' perceptions about refugees. I analyzed several examples of such print media to reveal how messages regarding belonging and/or nationalism may appear embedded within the texts' style, language, and format. Finally, I explored the interaction of media, language, and religion to demonstrate the ways that these three phenomena are inextricably linked in refugees' lives, and also explained the role of media in maintaining or negotiating connections between refugees' families and friends.

While the narrators' keen insights have allowed this book to cover a good deal of ground, there was much that I was not able to do, and researchers whose interests lead them to this area of study will find several footholds throughout this work wherein they could begin or continue their own related investigations. Two areas of possible future research in particular made themselves apparent as I pursued this venture. First, useful both to the expansion of scholarly understanding of resettlement's relationship to media and to the understanding of individuals in positions of providing pre-resettlement resources to refugees would be a multisited, ethnographic account that examined not only what kinds of media are currently available in the world's refugee camps but also a political economy of who provides refugee camp media and why, who consumes refugee camp media, how frequently it is accessed, and for what purposes. Indeed, this addition to the scholarship could provide knowledge that would make clearer how refugee camp-based engagements with media vary from incoming forced migrants' encounters outside refugee camps.

Second, this work did not attempt to consider in any detail the relationship with media refugees pursuing U.S. citizenship have, but such an investigation promises to be fruitful for anyone willing to take it on. After five years of residence in the United States, refugees can apply for U.S. citizenship, and many resettlement organizations organize and host programs to aid with preparations for this naturalization process. The media refugees consume and respond to both during this preparation and throughout the naturalization process itself is riddled with proclamations regarding the nature of both U.S. citizens and the U.S. government that beg for critical attention. An interested researcher might start with the government-produced media provided to help potential citizens prepare for the necessary exam and go from there.[1] Certainly, there is more work to be done than just in these two areas. Any scholar compelled to investigate the interaction of media and migration will likely find that the trouble lies not in identifying a research project but rather in narrowing the seemingly endless potential ways one might approach such a study.

This work is one of memory. It asks the reader to look back with the narrators onto histories of transition. Around the world, eight people flee their homes each minute in an attempt to escape terror, persecution, or war.[2] Thus as I look back on the narrators' memories contained in these pages, I am compelled also to look forward and to remember Tek's question: How will my research help refugees? In the way of pragmatic recommendations, I have a few. I am well aware that there are many more people willing to offer recommendations about refugee resettlement than there are those willing to expend the energy to implement such recommendations. Still, out of respect for and gratitude to the resettlement personnel who requested my recommendations at the conclusion of this project, I offer the following: (1) Because of the discrepancy in lifestyle between the U.S. media refugees typically encounter before their arrival and their firsthand experiences in the United States, media's exaggeration of opulence (and possibly violence) should be addressed more directly and with more sustained attention in pre-departure orientations and orientation media. (2) Whenever possible, local U.S. resettlement agencies should provide a volunteer or staff member to guide refugees through post-arrival, resettlement-related media to gauge understanding and allow for interactive questioning and answering as a refugee processes the material. Such a practice cannot safeguard completely against misunderstandings or frustration, but instead may offer an opportunity for refugees to practice their language skills, share their concerns, or, as some of the narrators I interviewed mentioned, simply share in a safe environment one's concerns during what may otherwise be a lonely, disorienting time. (3) Although resettlement agencies are not required by the U.S. government to provide newly arriving refugees with televisions, cell phones, computers, or other media technologies, there should be a heightened awareness of the integral role these technologies, as well as English language acquisition, might play in establishing and negotiating refugees' sense of belonging. If, as is most likely to be the case, resettlement agencies do not have the funding to purchase multiples of these technologies for all of their incoming refugees, perhaps they could provide a space where refugees could access a communal television, computer, or other media during particular hours with the help of a volunteer who could, if needed, teach a basic working knowledge of these technologies to those who may want it. Alternately, resettlement agencies might consider providing refugees with information regarding venues where they might be able to purchase used or discounted media technologies. Newly arriving refugees who see these technologies as a necessity may be unsure of the most cost-effective ways of acquiring them and may run the risk of being compelled to spend more money than is necessary. I offer these recommendations with full knowledge that refugee resettlement administrators in the United States and abroad already manage to accomplish an almost impossible amount of work with shockingly limited resources.

For as long as wars are fought and natural disasters continue to increase in frequency, refugees will be forced from their homes into new, unfamiliar worlds where media will act as both help and hindrance. Likewise, media will continue to traverse international borders and find its way into the imaginations of individuals living in this increasingly migratory world. Though the perpetuation of these phenomena is sure, only careful interrogation can reveal the scope of their impact.

Notes

1 To find these materials, visit http://www.uscis.gov/citizenship/learners/study-test.
2 The United Nations Refugee Agency (UNHCR), *Refugee Dilemma Videos*, available at http://www.unhcr-centraleurope.org/en/news/2011/every-minute-eight-people-flee-their-homes-to-escape-conflict-or-persecution.html.

APPENDIX

Quoted Narrators by Surname

Abdulali, Dahabo. Interview by Sarah Bishop. San Diego, CA, November 21, 2013.
Abiyow, Said. Interview by Sarah Bishop. San Diego, CA, November 21, 2013.
Aden, Fatuma. Interview by Sarah Bishop. San Diego, CA, November 20, 2013.
Al Allaq, Fahad. Interview by Sarah Bishop. Los Angeles, CA, July 11, 2013.
Al Dohi, Hussain. Interview by Sarah Bishop. San Diego, CA, November 18, 2013.
Al Zehhawi, Wijdan. Interview by Sarah Bishop. Houston, TX, November 13, 2013.
Alba, Lily. Interview by Sarah Bishop. Los Angeles, CA, July 12, 2013.
Alhadithi, Saif. Interview by Sarah Bishop. San Diego, CA, November 18, 2013.
"Amira" (Name changed at the request of the narrator). Interview by Sarah Bishop. Los Angeles, CA, July 12, 2013.
Anonymous. Interview by Sarah Bishop. Los Angeles, CA, July 11, 2013.
Askar, Abdi. Interview by Sarah Bishop. San Diego, CA, November 18, 2013.
Barake, Abdikadir Abdiyow. Interview by Sarah Bishop. San Diego, CA, November 20, 2013.
Bayara, Abreer. Interview by Sarah Bishop. Houston, TX, November 13, 2013.
Bazikiam, Edwin. Interview by Sarah Bishop. Los Angeles, CA, July 9, 2013.
Boghossian, Moses. Interview by Sarah Bishop. Los Angeles, CA, July 12, 2013.
Chapagain, Bishnu Maya. Interview by Sarah Bishop. Buffalo, NY, August 6, 2013.
Chuwan, Nanda. Interview with Sarah Bishop. Erie, PA, February 7, 2013.
Eskander, Zahraa. Interview by Sarah Bishop. Los Angeles, CA, July 11, 2013.
Estefan, Linda. Interview by Sarah Bishop. Los Angeles, CA, July 12, 2013.
Esther (Last name removed at the request of the narrator). Interview by Sarah Bishop. Buffalo, NY, August 6, 2013.
Gurung, Balaram. Interview by Sarah Bishop. Pittsburgh, PA, March 22, 2013.
Gurung, Bishnu. Interview by Sarah Bishop. Austin, TX, November 15, 2013.

Hsa, Hsit. Interview by Sarah Bishop. San Diego, CA, November 18, 2013.
Htoo, Kler. Interview by Sarah Bishop. Buffalo, NY, August 6, 2013.
Ibraheem, Fadhail. Interview by Sarah Bishop. Erie, PA, February 7, 2013.
Ibrahim, Kalsumo. Interview by Sarah Bishop. San Diego, CA, November 20, 2013.
Issa, Iptisam. Interview by Sarah Bishop. Los Angeles, CA, July 9, 2013.
Jackson, Dylanna. Interview by Sarah Bishop. Erie, PA, February 7, 2013.
Jama, Habiba. Interview by Sarah Bishop. San Diego, CA, November 20, 2013.
Januke, Darjee. Interview by Sarah Bishop. Houston, TX, November 13, 2013.
Kari, Laxmi Adhi. Interview with Sarah Bishop. Buffalo, NY, August 6, 2013.
Khanal, Bishnu. Interview by Sarah Bishop. Buffalo, NY, August 6, 2013.
Khanal, Govinda. Interview by Sarah Bishop. Buffalo, NY, August 6, 2013.
Khanal, Nirmala. Interview by Sarah Bishop. Buffalo, NY, August 6, 2013.
Mahmod, Mohammed. Interview by Sarah Bishop. Pittsburgh, PA, March 4, 2013.
Marip, Zau Aung. Interview by Sarah Bishop. Houston, TX, November 14, 2013.
Maya, Mon. Interview by Sarah Bishop. Houston, TX, November 13, 2013.
Mbere, Sitay. Interview by Sarah Bishop. San Diego, CA, November 20, 2013.
Meh, OO. Interview by Sarah Bishop. Houston, TX, November 14, 2013.
Minasaqen, Shiraz. Interview by Sarah Bishop. Los Angeles, CA, July 11, 2013.
Mohmmed, Abdirahim. Interview by Sarah Bishop. San Diego, CA, November 21, 2013.
Monger, Bhim "John." Interview by Sarah Bishop. Austin, TX, November 15, 2013.
Mugwaneza, Kheir. Interview with Sarah Bishop. Pittsburgh, PA, March 18, 2013.
Myae, Chan. Interview by Sarah Bishop. Buffalo, NY, August 7, 2013.
Nor, Sahro. Interview by Sarah Bishop. San Diego, CA, November 21, 2013.
Perry, Meghann. Interview by Sarah Bishop. Buffalo, NY, August 7, 2013.
Pradhan, Indra. Interview by Sarah Bishop. Austin, TX, November 15, 2013.
Rai, Bal Baduj. Interview by Sarah Bishop. Houston, TX, November 14, 2013.
Rai, Buddhi. Interview by Sarah Bishop. Pittsburgh, PA, February 20, 2013.
Rai, Sancha. Interview by Sarah Bishop. Pittsburgh, PA, February 5, 2013.
Rand (Iraq. Last name removed at the narrator's request). Interview by Sarah Bishop. Houston, TX, November 13, 2013.
Raw, Paw Htoo. Interview by Sarah Bishop. Austin, TX, November 15, 2013.
Rimal, Tek. Interview with Sarah Bishop. Pittsburgh, PA, March 18, 2013.
Saeed, Hiba. Interview by Sarah Bishop. San Diego, CA, November 18, 2013.
Seymo, Jasmine. Interview by Sarah Bishop. San Diego, CA, November 18, 2013.
Sheighei, Hassan. Interview by Sarah Bishop. San Diego, CA, November 21, 2013.
Wee, Ya. Interview by Sarah Bishop. Buffalo, NY, August 6, 2013.
Yaqo, Jala. Interview by Sarah Bishop. San Diego, CA, November 18, 2013.
"Zanuba" (Name changed at the request of the narrator). Interview by Sarah Bishop. San Diego, CA, November 21, 2013.

REFERENCES

Abrahamson, Jennie A., and Karen E. Fisher. "Modeling the Information Behavior or Lay Mediaries." *Proceedings of the American Society for Information Science and Technology* 43, no. 1 (2006): 1–4.
Alasuutari, Pertti, ed. *Rethinking the Media Audience: The New Agenda*. London: Sage, 1999.
Alibhai-Brown, Yasmin. "No Room at the Inn: Racism Underpins Current Attitudes towards Refugees and Asylum Seekers—And a Precious Heritage Is Being Lost." *New Internationalist*, October 1, 2002. http://newint.org/features/2002/10/01/racism/.
Althusser, Louis. "Ideology and Ideological State Apparatuses." In *Lenin and Philosophy, and Other Essays*, 127–86. New York: Monthly Review Press, 1971.
Amin, Samir. *Modern Migrations in Western Africa*. London: Oxford University Press, 1974.
Ana, Otto Santa. "'Like an Animal I Was Treated': Anti-Immigrant Metaphor in U.S. Public Discourse." *Discourse and Society* 10, no. 2 (1999): 191–224.
Anderson, Benedict R. *Imagined Communities: Reflections on the Origin and Spread of Nationalism*. London: Verso, 1983.
———. *Imagined Communities: Reflections on the Origin and Spread of Nationalism*. New York: Verso, 2006.
Ang, Ien. *Watching Dallas: Soap Opera and the Melodramatic Imagination*. London: Methuen, 1985.
Appadurai, Arjun. *Modernity at Large: Cultural Dimensions of Globalization*. Vol. 1. Minneapolis: University Of Minnesota Press, 1996.
Appiah, Kwame Anthony. *Cosmopolitanism: Ethics in a World of Strangers*. New York: Norton, 2007.
Augé, Marc. *Non-Places: Introduction to an Anthropology of Supermodernity*. New York: Verso, 1995.
Ausubel, David P. "Adults versus Children in Second-Language Learning: Psychological Considerations." *Modern Language Journal* 48, no. 7 (1964): 420–4.
Bailey, Olga. "Journalism and the 'Politics Of Naming' the Other." Paper presented at the annual meeting of the International Communication Association, New York, February 2, 2005.

Baker, Ahmed M. "Informal Education Programmes." *Journal of Refugee Studies* 2, no. 1 (1989): 98–107.

Barthes, Roland. *Image, Music, Text*. New York: Hill and Wang, 1978.

Batziou, Athanasia. *Picturing Immigration: Photojournalistic Representation of Immigrants in Greek and Spanish Press*. Bristol: Intellect, 2011.

Baynham, Mike. "Agency and Contingency in the Language Learning of Refugees and Asylum Seekers." *Linguistics and Education* 17, no. 1 (2006): 24–39.

Bekerman, Zvi, Nicholas C. Burbules, and Diana Silberman-Keller. *Learning in Places: The Informal Education Reader*. New York: Peter Lang, 2006.

Bellinger, Goli Amin. "Negotiation of Gender Responsibilities in Resettled Refugee Populations through Relationship Enhancement Training." *Transcultural Psychiatry* 50, no. 3 (2013): 455–71.

Berry, John. W. "Immigration, Acculturation, and Adaptation." *Applied Psychology: An International Review* 46 no. 1 (1997): 5–68.

Billig, Michael. "The Argumentative Nature of Holding Strong Views: A Case Study." *European Journal of Social Psychology* 19, no. 3 (1989): 203–23.

Bishop, Anne Peterson, and Lassana Magassa. "Using Design Thinking to Empower Ethnic Minority Immigrant Youth in the Roles as Technology and Information Mediaries." In *CHI '13 Extended Abstracts on Human Factors in Computing Systems*, 361–66. New York: ACM, 2013.

Black Hawk Down. DVD. Directed by Ridley Scott. Culver City: Columbia TriStar Entertainment, 2001.

Black, Richard, and Khalid Koser. *The End of the Refugee Cycle?: Refugee Repatriation and Reconstruction*. New York: Berghahn Books, 1998.

Blumer, Markie L. C. "And Action! Teaching and Learning through Film." *Journal of Feminist Family Therapy* 22, no. 3 (2010): 225–35.

Boniface, Bosire. "Trade Booms in Dadaab Refugee Camps." *Sabahi*, May 14, 2012. http://sabahionline.com/en_GB/articles/hoa/articles/features/2012/05/14/feature-02.

Borland, Katharine. "'That's Not What I Said': Interpretive Conflict in Oral Narrative Research." In *Women's Words: The Feminist Practice of Oral History*, edited by Sherna Berger Gluck and Daphne Patai, 63–75. New York: Routledge, 1991.

Boyd, Monica. "Gender, Refugee Status and Permanent Settlement." *Gender Issues* 17, no. 1 (2010): 5–25.

Bradimore, Ashley, and Harald Bauder. "Mystery Ships and Risky Boat People: Tamil Refugee Migration in the Newsprint Media." *Canadian Journal of Communication* 36, no. 4 (2011): 637–61.

Bradley, Megan. *Refugee Repatriation: Justice, Responsibility and Redress*. Cambridge: Cambridge University Press, 2013.

Branton, Regina, and Johanna Dunaway. "English- and Spanish-Language Media Coverage of Immigration: A Comparative Analysis." *Social Science Quarterly* 89, no. 4 (2008): 1006–22.

Briggs, Charles L. "Why Nation-States and Journalists Can't Teach People to be Healthy: Power and Pragmatic Miscalculation in Public Discourses on Health." *Medical Anthropology Quarterly* 17, no. 3 (2003): 287–321.

Brown, Jill, Jenny Miller, and Jane Mitchell. "Interrupted Schooling and the Acquisition of Literacy: Experiences of Sudanese Refugees in Victorian Secondary Schools." *Australian Journal of Language and Literacy* 29, no. 2 (2006): 150–62.

Burma Refugee Family Network. "Mission Statement." http://www.brfn.org/about-us.html.

Burrell, Jenna, and Ken Anderson. "'I Have Great Desires to Look Beyond My World': Trajectories of Information and Communication Technology Use among Ghanaians Living Abroad." *New Media and Society* 10, no. 2 (2008): 203–24.

Cambridge, Vibert C. *Immigration, Diversity, and Broadcasting in the United States, 1990–2001.* Athens: Ohio University Press, 2005.

Cameron, Lindsey, Adam Rutland, Rupert Brown, and Rebecca Douch. "Changing Children's Intergroup Attitudes toward Refugees: Testing Different Models of Extended Contact." *Child Development* 77, no. 5 (2006): 1208–19.

Carey, James W. *Communication as Culture: Essays on Media and Society.* New York: Routledge, 2009.

Carroll, Susan. "Refugees Struggle to Find Work As Houston Economy Slows." *The Houston Chronicle*, February 25, 2009. http://www.chron.com/default/article/Refugees-struggle-to-find-work-as-Houston-economy-1745961.php#photo-1296743.

Centers for Disease Control and Prevention. "Resources for Entertainment Education Content Developers: Preventive Health Care—What's the Problem?" Last modified June 12, 2013. http://www.cdc.gov/healthcommunication/ToolsTemplates/EntertainmentEd/Tips/PreventiveHealth.html.

———. "Bhutanese Refugee Health Profile." Last modified February 24, 2014. http://www.cdc.gov/immigrantrefugeehealth/profiles/bhutanese/background/index.html#four.

Chan, Wai Meng. *Media in Foreign Language Teaching and Learning.* Boston: De Gruyter Mouton, 2011.

Charland, Maurice. "Constitutive Rhetoric: The Case of the Peuple Québécois." *Quarterly Journal of Speech* 73, no. 2 (1987): 133–50.

Cheung, Sin Yi, and Jenny Phillimore. "Social Networks, Social Capital and Refugee Integration." Research Report, *Nuffield Foundation*, 2013.

Chia, Joyce, and Susan Kenny. "The Children of Mae La: Reflections on Regional Refugee Cooperation." *Melbourne Journal of International Law* 13, no. 2 (2012): 838–58.

Cho, Jaeho, Homero Gil De Zuniga, Dhavan V. Shah, and Douglas M. McLeod. "Cue Convergence: Associative Effects on Social Intolerance." *Communication Research* 33, no. 3 (2006): 136–54.

Choi, Chul-Byung. "Local Collective Identity Enculturation within a Global Media Consumption Culture." *Asia Pacific Education Review* 3, no. 1 (2002): 1–17.

Cisneros, J. David. "Contaminated Communities: The Metaphor of 'Immigrant as Pollutant' in Media Representations of Immigration." *Rhetoric and Public Affairs* 11, no. 4 (2008): 569–602.

Clark, Lynn Schofield, and Lynn Sywyj. "Mobile Intimacies in the U.S.A. among Refugee and Recent Immigrant Teens and Their Parents." *Feminist Media Studies* 12, no. 4 (2012): 485–95.

Clifford, James, George E. Marcus, Kim Fortun, and the School of American Research (Santa Fe, NM). *Writing Culture: The Poetics and Politics of Ethnography.* Berkeley: University of California Press, 2010.

Condit, Celeste M. "The Rhetorical Limits of Polysemy." *Critical Studies in Mass Communication* 6, no. 2 (1989): 103–22.

Cook, Robinson. "Dadaab Cultural Orientation–What Do Refugees Know about the U.S. before Coming?" Presentation given at the Mankato Rotary Club, Mankato, Minnesota, 2009.

Cooper-Chen, Anne. *Global Entertainment Media: Content, Audiences, Issues.* New York: Lawrence Erlbaum Associates, Inc., 2005.

Couldry, Nick. *Media, Society, World: Social Theory and Digital Media Practice*. Cambridge: Polity, 2012.
Crenshaw, Kimberle. "Mapping the Margins: Intersectionality, Identity Politics, and Violence against Women of Color." *Stanford Law Review* 43 (1993): 1241–99.
Crumlish, Niall, and Killian O'Rourke. "A Systematic Review of Treatments for Post-Traumatic Stress Disorder among Refugees and Asylum-Seekers." *Journal of Nervous and Mental Disease* 198, no. 4 (2010): 237–51.
Crystal, David. *Linguistics, Language, and Religion*. New York: Hawthorn Books, 1965.
Cultural Orientation Resource Center. "Domestic CO [Cultural Orientation] Delivery." http://www.culturalorientation.net/providing-orientation/domestic/delivery.
———. "Images from RSC MENA." Last modified 2013. http://www.culturalorientation.net/providing-orientation/overseas/programs/rsc-mena/images.
———. "Overseas CO [Cultural Orientation]." http://www.culturalorientation.net/providing-orientation/overseas.
———. "Providing Orientation and Training." http://www.culturalorientation.net/providing-orientation/.
Currie, Cheryl L., T. Cameron Wild, Donald P. Schopflocher, Lory Laing, Paul J. Veugelers, Brenda Parlee, and Daniel W. McKennitt. "Enculturation and Alcohol Use Problems among Aboriginal University Students." *Canadian Journal of Psychiatry* 56, no. 12 (2011): 735–42.
da Silva, Marisa Torres. "Online Forums, Audience Participation and Modes of Political Discussion: Readers' Comments on the Brazilian Presidential Election as a Case Study." *Comunicación Y Sociedad* 26, no. 4 (October 2013): 175–93.
Dabkowski, Colin. "Multivenue Show in Allentown Highlights Faces of Buffalo Refugees." *The Gusto Blog*, February 20, 2014. http://www.buffalonews.com/gusto/art-previews/multivenue-show-in-allentown-highlights-faces-of-buffalo-refugees-20140220.
Dallas. Television. Directed by David Jacobs. CBS: 1978–91.
Debouzy, Marianne. *In the Shadow of the Statue of Liberty: Immigrants, Workers, and Citizens in the American Republic, 1880–1920*. Urbana: University of Illinois Press, 1992.
Deegan, Mary Jo. *Jane Addams and the Men of the Chicago School 1892–1918*. New Brunswick, NJ: Transaction Publishers, 2005.
del Carpio, Leena. "Bridging the Gap: Immigrant Children as Language and Culture Brokers." Masters Thesis, Ryerson University, 2007.
Dennison, W.F., and Roger Kirk. *Do, Review, Learn, Apply: A Simple Guide to Experiential Learning*. Oxford: Blackwell Education, 1990.
DeWalt, Kathleen Musante, and Billie R. DeWalt. *Participant Observation: A Guide for Fieldworkers*. Lanham, MD: Rowman & Littlefield, 2011.
Dewey, John. *Experience and Education*. West Lafayette, IN: Kappa Delta Pi, 1938.
d'Haenens, Leen, and Marielle de Lange. "Framing of Asylum Seekers in Dutch Regional Newspapers." *Media, Culture and Society* 23, no. 6 (2001): 847–60.
Douai, Aziz, and Hala K. Nofal. "Commenting in the Online Arab Public Sphere: Debating the Swiss Minaret Ban and the 'Ground Zero Mosque' Online." *Journal of Computer-Mediated Communication* 17, no. 3 (April 2012): 266–82.
Downes, William. *Language and Religion: A Journey into the Human Mind*. Cambridge: Cambridge University Press, 2011.
Drewett, Michael, and Martin Cloonan. *Popular Music Censorship in Africa*. Burlington, VT: Ashgate, 2006.
Du Bois, Christine M. *Images of West Indian Immigrants in Mass Media: The Struggle for a Positive Ethnic Reputation*. New York: LFB Scholarly Publishing LLC, 2004.

Dumenden, Iris E. "The Soft Bigotry of Low Expectations: The Refugee Student and Mainstream Schooling." *British Journal of Sociology of Education* 35, no. 3 (2014): 484–86.

Dunnigan, Timothy. "Processes of Identity Maintenance in Hmong Society." In *The Hmong in Transition*, edited by Glenn L. Hendricks, Bruce T. Downing, and Amos S. Deinard, 41–53. New York: Center for Migration Studies, 1986.

Durham, Meenakshi G. "Constructing the 'New Ethnicities': Media, Sexuality, and Diaspora Identity in the Lives of South Asian Immigrant Girls." *Critical Studies in Media Communication* 21, no. 2 (2004): 140–61.

Elias, Nelly, and Dafna Lemish. "Between Three Worlds: Host, Homeland, and Global Media in the Lives of Russian Immigrant Families in Israel and Germany." *Journal of Family Issues* 32, no. 9 (2011): 1245–74.

———. "Media Uses in Immigrant Families: Torn Between 'Inward' and 'Outward' Paths of Integration." *International Communication Gazette* 70, no. 1 (2008): 21–40.

Ellis, Beverley Heidi, Helen Z. Macdonald, Alisa K. Lincoln, and Howard J. Cabral. "Mental Health of Somali Adolescent Refugees: The Role of Trauma, Stress, and Perceived Discrimination." *Journal of Consulting and Clinical Psychology* 76, no. 2 (2008): 184–93.

Ellis, Beverley Heidi, Helen Z. MacDonald, Julie Klunk-Gillis, Alisa K. Lincoln, Lee Strunin, and Howard J. Cabral. "Discrimination and Mental Health and Mental Health among Somali Refugee Adolescents: The Role of Acculturation and Gender." *American Journal of Orthopsychiatry* 80, no. 4 (2010): 564–75.

Esses, Victoria M., Scott Veenvliet, Gordon Hodson, and Ljiljana Mihic. "Justice, Morality, and the Dehumanization of Refugees." *Social Justice Research* 21, no. 1 (2008): 4–25.

Evans Barnes, Ann. "Realizing Protection Space for Iraqi Refugees: UNHCR in Syria, Jordan and Lebanon." *New Issues in Refugee Research*. Geneva: United Nations Refugee Agency, 2009.

Facebook. "Burmese Community Support Center." http://www.facebook.com/pages/Burmese-Community-Support-Center/162466873944623.

Fadiman, Anne. *The Spirit Catches You and You Fall Down: A Hmong Child, Her American Doctors, and the Collision of Two Cultures*. New York: Noonday Press, 1998.

Falb, Kathryn L., Marie C. McCormick, David Hemenway, Katherine Anfinson, and Jay G. Silverman. "Violence against Refugee Women Along the Thai-Burma Border." *International Journal of Gynecology and Obstetrics* 120, no. 3 (2013): 279–83.

First Blood. Video. Directed by Ted Kotcheff. Santa Monica: LionsGate Home Entertainment, 1982.

Fish, Stanley Eugene. *Is There a Text in This Class?: The Authority of Interpretive Communities*. Cambridge, MA: Harvard University Press, 1980.

Fisher, Colleen. "Changed and Changing Gender and Family Roles and Domestic Violence in African Refugee Background Communities Post-Settlement in Perth, Australia." *Violence Against Women* 19, no. 7 (2013): 833–47.

Fiske, John. *Understanding Popular Culture*. Boston: Unwin.

———. *Television Culture*. London: Verso, 1987.

Foss, Sonja K. *Rhetorical Criticism: Exploration and Practice*. Long Grove, IL: Waveland Press, 2004.

Foucault, Michel. *Madness and Civilization: A History of Insanity in the Age of Reason*. New York: Vintage Books, 1988.

———. "Truth and Power: An Interview with Alessandro Fontana and Pasquale Pasquino." *L'Arc* 70 (1977): 16–22.

———. *Power/Knowledge: Selected Interviews and Other Writings 1972–1977*. Edited by Colin Gordon. New York: Pantheon, 1980.
Fried, Jane. *Transformative Learning Through Engagement: Student Affairs Practice as Experiential Pedagogy*. Sterling: Stylus Publishing, 2012.
Gabrielatos, Costas, and Paul Baker. "Fleeing, Sneaking, Flooding." *Journal of English Linguistics* 36, no. 1 (2008): 5–38.
Gaonkar, Dilip Parameshwar. "Toward New Imaginaries: An Introduction." *Public Culture* 4, no. 1 (2002): 1–19.
Geertz, Clifford. *The Interpretation of Cultures*. New York: Basic Books, 1973.
———. "Local Knowledge and Its Limits: Some Obiter Dicta." *Yale Journal of Criticism* 5, no. 2 (1992): 129–35.
Geiger, Vance. "Refugee Cognitive Expectations and Sociocultural Change Theory." *Selected Papers on Refugee Issues* 2 (1993): 67–80.
Georgiou, Myria. "Media and the City: Making Sense of Place." *International Journal of Media and Cultural Politics* 6, no. 3 (2011): 343–50.
German, Terence J. *Hamann on Language and Religion*. Oxford: Oxford University Press, 1981.
Gifford, Sandra M., and Raelene Wilding. "Digital Escapes?: ICTs, Settlement and Belonging Among Karen Youth in Melbourne, Australia." *Journal of Refugee Studies* 26, no. 4 (2013): 558–75.
Gjini, Klevest, Nash N. Boutros, Luay Haddad, Deane Aikins, Arash Javahbakht, Alireza Amirsadri, and Manuel E. Tancer. "Evoked Potential Correlates of Post-Traumatic Stress Disorder in Refugees with History of Exposure to Torture." *Journal of Psychiatric Research* 47, no. 10 (2013): 1492–98.
Glazer, Nathan, and Daniel P. Moynihan. *Beyond the Melting Pot: The Negroes, Puerto Ricans, Jews, Italians, and Irish of New York City*. Cambridge, MA: The MIT Press, 1970.
Gluck, Sherna. "What's So Special about Women? Women's Oral History." *Frontiers: A Journal of Women Studies* 2, no. 2 (1977): 3–17.
Gone with the Wind. Video. Directed by Victor Fleming. Burbank: Warner Home Video, 1939.
Goodall, Christine. "Moving Together: Involuntary Movement and the Universal Dynamics of Moving, Meeting and Mixing." *New Issues in Refugee Research*. Geneva: United Nations Refugee Agency, 2013.
Gordon, Milton M. *Assimilation in American Life: The Role of Race, Religion, and National Origins*. New York: Oxford University Press, 1964.
Gorman, Robert. "Refugee Repatriation in Africa." *The World Today* 40, no. 10 (1984): 436–43.
Grossberg, Lawrence. "Marxist Dialectics and Rhetorical Criticism." *Quarterly Journal of Speech* 65, no. 3 (1979): 235–49.
———. *Cultural Studies in the Future Tense*. Durham, NC: Duke University Press, 2010.
Gubrium, Jaber F., and James A. Holstein. "Life Course Malleability: Biographical Work and Deprivatization." *Sociological Inquiry* 65, no. 2 (1995): 207–23.
———. "Qualitative Inquiry and Deprivatization of Experience." *Qualitative Inquiry* 1, no. 2 (1995): 204–22.
Gudykunst, William B. *Theorizing About Intercultural Communication*. Thousand Oaks, CA: Sage, 2005.
———. "Individualistic and Collectivistic Perspectives on Communication: An Introduction." *International Journal of Intercultural Relations* 22 (1998): 7–34.

Guertin, Carolyn C. *Digital Prohibition: Piracy and Authorship in New Media Art*. London: Continuum International Publication Group, 2012.
Gumpert, Gary, and Susan J. Drucker. *The Huddled Masses: Communication and Immigration*. Cresskill, NJ: Hampton Press, 1998.
Hafften, Anne. "'Technical Difficulty' or Censorship?" *Washington Report on Middle East Affairs* 31, no. 2 (2012): 1–76.
Haines, David. *Safe Haven?: A History Of Refugees In America*. Sterling: Stylus Publishing, 2010.
Hall, Stuart. "Encoding/Decoding." In *Culture, Media, Language*, edited by Stuart Hall, Dorothy Hobson, Andrew Lowe, and Paul Willis, 128–38. London: Routledge, 1980.
Halpern, Peggy. "Refugee Economic Self-Sufficiency: An Exploratory Study of Approaches Used in Office of Refugee Resettlement Program." U.S. Department of Health and Human Services, 2008. http://aspe.hhs.gov/hsp/08/RefugeeSelfSuff/.
Hamilton, Richard J., and Dennis Moore. *Educational Interventions for Refugee Children: Theoretical Perspectives and Implementing Best Practice*. New York: Routledge, 2004.
Hammond, Laura. "History, Overview, Trends and Issues in Major Somali Refugee Displacements in the Near Region." *New Issues in Refugee Research*. Geneva: United Nations Refugee Agency, 2014.
Handlin, Oscar. *Boston Immigrants, 1790–1880: A Study in Acculturation*. Cambridge, MA: Harvard University Press, 1991.
Hansen, Art, and Anthony Oliver-Smith, eds. *Involuntary Migration and Resettlement: The Problems and Responses of Dislocated People*. Boulder, CO: Westview Press, 1982.
Hanson-Easey, Scott, and Martha Augoustinos. "Complaining about Humanitarian Refugees: The Role of Sympathy Talk in the Design of Complaints on Talkback Radio." *Discourse and Communication* 5, no. 3 (2011): 247–71.
Harindranath, Ramaswami. "Ethnicity and Cultural Difference. Some Thematic and Political Issues on Global Audience Research." *Participations* 2, no. 2 (2005): 1–17.
Harney, Nicolas. "Precarity, Affect and Problem Solving with Mobile Phones by Asylum Seekers, Refugees and Migrants in Naples, Italy." *Journal of Refugee Studies* 26, no. 4 (2013): 541–57.
Harper, Richard. *Inside the IMF: An Ethnography of Documents, Technology, and Organisational Action*. San Diego: Academic Press, 1998.
Harvey, David. *The Condition of Postmodernity: An Enquiry into the Origins of Cultural Change*. Hoboken, NJ: Wiley-Blackwell, 1991.
Haskill, Thomas. "Capitalism and the Origins of the Humanitarian Sensibility, Part 1." *American Historical Review* 9, no. 2 (1995): 339–61.
Hauser, Gerard A. *Vernacular Voices: The Rhetoric of Publics and Public Spheres*. Columbia: University of South Carolina, 1999.
Hawkins, Sean. *Writing and Colonialism in Northern Ghana: The Encounter between the Lodagaa and the 'World on Paper.'* Toronto: University of Toronto Press, 2002.
Hawley, Caroline. "Iraqi Refugees Flee Syrian Conflict to Return Home." *BBC News: Middle East*, October 29, 2012. http://www.bbc.co.uk/news/world-middle-east-20131033.
Hegde, Radha S. "Eyeing New Publics: Veiling and the Performance of Civic Visibility." In *Public Modalities: Rhetoric, Culture, Media, and the Shape of Public Life*, edited by Daniel Brouwer and Robert Asen, 154–72. Tuscaloosa: University of Alabama Press, 2010.
Heinze, Andrew R. *Adapting to Abundance: Jewish Immigrants, Mass Consumption, and the Search for American Identity*. New York: Columbia University Press, 1990.

Henkin, Alan B., and Carole A. Singleton. "Looking Forward: Indochinese Refugee Expectations for Post-Resettlement Change." *International Review of Modern Sociology* 22, no. 2 (1992): 45–56.

Hernes, Gudmund, and Knud Knudsen. "Norwegians' Attitudes toward New Immigrants." *Acta Sociologica* 35, no. 2 (1992): 123–39.

Higson, Andrew. "The Limiting Imagination of National Cinema." In *Cinema and Nation*, edited by Mette Hjort and Schott Mackenzie. London: Routledge, 2000.

Hirtzel, Ashley. "Community Led Non-Profit to Assist Buffalo's Burmese Population." *WSKG*, September 6, 2013. http://www.wskg.org/wskg_news/community-led-non-profit-assist-buffalos-burmese-population.

Horst, Cindy. "*Buufis* amongst Somalis in Dadaab: The Transnational and Historical Logics behind Resettlement Dreams." *Journal of Refugee Studies* 19, no. 2 (2006): 143–57.

Horst, Cindy, and Nick Van Hear. "Counting the Cost: Refugees, Remittances and the 'War Against Terrorism.'" *Forced Migration Review* 14 (2002): 32–4.

Horsti, Karina. "Global Mobility and the Media: Presenting Asylum Seekers as a Threat." *Nordic Research on Media and Communication* 24, no. 1 (2003): 41–55.

Hou, Feng, and Morton Beiser. "Learning the Language of a New Country: A Ten-Year Study of English Acquisition by South-East Asian Refugees in Canada." *International Migration* 44, no. 1 (2006): 135–65.

———. "Language Acquisition, Unemployment and Depressive Disorder among Southeast Asian Refugees: A 10-Year Study." *Social Science and Medicine* 53, no. 10 (2001): 1321–34.

Howell, Perry. "Got Worry? Missing Children Notices on Milk Cartons in the United States." *Interactions: Studies in Communication and Culture* 2, no. 1 (2012): 35–46.

Hugo, Graeme. *Migration, Development and Environment*. Geneva, Switzerland: International Organization for Migration, 2008.

Husarska, Anna. "Exile Off Main Street: Refugees and America's Ingratitude." *Current* 506 (2008): 27–30.

Hutt, Michael. "Things That Should Not Be Said: Censorship and Self-Censorship in the Nepali Press Media, 2001–02." *The Journal of Asian Studies* 65, no. 2 (2006): 361–92.

Independence Day. Video. Directed by Roland Emmerich. Beverly Hills: Twentieth Century Fox Film Corporation, 1996.

International Institute of Los Angeles. "Gallery." http://www.iilosangeles.org/about/gallery/.

International Organization for Migration. "Press Room." http://www.iom.int/cms/media.

———. "United States Cultural Orientation in Nepal: Preparing Refugees for a New Life in the U.S.A." Accessed October 19, 2013. http://www.iom.int/cms/united-states-cultural-orientation.

———. "Videos." http://www.iom.int/cms/en/sites/iom/home/news-and-views/video-vault.html.

International Rescue Committee. "From Surviving to Thriving, One Man's Journey." Accessed July 19, 2013. http://www.rescue.org/us-program/us-seattle-wa/surviving-thriving-one-man%E2%80%99s-journey.

———. "Iraqi Refugees." http://www.rescue.org/node/5678.

———. "Iraqi Refugees in the United States: In Dire Straits." http://www.rescue.org/sites/default/files/resource-file/irc_report_iraqcommission.pdf.

Iraqi Refugee Assistance: Improvements Needed in Measuring Progress, Assessing Needs, Tracking Funds, and Developing an International Strategic Plan: Report to Congressional Committees. Washington, DC: United States Government Accountability Office, 2009.

Iser, Wolfgang. *The Implied Reader: Patterns of Communication in Prose Fiction from Bunyan to Beckett*. Baltimore: John Hopkins University Press, 1978.

Iversen, Valentina C., John E. Berg, and Arne E. Vaaler. "Expectations of the Future: Immigrant, Asylum Seeker, or Refugee—Does it Matter?" *Journal of Psychiatric Intensive Care* 6, no. 1 (2010): 23–30.

Jack, Rachael E., Caroline Blais, Christoph Scheepers, Philippe G. Schyns, and Roberto Caldara. "Cultural Confusions Show That Facial Expressions Are Not Universal." *Current Biology* 19, no. 18 (2009): 1543–8.

Jack, Rachael E., Oliver G. B. Garrod, Hui Yu, Roberto Caldara, and Philippe G. Schyns. "Facial Expressions of Emotion Are Not Culturally Universal." *Proceedings of the National Academy of Sciences of the United States of America* 109, no. 19 (2012): 7241–44.

Jack, Rachael E., Roberto Caldara, and Philippe G. Schyns. "Internal Representations Reveal Cultural Diversity in Expectations of Facial Expressions of Emotion." *Journal of Experimental Psychology-General* 141, no. 1 (2012): 18–25.

Jaeckle, Tina, and Alexia Georgakopoulos. "Cultural Representations of Identity, Trauma, and Transnationalism among Dinka Refugees: Implications for Conflict Analysis and Resolution." *International Journal of Psychological Studies* 2, no. 2 (2010): 3–13.

Jamil, Hikmet, Julie Hakim-Larson, Mohamed Farrag, Talib Kafaji, Laith H. Jamil, and Adnan Hammad. "Medical Complaints among Iraqi American Refugees with Mental Disorders." *Journal of Immigrant Health* 7, no. 3 (2005): 145–52.

Jamil, Hikmet, Mohamed Farrag, Julie Hakim-Larson, Talib Kafaji, Husam Abdulkhaleq, and Adnan Hammad. "Mental Health Symptoms in Iraqi Refugees: Posttraumatic Stress Disorder, Anxiety, and Depression." *Journal of Cultural Diversity* 14, no. 1 (2007): 19–25.

Jin, Huimin. "British Cultural Studies, Active Audiences and the Status of Cultural Theory: An Interview with David Morley." *Theory, Culture and Society* 28, no. 4 (2011): 124–44.

Jones, Diana Nelson. "Carrick Home for Ethnic Nepali Refugees." *Pittsburgh Post-Gazette*, September 3, 2012. http://www.Post-Gazette.Com/Stories/Local/Neighborhoods-South/Carrick-Home-For-Ethnic-Nepali-Refugees-651673/.

Journey from the Fall. DVD. Directed by Ham Tran. Santa Monica: ImaginAsian Pictures, 2007.

Jurassic Park. Video. Directed by Steven Spielberg. Universal City: Universal Pictures, 1993.

Kaapa, Pietari, and Guan Wenbo. "Santa Claus in China and Wi xia in Finland: Translocal Reception of Transnational Cinema in Finnish and Chinese Film Cultures." *Journal of Audience and Reception Studies* 8, no. 2 (2011): 24–51.

Kammerer, Cornelia A. "Customs and Christian Conversion among Akha Highlanders of Burma and Thailand." *American Ethnologist* 17, no. 2 (1990): 277–91.

Karen News. "Home." http://karennews.org/.

Katz, Elihu. "The Two-Step Flow of Communication: An Up-To-Date Report on an Hypothesis." *Public Opinion Quarterly* 21, no. 1 (1957): 61–78.

Katz, Elihu, John Durham Peters, Tamar Liebes, and Avril Orloff. *Canonic Texts in Media Research: Are There Any? Should There Be? How About These?* Cambridge: Polity, 2002.

Kaur, Raminder, and William Mazzarella. *Censorship in South Asia: Cultural Regulation from Sedition to Seduction*. Bloomington: Indiana University Press, 2009.

Keeping Up with the Kardashians. Television. Directed by Chris Ray. Bunim-Murray Productions (BMP) and Ryan Seacrest Productions, 2013.

Kenny, James F. "TV Viewing among TV Set Ownders and Non-Owners in a Remote Philippine Province." *Journal of Broadcasting and Electronic Media* 40, no. 2 (1996): 227–42.

Keown-Bomar, Julie. *Kinship Networks among Hmong-American Refugees*. New York: LFB Scholarly Publications, 2004.

Kibreab, Gaim. "Citizenship Rights and Repatriation of Refugees." *International Migration Review* 37, no. 1 (2003): 24–73.

KhosraviNik, Majid. "The Representation of Refugees, Asylum Seekers and Immigrants in British Newspapers during the Balkan Conflict (1999) and the British General Election (2005)." *Discourse and Society* 20, no. 4 (2009): 477–98.

———. "The Representation of Refugees, Asylum Seekers and Immigrants in British Newspapers: A Critical Discourse Analysis." *Journal of Language and Politics* 9, no. 1 (2010): 1–28.

Kim, Youna. *Transnational Migration, Media and Identity of Asian Women: Diasporic Daughters.* New York: Routledge, 2011.

Kim, Young Y. *Becoming Intercultural: An Integrative Theory of Communication and Cross-Cultural Adaptation.* Thousand Oaks, CA: Sage Publications, 2001.

———. *Communication and Cross-Cultural Adaptation: An Integrative Theory.* Clevedon, UK: Multilingual Matters, 1988.

———. *Becoming Intercultural: An Integrative Theory of Communication and Cross-Cultural Adaptation.* Thousand Oaks, CA: Sage Publications, 2001.

Kiver, Phil. *182 Days in Iraq.* Pittsburgh: Word Association Publishers, 2006.

Klinger, Barbara. "Contraband Cinema: Piracy, Titanic, and Central Asia." *Cinema Journal* 39, no. 2 (2010): 106–24.

Kraidy, Marwan M. *Reality Television and Arab Politics: Contention in Public Life.* Cambridge: Cambridge University Press, 2010.

Kroll, Jerome, Ahmed Ismail Yusuf, and Koji Fujiwara. "Psychoses, PTSD, and Depression in Somali Refugees in Minnesota." *Social Psychiatry and Psychiatric Epidemiology* 46, no. 6 (2011): 481–93.

Krumov, Krum, and Knud S. Larsen. *Cross-Cultural Psychology: Why Culture Matters.* Charlotte, NC: Information Age Publications, 2013.

Kulick, Don, and Margaret Willson. "Rambo's Wife Saves the Day: Subjugating the Gaze and Subverting the Narrative in a Papua New Guinean Swamp." *Visual Anthropology Review* 10, no. 2 (1994): 1–13.

Lænkholm, Christer. "Resettlement for Bhutanese Refugees." *Forced Migration Review* 29 (2007): 59–60.

Lang, H. J. "Women as Refugees: Perspectives from Burma." *Cultural Survival Quarterly* 19, no. 1 (1995): 54–58.

Latour, Bruno. *The Pasteurization of France.* Cambridge: Harvard University Press, 1993.

Lazarsfeld, Paul, and Robert K. Merton. "Mass Communication, Popular Taste, and Organized Social Action." In *The Communication of Ideas*, edited by Lyman Bryson. New York: Institute for Religious and Social Studies, 1948.

Lee, Yew Liang, and Barry R. Chiswick. "Parents and Children Talk: English Language Proficiency within Immigrant Families." *Review of Economics of the Household* 3, no. 3 (2005): 243–68.

Leibes, Tamar, and Elihu Katz. *The Export of Meaning: Cross Cultural Readings of Dallas.* New York: Oxford University Press, 1990.

Leudar, Ivan, Jacqueline Hayes, Jiří Nekvapil, and Johanna Turner Baker. "Hostility Themes in Media, Community and Refugee Narratives." *Discourse and Society* 19, no. 2 (2008): 187–221.

Leung, Linda, Cath Finney Lamb, and Liz Emrys. *Technology's Refuge: The Use of Technology by Asylum Seekers and Refugees.* Sydney: University of Technology Sydney Press, 2009.

Lichtman, Karen Melissa. "Child-Adult Differences in Implicit and Explicit Second Language Learning." PhD diss., University of Illinois at Urbana-Champaign, 2012.

Lie, Rico. *Spaces of Intercultural Communication: An Interdisciplinary Introduction to Communication, Culture, and Globalizing/Localizing Identities*. Cresskill, NJ: Hampton Press, 2003.

Lincoln, Yvonna S., and Egon G. Guba. *Constructivist Credo*. Walnut Creek, CA: Left Coast Press, 2013.

Lindley, Anna. *The Early Morning Phone Call: Somali Refugees' Remittances*. New York: Berghahn Books, 2010.

Livingstone, Sonia. "The Influences of Personal Influence on the Study of Audiences." *Annals of the American Academy of Political and Social Science* 608, no. 1 (2006): 233–50.

Loke, Jaime. "Readers' Debate a Local Murder Trial: 'Race' in the Online Public Sphere." *Communication, Culture and Critique* 6, no. 1 (2013): 179–200.

Lopes-Cardozo, Barbara, Sharmila Shetty, Trong Ao, Eboni Taylor, Emily Lankau, Teresa I. Sivilli, and Curtis Blanton. "An Investigation into Suicides among Bhutanese Refugees in the U.S. 2009–2012: Stakeholders Report." *Centers for Disease Control and Prevention*, 2012. http://www.azdhs.gov/phs/edc/odis/refugee/documents/bhutanese-suicide-stakeholder-report-oct12.pdf.

Making Your Way: A Reception and Placement Orientation Curriculum. Washington, DC: Center for Applied Linguistics and the Cultural Orientation Resource Center, 2013.

Manovich, Lev. *The Language of New Media*. Cambridge, MA: MIT Press, 2001.

Manzo, Ula Casale, Anthony V. Manzo, and Matthew M. Thomas. *Content Area Literacy: A Framework for Reading-Based Instruction*. Hoboken, NJ: John Wiley and Sons, 2009.

Martin, Daniel C., and James E. Yankay. "Annual Report: Refugees and Asylees 2012." *Department of Homeland Security*, 2012. Accessed April 13, 2013. http://www.dhs.gov/sites/default/files/publications/ois_rfa_fr_2012.pdf.

Martin, Judith N., and Thomas K. Nakayama. *Intercultural Communication in Contexts*. Boston: McGraw-Hill, 2007.

Masterson, Daniel. "An American Dream: The Broken Iraqi Refugee Resettlement Program and How to Fix It." *Kennedy School Review* 10 (2010): 4.

Mateen, Farrah J., Marco Carone, Sayre Nyce, Jad Ghosn, Timothy Mutuerandu, Huda Al-Saedy, Daniel H. Lowenstein, and Gilbert Burnham. "Neurological Disorders in Iraqi Refugees in Jordan: Data from The United Nations Refugee Assistance Information System." *Journal of Neurology* 259, no. 4 (2012): 694–701.

McCarthy, Florence E., and Margaret H. Vickers. *Refugee and Immigrant Students: Achieving Equity in Education*. Charlotte, NC: Information Age Publications, 2012.

McCluskey, Michael, and Jay Hmielowski. "Opinion Expression during Social Conflict: Comparing Online Reader Comments and Letters to the Editor." *Journalism* 13, no. 3 (April 2012): 303–19.

McCombs, Maxwell E., and Donald L. Shaw. "The Agenda-Setting Function of Mass Media." *Public Opinion Quarterly* 36, no. 2 (1972): 176–87.

McDonald, Theodore W., and Jaime N. Sand. *Post-Traumatic Stress Disorder in Refugee Communities: The Importance of Culturally Sensitive Screening, Diagnosis, and Treatment*. New York: Nova Science, 2010.

McGee, Michael C. "In Search Of 'The People': A Rhetorical Alternative." *Quarterly Journal of Speech* 61, no. 3 (1975): 235–49.

McKay, Fiona H., Samantha L. Thomas, Kate Holland, R. Warwick Blood, and Susan Kneebone. "'AIDS Assassins': Australian Media's Portrayal of HIV-Positive Refugees Who Deliberately Infect Others." *Journal of Immigrant and Refugee Studies* 9, no. 1 (2011): 20–37.

McKerrow, Raymie E. "Critical Rhetoric: Theory and Praxis." *Communication Monographs* 56, no. 2 (1989): 91–111.

McKinnon, Sara. "Rhetorical Dimensions of Forced Migration: Using Transnational Feminist Theory to Make Rhetoric Relevant." Paper presented at the annual meeting of the National Communication Association, November 21–24, 2008, San Diego, California.

———. "'Bringing New Hope and New Life': The Rhetoric of Faith-Based Refugee Resettlement Agencies." *Howard Journal of Communications* 20, no. 4 (2009): 313–32.

———. "(In)Hospitable Publics: Theorizing Modalities of Access to U.S. Publics." *Public Modalities*, edited by R. Asen and D.C. Brouwer, 132–53. Tuscaloosa: University of Alabama Press, 2010.

McLuhan. Marshall. *Understanding Media: The Extensions of Man*. New York: Signet, 1964.

Mediascribe. "Transcription Services: Oral History is Our Specialty." http://www.mediascribe.us/.

Mehrotra, Ateev, Alan M. Zaslavsky, and John Z. Ayanian. "Preventive Health Examinations and Preventive Gynecological Examinations in the United States." *Journal of the American Medical Association* 167, no. 17 (2007): 1876–83.

Michel, Eva. "The Role of Individual Differences in Cognitive Skills in Children's Learning through Film." *Journal of Media Psychology* 22, no. 3 (2010): 105–13.

Miller, J. M., S. P. Wahlquist, L. H. Weld, R. B. Wainwright, B. D. Gushulak, M. S. Cetron, H. A. Boyd, S. R. Ostrowski, S. T. Cookson, M. E. Parise, P. S. Gonzaga, D. G. Addiss, M. Wilson, and P. Nguyen-Dinh. "Malaria, Intestinal Parasites, and Schistosomiasis among Barawan Somali Refugees Resettling to the United States: A Strategy to Reduce Morbidity and Decrease the Risk of Imported Infections." *American Journal of Tropical Medicine and Hygiene* 62, no. 1 (2000): 115–21.

Miller, Toby. *Cultural Citizenship: Cosmopolitanism, Consumerism, and Television in a Neoliberal Age*. Philadelphia: Temple University Press, 2006.

Mills, Charles. "White Ignorance." In *Race And Epistemologies of Ignorance*, edited by Shannon Sullivan and Nancy Tuana, 11–38. Albany: State University of New York Press, 2007.

Mirici, Ismail Hakkı, Rebecca Galleano, and Kelly Torres. "Immigrant Parent vs. Immigrant Children: Attitudes toward Language Learning in the U.S." *Novitas-Royal* 7, no. 2 (2013): 137–46.

Mowafi, Hani, and Paul Spiegel. "The Iraqi Refugee Crisis: Familiar Problems and New Challenges." *JAMA: The Journal of the American Medical Association* 299, no. 14 (2008): 1713–15.

Mukherjee, Sipra. "Reading Language and Religion Together." *International Journal of the Sociology of Language*, no. 220 (2013): 1–6.

Mukti. Video. Directed by Kishor Subba. Produced by Jenita Movie Makers P. Ltd., jointly made by Southern Ilam Christian Society and Gospel for Asia Publications.

Mummery, Jane, and Debbie Rodan. "Discursive Australia: Refugees, Australianness, and the Australian Public Sphere." *Continuum: Journal of Media and Cultural Studies* 21, no. 3 (2007): 347–60.

Naficy, Hamid. *Home, Exile, Homeland: Film, Media, and the Politics of Place*. New York: Routledge, 1999.

Nawyn, Stephanie J. "Institutional Structures of Opportunity in Refugee Resettlement: Gender, Race Ethnicity, and Refugee NGOs." *Journal of Sociology and Social Welfare* 37, no. 1 (2010): 149–67.

———. "Faith, Ethnicity, and Culture in Refugee Resettlement." *American Behavioral Scientist* 49, no. 11 (2006): 1509 27.

———. *Faithfully Providing Refuge: The Role of Religious Organizations in Refugee Assistance and Advocacy*. San Diego: University of California, San Diego, and the Center for Comparative Immigration Studies, 2005.

Nezer, Melanie. *Resettlement at Risk: Meeting Emerging Challenges to Resettlement in Local Communities*. New York: Hebrew Immigrant Aid Society, 2013.
Niles, Chris. "Somali Refugees Crowd Camps in Kenya amid Record-Setting Drought." *UNICEF*, July 13, 2011. http://www.unicefusa.org/news/news-from-the-field/drought-somali-refugees.html.
Nord, David Paul. *Communities of Journalism: A History of American Newspapers and Their Readers*. Chicago: University of Illinois Press, 2006.
Office of Temporary and Disability Assistance in New York State. "Electronic Benefits Transfer." Last modified June 2013. http://otda.ny.gov/programs/ebt/.
Oh, David C. "Viewing Identity: Second-Generation Korean American Ethnic Identification and the Reception of Korean Transnational Films." *Communication, Culture and Critique* 4, no. 2 (2011): 184–204.
Olson, David R. *The World on Paper: The Conceptual and Cognitive Implications of Writing and Reading*. Cambridge: Cambridge University Press, 1994.
Omoniyi, Tope. *The Sociology of Language and Religion: Change, Conflict and Accommodation*. Basingstoke: Palgrave Macmillan, 2010.
Omoniyi, Tope, and Joshua A. Fishman. *Explorations in the Sociology of Language and Religion*. Philadelphia: John Benjamin's Publishing Company, 2006.
Ong, Aihwa. *Buddha is Hiding: Refugees, Citizenship, and the New America*. Berkeley: University of California Press, 2003.
Ong, Aihwa, Virginia R. Dominguez, Jonathan Friedman, Nina Glick Schiller, Verena Stolcke, David Y. H. Wu, and Hu Ying. "Cultural Citizenship as Subject-Making: Immigrants Negotiate Racial and Cultural Boundaries in the United States." *Current Anthropology* 37, no. 55 (1996): 737–62.
Ong, Jonathan Corpus. "Watching the Nation, Singing the Nation: London-Based Filipino Migrants' Identity Constructions in News and Karaoke Practices." *Communication, Culture and Critique* 2, no. 2 (2009): 160–81.
Ono, Kent A., and John M. Sloop. *Shifting Borders: Rhetoric, Immigration, and California's Proposition 187*. Philadelphia: Temple University Press, 2002.
Ono, Kent A., and Vincent N. Pham. *Asian Americans and the Media*. Cambridge: Polity, 2009.
Oral History Association. "About OHA." Last modified October 2009. Accessed March 4, 2013. http://www.oralhistory.org/about/.
———. "Introduction." Last modified October 2009. Accessed March 4, 2013. http://www.oralhistory.org/about/principles-and-practices/#intro.
———. "Principles and Best Practices." Last modified October 2009. http://www.oralhistory.org/about/principles-and-practices/.
Ortiz, Fernando. *Cuban Counterpoint, Tobacco and Sugar*. New York: Alfred Knopf, 1947.
O'Toole, Christine. "Pittsburgh's New Immigrants Equal Brain Gain." *Pittsburgh Post-Gazette*, May 27, 2012. http://www.post-gazette.com/local/region/2012/05/27/Pittsburgh-s-new-immigrants-equal-brain-gain/stories/201205270140.
Oxford, Rebecca, Sukero Ito Young Park-Oh, and Malenna Sumrall. "Learning a Language by Satellite Television: What Influences Student Achievement?" *System* 21, no. 1 (1993): 31–48.
Paganos, Jennifer. "Nepal: Generous U.S. Resettlement Offer May Help Break Bhutanese Deadlock." *UNHCR Briefing Notes*, October 6, 2006. http://www.unhcr.org/45262b462.html.
Parameswaran, Radhika. "Reading Fictions of Romance: Gender, Sexuality, and Nationalism in Postcolonial India." *Journal of Communication* 52, no. 4 (2002): 832–51.

"Part 7." In *Risks and Reconstruction: Experiences of Resettlers and Refugees*, edited by Michael M. Cernea and Chris McDowell, 291–362. Washington, DC: World Bank Publications, 2000.

Paterson, Ashley D., and Julie Hakim-Larson. "Arab Youth in Canada: Acculturation, Enculturation, Social Support, and Life Satisfaction." *Journal of Multicultural Counseling and Development* 40, no. 4 (2012): 206–15.

Penfield, Joyce. *The Media: Catalysts for Communicative Language Learning*. Reading, MA: Addison-Wesley, 1987.

Pessar, Patricia R., and Pamela M. Graham. "The Dominicans: Transnational Identities and Local Politics." In *New Immigrants in New York*, edited by Nancy Foner, 251–74. New York: Columbia University Press, 2001.

Peters, John Durham. *Speaking into the Air: A History of the Idea of Communication*. Chicago: University of Chicago Press, 1999.

Peterson, Mark. *Computer Games and Language Learning*. New York: Palgrave Macmillan, 2013.

Peterson, William. "A General Typology of Migration." *American Sociological Review* 23, no. 3 (1958): 256–66.

Philipsen, Gerry. "A Theory of Speech Codes." In *Developing Communication Theories*, edited by Terrance L. Albrecht and Gerry Philipsen, 119–56. Albany, NY: Tate University of New York Press, 1997.

Phillips, Melissa Anne. "Re-Visualising New Arrivals in Australia: Journey Narratives of Pre-Migration and Settlement." PhD Diss., the University of Melbourne, 2012.

Pinter, Annamaria. *Children Learning Second Languages*. New York: Palgrave Macmillan, 2011.

Podber, Jacob J. *The Electronic Front Porch: An Oral History of the Arrival of Modern Media in Rural Appalachia and the Melungeon Community*. Macon, GA: Mercer University Press, 2007.

———. "Early Radio in Rural Appalachia: An Oral History." *Journal of Radio Studies* 8, no. 2 (2001): 388–410.

Poole, Amanda. "Ransoms, Remittances, and Refugees: The Gatekeeper State in Eritrea." *Africa Today* 60, no. 2 (2013): 67–82.

Portelli, Alessandro. "The Peculiarities of Oral History." *History Workshop*, 12 (1981): 96–107.

Radway, Janice. *Reading the Romance: Women, Patriarchy, and Popular Literature*. Chapel Hill: University of North Carolina Press, 1984.

Ramsden, Robyn. "'It Was the Most Beautiful Country I Have Ever Seen': The Role of Somali Narratives in Adapting to a New Country." *Journal of Refugee Studies* 26, no. 2 (2013): 226–46.

Razavi, Minoo. "Navigating New National Identity Online: On Immigrant Children, Identity, and the Internet." MA Thesis, Georgetown University, 2013.

"Refugee Journalists Emphasize the Importance of Community Radio in Dadaab at a High Profile United Nations Panel in Geneva." *Internews*, August 13, 2013. http://internews.org/our-stories/project-updates/radio-you-can-reach-everyone-camps-everyone-will-listen.

"Resettlement by Country." In *World Refugee Survey 2009*, 29. United States Committee for Refugees and Immigrants: 2009.

Rey, Jay. "Refugees Get First Taste of Thanksgiving Traditions." *The Buffalo News*, November 23, 2013. http://www.buffalonews.com/city-region/refugees-get-first-taste-of-thanksgiving-traditions-20131123.

Riles, Annelise. *Documents: Artifacts of Modern Knowledge*. Ann Arbor: University of Michigan Press, 2006.

Rinchon, Kinley. "Media and Public Culture: Media Whitewashing." In *Proceedings of the Second International Seminar on Bhutan Studies*, 221–35. Thimphu, Bhutan: Center for Bhutanese Studies, 2007.

Robertson, Cheryl Lee, Linda Halcon, Kay Savik, David Johnson, Marline Spring, James Butcher, Joseph Westermeyer, and James Jaranson. "Somali and Oromo Refugee Women: Trauma and Associated Factors." *Journal of Advanced Nursing* 56, no. 6 (2006): 577–87.

Robins, Melinda B. "'Lost Boys' and the Promised Land: U.S. Newspaper Coverage of Sudanese Refugees." *Journalism* 4, no. 1 (2003): 29–49.

Rocky. Video. Directed by John G. Avildsen. Santa Monica: MGM Home Studios, 1976.

Rollins, Peter C. *Benjamin Lee Whorf: Lost Generation Theories of Mind, Language, and Religion*. Ann Arbor, MI: University Microfilms International, 1980.

Romer, Daniel, Kathleen Hall Jamieson, and Sean Aday. "Television News and the Cultivation of Fear of Crime." *Journal of Communication* 53, no. 1 (2003): 88–104.

Rugunanan, Pragna, and Ria Smit. "Seeking Refuge in South Africa: Challenges Facing a Group of Congolese and Burundian Refugees." *Development Southern Africa* 28, no. 5 (2011): 705–18.

Rushing, Janice Hocker. "Power, Other, and Spirit in Cultural Texts." *Western Journal of Communication* 57, no. 2 (1993): 159–68.

Russeau, Cecile, Taher M. Said, Marie-Jose Gagne, and Gilles Bibeau. "Between Myth and Madness: The Premigration Dream of Leaving Among Young Somali Refugees." *Culture, Medicine and Psychiatry* 22, no. 4 (1998): 385–411.

Sabah, Zaid. "Pirated DVDs among Hottest Items on Shelves," *U.S.A. Today*, January 20, 2006.

Saghaye-Biria, Hakimeh. "American Muslims as Radicals? A Critical Discourse Analysis of the U.S. Congressional Hearing on 'The Extent of Radicalization in the American Muslim Community and That Community's Response'." *Discourse and Society* 25, no. 5 (2012): 508–24.

Said, Edward W. *Orientalism*. London: Penguin, 2003.

Salomone, Rosemary C. *True American: Language, Identity, and the Education of Immigrant Children*. Cambridge: Harvard University Press, 2010.

Schweitzer, Robert, Fritha Melville, Zachary Steel, and Philippe Lacherez. "Trauma, Post-Migration Living Difficulties, and Social Support as Predictors of Psychological Adjustment in Resettled Sudanese Refugees." *Australian and New Zealand Journal of Psychiatry* 40, no. 2 (2006): 179–87.

Schweitzer, Robert, Shelley Perkoulidis, Sandra Krome, Christopher Ludlow, and Melanie Ryan. "Attitudes Towards Refugees: The Dark Side of Prejudice in Australia." *Australian Journal of Psychology* 57, no. 3 (2005): 170–79.

Scollon, Ronald, Suzanne B.K. Scollon, and Rodney H. Jones. *Intercultural Communication: A Discourse Approach*. Malden, MA: Blackwell Publishers, 2001.

Scott Jr., George M. "The Lao Hmong Refugees in San Diego: Their Religious Transformation and its Implications for Geertz's Thesis." *Ethnic Studies Report* 5 (1987): 32–46.

Sherstha, Christie. *Power and Politics in Resettlement: A Case Study of Bhutanese Refugees in the U.S.A.* Geneva: United Nations High Commissioner for Refugees, 2011.

Simon, Rita J. *Public Opinion and the Immigrant: Print Media Coverage, 1880–1980*. Lexington, MA: Lexington Books, 1985.

Slade, Christina. "Media and Citizenship: Transnational Television Cultures Reshaping Political Identities in the European Union." *Journalism* 11, no. 6 (2010): 727–33.

Smith-Hefner, Nancy J. "Ethnicity and the Force of Faith: Christian Conversion among Khmer Refugees." *Anthropological Quarterly* 67, no. 1 (1994): 24–38.

Sollors, Werner. *Beyond Ethnicity: Consent and Descent in American Culture*. London: Oxford University Press, 1987.
Sommer, Mark. "Refugees Turn Hard Work into Better Future through Programs Here." *The Buffalo News*, December 2, 2013. http://www.buffalonews.com/business/refugees-turn-hard-work-into-better-future-through-programs-here-20131202#comment-1148818119.
Sooyoungand, Cho, and Hong Youngshin. "Netizens' Evaluations of Corporate Social Responsibility: Content Analysis of CSR News Stories and Online Readers' Comments," Paper presented at the annual meeting of the National Communication Association, Chicago, IL, November 2007.
Sophocles. *The Dramas of Sophocles*. New York: E. P. Dutton, 1906.
Souter, James. "Refugee Studies: The Challenge of Translating Hope into Reality." *Open Democracy*, January 8, 2013. http://www.opendemocracy.net/5050/james-souter/refugee-studies-challenge-of-translating-hope-into-reality.
Speare, Alden. "The Relevance of Models of Internal Migration for the Study of International Migration. In *International Migration: Proceedings of a Seminar on Demographic Research in Relation to International Migration*, edited by G. Tapinos. Buenos Aires, Argentina: CICRED, 1974.
Spitulnik, Deborah. "Anthropology and Mass Media," *Annual Review of Anthropology* 22 (1993): 293–315.
Steimel, S. J. "Refugees as People: The Portrayal of Refugees in American Human Interest Stories." *Journal of Refugee Studies* 23, no. 2 (2010): 219–37.
Stevenson, Nick. *Cultural Citizenship: Cosmopolitan Questions*. Maidenhead, UK: Open University Press Maidenhead, 2003.
Strauss, Harry L., and J. R. Kidd. *Look, Listen, and Learn: A Manual on the Use of Audio-Visual Materials in Informal Education*. New York: Association Press, 1948.
Subramanian, Ramesh. "The Growth of Global Internet Censorship and Circumvention: A Survey." *Communications of the IIMA* 11, no. 2 (2011): 69–90.
Sulaiman-Hill, Cheryl R., Sandra C. Thompson, Rita Afsar, and Toshi L. Hodliffe. "Changing Images of Refugees: A Comparative Analysis of Australian and New Zealand Print Media 1998–2008." *Journal of Immigrant and Refugee Studies* 9, no. 4 (2011): 345–66.
Sunoo, Don H., Edgar P. Trotter, and Ronald L. Aames. "Media Use and Learning of English by Immigrants." *Journalism Quarterly* 57, no. 22 (1980): 330–33.
Svenberg, Kristian, Carola Skott, and Margret Lepp. "Ambiguous Expectations and Reduced Confidence: Experience of Somali Refugees." *Journal of Refugee Studies* 24, no. 4 (2011): 690–705.
Taft, Julia Vadala, David S. North, David A. Ford, and the United States Social Security Administration. *Refugee Resettlement in the U.S.: Time for a New Focus*. Washington DC: New TransCentury Foundation, 1979.
The Ellen DeGeneres Show. Television. Burbank: Telepictures, 2003–present.
The Great Gatsby. Video. Directed by Jack Clayton. Hollywood: Paramount Pictures, 1974.
The Pursuit of Happyness. DVD. Directed by Gabriele Muccino. Culver City: Sony Pictures Home Entertainment, 2006.
The State of the World's Refugees 2012: In Search of Solidarity. Geneva: United Nations High Commissioner for Refugees, 2012.
The Terminator. Video. Directed by James Cameron. Santa Monica: MGM Home Entertainment, 1984.
Thomas, William G. "Experiential Education: A Rationale for Creative Problem Solving." *Education and Urban Society* 7, no. 2 (1975): 1972–81.

Thomas, William Isaac, Florian Znaniecki, and Eli Zaretsky. *The Polish Peasant in Europe and America: A Classic Work in Immigration History*. Urbana: University Of Illinois Press, 1996.
Thomson, Alistair. "Four Paradigm Transformations in Oral History." *Oral History Review*, 34, no. 1 (2007): 49–70.
Thweatt, Tatyana S. "Attitudes towards New Americans in the Local Press: A Critical Discourse Analysis." *North Dakota Journal of Speech and Theatre* 18 (2005): 25–43.
Titanic. Video. Directed by James Cameron. Hollywood: Paramount Pictures, 1997.
Trebbe, Joachim, and Philomen Schoenhagen. "Ethnic Minorities in the Mass Media: Always the Same and Always Negative." Paper presented at the annual meeting for the International Communication Association, Montreal, Quebec, Canada, May 21, 2008.
Trevorton, Gregory F. *Film Piracy, Organized Crime, and Terrorism*. Santa Monica, CA: Rand Corporation, 2008.
Turner, James. *Language, Religion, Knowledge: Past and Present*. Notre Dame, IN: University of Notre Dame Press, 2003.
Turner, Rhiannon N., and Rupert Brown. "Improving Children's Attitudes toward Refugees: An Evaluation of a School-Based Multicultural Curriculum and an Anti-Racist Intervention." *Journal of Applied Social Psychology* 38, no. 5 (2008): 1295–328.
United Nations High Commissioner for Refugees (UNHCR). "1951 Convention on the Status of Refugees." Last modified 2010. http://www.unhcr.org/3b66c2aa10.html.
———. "2013 UNHCR Country Operations Profile—Somalia." Accessed June 20, 2013. http://www.unhcr.org/pages/49e483ad6.html.
———. "2014 UNHCR Country Operations Profile–Myanmar." Last modified 2014. http://www.unhcr.org/pages/49e4877d6.html.
United States Citizenship and Immigration Services. "Iraqi Refugee Processing Fact Sheet." Last modified June 6, 2013. Accessed June 20, 2013. http://www.Uscis.Gov/Portal/Site/Uscis/Menuitem.5af9bb95919f35e66f614176543f6d1a/?Vgnextchannel=68439c7755cb9010vgnvcm10000045f3d6a1rcrd&Vgnextoid=Df4c47c9de5ba110vgnvcm1000004718190arcrd.
United States Committee for Refugees and Immigrants. "Frequently Asked Questions." Last modified 2011. http://www.refugees.org/about-us/faqs.html.
United States for Refugees and Immigrants. "World Refugee Survey 2009: Nepal." Last modified 2009. http://www.refugees.org/resources/refugee-warehousing/archived-world-refugee-surveys/2009-wrs-country-updates/nepal.html.
United States Department of Health and Human Services: Administration for Children and Families, Office of Refugee Resettlement. "History." http://www.acf.hhs.gov/programs/orr/about/history.
———. "Refugee Arrival Data." http://www.acf.hhs.gov/programs/orr/resource/refugee-arrival-data.
———. "Report to Congress 2009." http://www.acf.hhs.gov/programs/orr/resource/annual-orr-reports-to-congress.
United States Department of Homeland Security. "Definition of Terms." http://www.dhs.gov/definition-terms#15.
United States Department of State. "Posttraumatic Stress Disorder." http://www.state.gov/m/med/dsmp/c44953.htm.
United States Department of State, Bureau of Consular Affairs. "Special Immigrant Visas for Iraqis Who Were Employed by/on Behalf of the U.S. Government: Iraqi SIV Program Extended." Last modified 2014. http://travel.state.gov/content/visas/english/immigrate/types/iraqis-work-for-us.html?cq_ck=1337693754375.

United States Department of State, Bureau of Population, Refugees and Migration. "The U.S. Refugee Admissions Program Report on Recent Progress and Challenges, Including Security Screening Procedures." Last modified July 26, 2011. http://www.state.gov/j/prm/releases/letters/2011/181130.htm.

United States Department of State, Bureau of Population, Refugees, and Migration (PRM), Worldwide Refugee Admissions Processing System (WRAPS). "Annual Flow Report 2012." Accessed June 1, 2013. http://www.dhs.gov/sites/default/files/publications/ois_rfa_fr_2012.pdf.

United States Department of State, United States Department of Homeland Security, United States Department of Health and Human Services. "Proposed Refugee Admissions for Fiscal Year 2012: Report to the Congress." http://www.state.gov/documents/organization/181378.pdf.

United States of America, Department of State, Bureau for Population, Refugees, and Migration, Cultural Orientation Resource Center. *Welcome to the United States: A Guidebook for Refugees*. Washington, DC: Cultural Orientation Resource Center and Center for Applied Linguistics, 2012. http://www.culturalorientation.net/resources-for-refugees/welcome-set.

Vallejo, Mari-Luisa, Peter Simon, and Jiachen Zou. "Resettlement of Refugees from Africa and Iraq in Rhode Island: The Impact of Violence and Burden of Disease." *Medicine and Health, Rhode Island* 92, no. 9 (2009): 318–19.

van Dijk, Teun A. "New(s) Racism: A Discourse Analytic Approach." In *Ethnic Minorities and the Media*, edited by S. Cottle, 33–49. Buckingham, UK: Open University Press, 2000.

———. *News Analysis: Case Studies of International and National News in the Press*. Hillsdale: L. Erlbaum, 1987.

Vize, Anne. "Engaging ESL Students in Media Literacy." *Screen Education* 61 (2011): 78–81.

Waisanen, Don. "Bordering Populism in Immigration Activism: Outlaw–Civic Discourse and a (Counter)Public." *Communication Monographs* 79, no. 2 (2012): 232–55.

Walker, Doug. "The Media's Role in Immigrant Adaption: How First-Year Haitians in Miami use the Media." *Journalism and Communication Monographs* 1, no. 3 (1999): 159–96.

Walsh, Christine A., Dave Este, and Brigette Krieg. "The Enculturation Experience of Roma Refugees: A Canadian Perspective." *British Journal of Social Work* 38, no. 5 (2008): 900–17.

Walsh, Kevin. "Victims of a Growing Crisis: A Call for Reform of the United States Immigration Law and Policy Pertaining to Refugees of the Iraq War." *Villanova Law Review* 53 (2008): 421–973.

Wander, Philip. "The Rhetoric of American Foreign Policy." *Quarterly Journal of Speech* 70, no. 4 (1984): 339–61.

Wasserman, Herman, and Patrice Kayeya-Mwepu. "Creating Connections: Exploring the Intermediary Use of ICTs by Congolese Refugees at Tertiary Educational Institutions in Cape Town." *African Journal of Information and Communication* 6 (2005): 94–103.

Webb, Stuart. "Pre-Learning Low-Frequency Vocabulary in Second Language Television Programmes." *Language Teaching Research* 14, no. 4 (2010): 501–15.

Welcome to the United States. DVD. Washington, DC: Cultural Orientation Resource Center, 2012.

What Lies Beneath. Video. Directed by Robert Zemeckis. Glendale: Dreamworks SKG, 2000.

White, James Boyd. *Heracles' Bow*. Madison: University of Wisconsin, 1985.

Wilding, Raelene. "'Virtual' Intimacies? Families Communicating across Transnational Contexts." *Global Networks* 6, no. 2 (2006): 125–42.

Williams, Tennessee. *The Cat on a Hot Tin Roof: A Play in Three Acts*. New York: Dramatists Play Service, 1983.

Witteborn, Saskia. "Identity Mobilization Practices of Refugees: The Case of Iraqis in the United States and the War in Iraq." *Journal of International and Intercultural Communication* 1, no. 3 (2008): 202–20.

Wodak, Ruth. "The Genesis of Racist Discourse in Austria since 1989." In *Texts and Practices: Readings on Discourse Analysis*, edited by C. R. Caldas-Coulthard and M. Coulthard, 107–28. London: Routledge, 1996.

Young, Wendy, Sandee Pyne, Diana Quick, and Megan McKenna. *Abuse without End: Burmese Refugee Women and Children at Risk of Trafficking*. New York: Women's Commission for Refugee Women and Children, 2006. http://www.refworld.org/docid/48aa82ff0.html.

Yow, Valerie Raleigh. *Recording Oral History: A Guide for the Humanities and Social Sciences*. Walnut Creek, CA: Altamira Press, 2005.

Zboray, Ronald. *A Fictive People: Antebellum Economic Development and the American Reading Public*. Oxford: Oxford University Press, 1993.

Zhimei, Xu, and Ratha Dilip. *Migration and Remittances Factbook 2008*. Washington: World Bank Publications, 2008.

INDEX

Abiyow, Said 55, 70, 76
acculturation 21, 78, 79, 134, 143, 144, 152
acquisition 104–9
active audiences 48, 54note79, 90, 172
Aden, Fatuma 97, 98, 115
Alasuutari, Pertti 58
Alba, Lily 102, 150
Aldonco 147–8
Alhadithi, Saif 114, 115
Alhasani, Anmar 88–9, 123
Al Zehhawi, Wijdan 165–6
America's Funniest Home Videos 179note79
Amira 96–7, 105, 109, 163
Ana, Otto Santa 146
Anderson, Benedict 156; *Imagined Communities* 77
Appadurai, Arjun 43

Ba'ath 30
Baker, Johanna Turner 152
Barake, Abdikadir Abdiyow 55–6
Barthes, Roland 6
Bayara, Abreer 44, 74, 106, 165–7
Bazikiam, Edwin 39, 41, 52note54, 52note56
BBC 35, 52note56
Beldangi II Extension refugee camp 35, 91note19
Berry, John 134
Bhanu, Phuyel 154

Bhutan 4, 9, 24, 31–2; beautiful 31; eviction of Nepalese people 20, 153; language 31; media 34–5; media censorship 32
Bhutanese Citizenship Act 20
Bhutanese refugees 9, 11, 20, 26, 48note3, 69, 180; airplane travel 97; interaction with children 79; ongoing resettlement 158–9, 167, 168, 170, 172; post-arrival media acquisition 104, 106, 110; pre-arrival orientation 22, 64, 73, 74, 75, 79, 85, 100–1, 102; pre-arrival media encounters 24, 28, 31, 34, 35; religion 167, 168
Bieber, Justin 29
Black Hawk Down 21, 35
Blose, Amy: *Reception and Placement* 117–21, 130
Boghossian, Moses 47–8, 113, 114, 115, 162
Briggs, Charles 68, 132
Buffalo News 148; "Refugees Get First Taste of Thanksgiving Traditions" 147; "Refugees Turn Hard Work into Better Future through Programs Here" 147
Bureau of Population, Refugees, and Migration *see* U.S. Department of State: Bureau of Population, Refugees, and Migration

Index

Burma (Myanmar) 9, 26, 27, 28, 36, 40, 62, 73, 79, 84, 98, 104, 105, 115, 127–8, 142, 163, 180; employment 128; Karen 173note1; language 51note32, 173note1
Burmese Community Support Center 127, 142–43

Cambridge, Vibert 144
Carroll, Susan 160
cartoons 46–7, 109
Cat on a Hot Tin Roof 28
Center for Global Culture and Communication 60
Centers for Disease Control and Prevention 77
Champaign, Bishnu 86
Chappel, Jonathan 155
Child Protective Services 117
Chin 40
Christianity 165, 166, 167, 168
Clifford, James 14
CNN 35, 52note56, 146
communication 6, 12, 27, 36, 68, 92note39, 106, 137note42; intercultural 78; mediated 67, 164 "two-step flow" 33
Community Assistance and Refugee Resettlement 149
Cook, Robinson 71
Costner, Kevin 37
Couldry, Nick 68
Cultural Orientation Resource (COR) Center 13–14, 52note40, 60, 72, 84, 85, 116; *Making Your Way* 105, 107, 125–6, 127, 128–9, 133; *Welcome to the United States: A Guidebook for Refugees* 14, 56, 61, 62, 69, 70, 71, 72, 73, 74, 76, 79–82, 83, 87, 92note44, 97, 103, 105, 116, 121, 168, 181

Dadaab refugee camp 27, 32, 55, 65, 71, 99
Dallas 47, 54note77
Department of Homeland Security 18note26, 19note28, 82
deprivatization government 16; refugee 16, 98, 131–4, 141note101, 181
Dewey, John 98
Dohi, Hussein Al 37

Ellen DeGeneres Show 28
emotions 70, 78–82, 153
employment 4, 23, 41, 46, 53note62, 74–5, 102, 104, 106, 116, 123, 125–6, 137note32, 144, 153

enculturation 3, 21, 23, 26, 28, 43–8, 49note9, 56, 78–9, 82, 106, 152, 166, 173
England, Jennifer 157
Ernst, Jim 156
Eskander, Zahraa 27, 73, 162
Estefan, Linda 46–7, 48, 89
Esther 40–1, 43

Farrag, Mohamed 111
Fiske, John 28
forced migration 3, 4, 15, 16, 17note1, 174note16
Foreigners Act 48note3
formal cultural orientations 24, 49note11
Forum 146
Foss, Sonja K. 12
Foucault, Michel 61, 129
Fox News 146

Georgie! 105, 136note26
Great Gatsby, The 28, 35, 41, 45, 48
Gluck, Sherna 5
Goankar, Dilip Parameshwar 60
Gone with the Wind 46, 54note75
government agency self-representation 125–9
Gregory, Michelle Soski 156
Gubrium, Jaber 132
Gurung, Balaram 34, 36, 64–5, 158–9
Gurung, Bishnu 110

Hagio Studio Production 170
Harvey, David 6
Hauser, Gerard 148, 155
Hawa 86
Hayes, Jacqueline 152
Health and Human Services 8
Heinze, Andrew 2
Holstein, James 132
Hsa, Hsit 63–4, 70
Htoo, Kler 27
Htoo, Paw 36, 37
Hussain, Saddam 30

Ibraheem, Fadhail 38, 56
Ibrahim, Kalsumo 85, 103–4, 131
ideological criticism 12
Independence Day 40
informal education 20, 21, 22, 23, 28, 42, 48, 49note6
International Institute of Los Angeles 39, 102, 103, 130, 132, 150

International Organization for Migration (IOM) 17note1, 21, 32, 33, 49note5, 50note16, 51note38, 52note39, 56, 61, 62, 64–5, 69, 70, 73, 96, 100, 103, 115
International Rescue Committee 63
Internews 27
interpretive research 19note36
Iraq 4, 9; special immigrants 53note67
Iraq Communications and Media Commission 30
Iraqi refugees 9, 11, 52note54, 113, 180; audiences of U.S. media 29–30, 35, 37, 38, 39, 41, 44, 45, 46–7, 49note15, 50note16; ongoing resettlement 160–1, 162–5, 166, 169; post-arrival media acquisition 104, 105, 106, 107; post-arrival media encounters 96, 97, 102, 110, 111, 112, 113, 114–15, 123; pre-arrival media encounters 24, 28; predeparture U.S. media encounters 60, 65–6, 69, 73, 74, 75, 85, 88, 89; refugee camps 27; resettled in the United States 27
Iraq War 89
IRB 18note8
Iser, Wolfgang 68, 125
Izawa, Mann 136note26

Jackson, Dylanna 110
Jackson, Michael 29, 37, 42
Jama, Habiba 33–4, 36, 51note38, 52note39, 84, 104–5
Jewish Family and Children's Services 22
Jones, Diana Nelson: "Carrick Home for Ethnic Nepali Refugees" 153, 154, 159, 176note37
Journal of the American Medical Association 77
Journey from the Fall 21
Journey's End Refugee Services 13, 39, 121, 139note70, 146
Jurassic Park 35

Kakuma refugee camp 32, 33, 57
Karen 63, 142, 173note1
Kari, Laxmi Adhi 34, 74, 93note61
Katz, Elihu 33
Khanal, Govinda 28–9, 34, 36, 45
Khanal, Nirmala 28, 100–1
KhosraviNik, Majid 148
Khudunabari 20, 26, 48note3
Klien, Ramona 154
Kraidy, Marwan 30
Kulick, Don 28, 30

Latour, Bruno 128
Leudar, Ivan 151–2
living arrangements and media access, American 98–104
Loke, Jaime 153
"Lost Boys" 145
luggage 53note61, 69
Lutheran Immigration and Refugee Services 71

Madonna 37, 42
Mahmod, Mohammed 44
Making Your Way 105, 107, 125–6, 127, 128–9, 133
Mbere, Sitay 57
McKinnon, Sara 154
media about refugees in the United States 144–5
media and refugees' ongoing resettlement 142–79; friends and family 169–71; language and religion 164–8; media about refugees in the United States 144–5; refugees and Americans respond to news about refugees in the United States 151–64; refugees in U.S. news 145–51
Meh, OO 131, 133
Miller, Toby 67–8, 76, 106, 135note21
Minasaqen, Shiraz, 29–30, 36, 41, 43, 45, 113, 115
missing children notices 137note42
Mohammed, Abdikadir 123–4, 125
Monger, Bhim "John" 167
movies 24, 30, 35, 42, 51note38, 85, 96, 163, 168; action 37; American 25, 29, 34, 36, 38, 29–41, 44, 47, 110, 114; cowboys 47; depicting seasons 99; English 105; IOM 33; luxury portrayed in the United States 112; ordinary people in the United States 20; social system in the United States 44, 45–6, 75, 89, 111, 112, 113; State of Liberty 96–7; *see also* cartoons; orientation videos/films
Mugwaneza, Kheir 149–50, 157
Mukti 168, 178note70
Myae, Chan 105, 127–8, 142

Nekvapil, Jiri 152
Nor, Sahro 24–6, 79, 101, 108, 168, 170–2
Northern Area Multi-Service Center 34
Nyo, Yin 83

Onega, Matthew 153
Oral History Association (OHA) 5, 9
orientation content and context 61, 64–7, 69, 70, 129
orientation media, power of 67–9
orientation videos/films 42, 51note38, 61, 63, 66, 69, 85, 97, 98, 100; *see also Welcome to the United States*
Osmani, Khadija 115
O'Toole, Christine: "Pittsburgh's New Immigrants Equal Brain Gain" 157

Parameswaran, Rahika 28
Perhach, Robyn Juergen 157
Perry, Meghann 39, 40, 87, 113, 121, 139note70, 146–7, 148–9, 150
Peters, John Durham 44
Peterson, Mark 105
Pittsburgh Post-Gazette 153, 154, 155, 157, 176note37
Portelli, Alessandro 6
post-arrival orientations and orientation media 15, 98, 105, 107, 116–25, 126, 134, 141note97, 142, 143; *see also Making Your Way*; print media as a means to develop, standardize, and ensure fulfillment of orientation
predeparture orientation 13, 34, 57–63, 66, 67, 69, 70, 71, 73, 75, 79, 83, 84, 85, 86, 87, 90, 97, 98, 102, 116, 120, 121, 122, 131, 133, 181, 182
pre-relocation phase 23, 56
print media as a means to develop, standardize, and ensure fulfillment of orientation 129–31
Puerto Ricans 72
Pursuit of Happyness, The 20, 21, 23, 35, 113

Rai, Buddhi 41, 73
Rai, Sancha 20–3, 26, 36, 41, 48note3, 58, 79, 113, 150–1, 172, 179note79
Ramazani, Megeney 32, 33, 36, 51note38, 99–100, 101, 109
Rambo 34, 48
Rand 111–13, 129, 160–2, 173, 176note48
Raw, Paw Htoo 36
refugee anchor 54note73
refugee camps 1, 60, 64, 84, 101, 155, 169, 181–2; Beldangi II Extension 35; Dadaab 27, 32, 55, 65, 71, 99; Ethiopia 85; films 34, 51note38; Kakuma 32, 33, 57; Kenya 24, 27, 32, 55, 57, 99; Khudunabari 20, 26, 48note3; Malaysia 98–9; Nepal 20, 26, 29, 34, 35, 36, 48note3, 100; Sanischare 91note19; television 34; Thailand 26, 36, 63, 105–6, 135note11; *see also* orientation videos
refugee resettlement *see* media and refugees' ongoing resettlement
Refugee Resettlement Progress 70, 73
refugees and Americans respond to news about refugees in the United States 151–64
refugees as audiences of U.S. media in pre-arrival context 20–54; complicating enculturation through media 43–8; gaining access to U.S. media 28–37; sorting fact from fiction 37–43
refugees in U.S. news 145–51; refugees and Americans respond to news about 151–64
refugees' post-arrival U.S. media encounters 96–141; airplane travel 97; deprivatization 131–4; first days in the United States 109–16; government agency self-representation 125–9; making sense of American living arrangements and media access 98–104; perspectives on the importance of acquisition 104–9; post-arrival orientations and orientation media 116–25; print media as a means to develop, standardize, and ensure fulfillment of orientation 129–31
refugees' use of media in predeparture preparation and orientations 55–95; importance of visuality in orientation media 63–4; limited access to and disappointment with orientations and their media 84–7; power of orientation media 67–9; predeparture overseas orientations 58–63; relationship between orientation content and context 64–7; relocation preparation outside of orientation 88–90; *Welcome to the United States* 69–83
relocation preparation outside of orientation 88–90
repatriation 139note59
Resettlement Support Center 65–6; Cultural Orientation programs 60
Richards, Candi 156
Rimal, Tek 4, 31, 35–6, 38, 52note56, 62, 106, 157–8, 159, 182

Rinchen, Kinley: *Media and Public Culture in Bhutan* 31
Robins, Melinda B. 145–6
Rocky 29
RSC Thailand 63
Rudiak, Natalia 153

Said, Edward 151
San Diego Refugee Council 13
Sanischare refugee camp 91note19
Sauerbrey, Ellen 21
Schoenhagen, Philomen 144, 148
Seymo, Jasmine 62–3, 79, 105–6
Sheeko Gaaban 170–1, 172
Sheik, Mohamed Bashir 27
Shōjo Comic 136note26
Somalia 4, 8, 9, 11, 25–6, 32; civil war 24, 42, 55, 124; cockroaches 42
Somali Bantu Association of America 55, 124
Somali Bantu Organization of America 76
Somali refugees 9, 11, 24, 27, 28, 32, 33, 42, 55, 57, 65, 69, 71, 73, 76, 79, 84, 86, 97, 99, 101, 102–3, 104, 109, 110, 115, 123–4, 131, 147, 163, 170, 171, 180
Sophocles: *Trachiniae* 98
Special Immigrant Visa 53note67
Statue of Liberty 59, 96–7
Subba, Kishor: *Mukti* 178note70
Sullivan, Shannon: "White Ignorance and Colonial Oppression, or, Why I Know So Little about Puerto Rico" 72
Syria Civil War 50note16

Taylor, Elizabeth 46, 54note75
Terminator, The 29, 35, 40
Thweatt, Tatyana S. 148
third wave of audience 58, 91note8
Thu, Chan 105, 127–8, 142
Titanic 29, 34
Tokyo Movie Shinsha 136note26
Trebbe, Joachim 144, 148
Trzeciak, Daniel 155

UNHCR *see* United Nations High Commissioner for Refugees
United Nations High Commissioner for Refugees (UNHCR) 17note2, 20, 28, 90, 143
United Nations Refugee Agency 3

University of Pittsburg 18note8
Untouchables, The 37
U.S. Committee for Refugees and Immigrants (USCRI) 11, 120, 130; "Violence in the Home" 121
USCRI *see* U.S. Committee for Refugees and Immigrants
U.S. Department of State 69, 116, 121; Bureau of Population, Refugees, and Migration 9, 21, 58, 82, 125; Deployment Stress Management Program 124; *Making Your Way* 105, 107, 125–6, 127, 128–9, 133; *Welcome to the United States: A Guidebook for Refugees* 14, 56, 61, 62, 69, 70, 71, 72, 73, 74, 76, 79–82, 83, 87, 92note44, 97, 103, 105, 116, 121, 167, 181
"U.S. Department of State, Bureau of Population, Refugees, and Migration (PRM), Worldwide Refugee Admissions Processing System (WRAPS)" 19note28
U.S. Government Accountability Office 111

van Dijk, Teun A. 152
visuality in orientation media 63–4, 118

Waleed 85, 114, 115
Walker, Doug: "The Media's Role in Immigrant Adaption" 105
Warner, Michael 68
Wee, Ya 73–4, 98–9, 101, 135note11
Welcome to the United States: A Guidebook for Refugees 14, 56, 61, 62, 69, 70, 71, 72, 73, 74, 76, 79–82, 83, 87, 92note44, 97, 103, 105, 116, 121, 167, 181
What Lies Beneath 38–9
White, James Boyd 78
Willson, Margaret 28, 30
Worldwide Refugee Admissions Processing System 9, 19note28

Yaqo, Jala 30, 36, 75, 114–15
YMCA Houston, Texas 13; *Reception and Placement* 117–18, 121, 130, 133
YMCA International Services 89, 123

Zanuba 42–3, 110
Zau Aung Marip 84–5, 115

CPSIA information can be obtained
at www.ICGtesting.com
Printed in the USA
FFOW01n1307010617
36288FF